Expressing Silence

Expressing Silence

Where Language and Culture Meet in Japanese

Natsuko Tsujimura

LEXINGTON BOOKS
Lanham • Boulder • New York • London

Published by Lexington Books
An imprint of The Rowman & Littlefield Publishing Group, Inc.
4501 Forbes Boulevard, Suite 200, Lanham, Maryland 20706
www.rowman.com

86-90 Paul Street, London EC2A 4NE

Copyright © 2022 by The Rowman & Littlefield Publishing Group, Inc.

All rights reserved. No part of this book may be reproduced in any form or by any electronic or mechanical means, including information storage and retrieval systems, without written permission from the publisher, except by a reviewer who may quote passages in a review.

British Library Cataloguing in Publication Information Available

Library of Congress Cataloging-in-Publication Data

Names: Tsujimura, Natsuko, author.
Title: Expressing silence : where language and culture meet in Japanese / Natsuko Tsujimura.
Description: Lanham : Lexington Books, [2022] | Includes bibliographical references and index.
Identifiers: LCCN 2021051321 (print) | LCCN 2021051322 (ebook) | ISBN 9781498569248 (cloth) | ISBN 9781498569255 (ebook) | ISBN 9781498569262 (pbk.)
Subjects: LCSH: Japanese language—Discourse analysis. | Japanese language—Rhetoric. | Silence.
Classification: LCC PL640.5 .T78 2022 (print) | LCC PL640.5 (ebook) | DDC 495.61/501—dc23/eng/20211206
LC record available at https://lccn.loc.gov/2021051321
LC ebook record available at https://lccn.loc.gov/2021051322

Contents

Preface		vii
1	Expressing Voids	1
2	The Sound of Silence	13
3	Mimetics and Silence	85
4	Epilogue	143
References		147
Index		159
About the Author		163

Preface

Trained in formal linguistics, I never imagined conducting research on how silence is expressed and portrayed, let alone write a book on it. Like many people, I took (and still take) sound and silence for granted. As much as I enjoyed the movie *The Graduate* and its soundtrack, even Simon and Garfunkel's *The Sound of Silence* remained to be no more than a title of a song. So, working on this book has turned out to be a serendipitous project that has given me an opportunity to go beyond my comfort zone of being a linguist. And, indeed, it has been a long journey. In the process, though, various levels of inquiries have greatly informed me about my own language and culture, and it has been most assuring to me as a linguist that linguistic analysis has much to contribute to analyzing how silence is conceptualized and represented in Japanese.

Throughout this research, I have benefited from discussing the topic with many people. My colleagues in the humanities offered me tremendous guidance. I thank Yasuko Akiyama, Bob Eno, Edie Sarra, Yasuko Watt, and Tie Xiao for their comments and suggestions, which helped me look at conceptual and practical issues in a variety of ways to which I was not accustomed. In particular, Bob Eno's critical feedback, which he delivered very judiciously (so as not to offend me), put me on track when I was clearly going the wrong way. I took pleasure in discussing Japanese poetry with tanka poets, Yasuko Watt, Kozue Uzawa, and Fumiko Sakai, who opened my eyes to a creative world. I am deeply indebted to scholars of ASL, Janis Cole, Brenda Nicodemus, Daniel Roush, and Donna Jo Napoli, for sharing their expertise in ASL and their thoughts on expressing silence in the Deaf culture. Donna Jo Napoli has been an inspiration and role model throughout my career as a linguist. Offered through the lens of a linguist, ASL researcher, and creative writer,

Donna Jo's insight into linguistic and rhetorical matters regarding silence has been of great value to this project.

I am indebted to two anonymous reviewers for their professional assessments. Challenging but very useful, their critiques have shown me different perspectives to consider for improvement on earlier versions of my analysis. This book project has been partially funded by Indiana University's College Arts and Humanities Institute (CAHI) through a CAHI Research Fellowship during the academic year of 2019–2020. Without their generous support, I would not have been able to complete this book.

My sincere thanks go to staff at Lexington Books, Jana Hodges-Kluck, Senior Acquisitions Editor, and Sydney Wedbush, Assistant Acquisitions Editor. They have been a pleasure to work with. Ever since Jana reached out to me about a possible book plan on the topic, she has been exceptionally attentive to every aspect of production. Sydney ever patiently answered numerous logistical questions that I raised. For both of them it was not an easy (or normal) task to oversee the publication process especially given this extraordinary time of pandemic and uncertainty.

Family members, Howard Davis, Kazuto Tsujimura, and Mariko Tsujimura, to my surprise, showed interest in this research. Although reluctantly at first, discussing it with them led me to include some complementary materials. Finally, I cannot complete this list of thanks without acknowledging Stuart Davis, who served as my discussion partner for the project, careful reader and critic of numerous drafts, serious cheerleader for this book, and sole domestic comedian. My first teacher in linguistics, John Underwood, and my first and eternal teacher in life, Miyo Tsujimura, departed without seeing the end of this project. I dedicate this book for their memory.

Chapter One

Expressing Voids

The language we use on a daily basis richly affords us the opportunity to describe our perceptual experiences. There are endless ways to express through language what we see, hear, smell, taste, and feel by touch; and through language we are able to share these tangible experiences with whomever we wish to communicate. Upon talking about expressing our perceptual experiences, we generally refer to the presence of what gives us these perceptual sensations, and not so much to what we do not see, hear, smell, taste, and feel by touch. There are actually a number of situations in which we choose to portray a void in each of our five senses. Adjectives like "invisible," "silent," "odorless," "tasteless," and "numb" are available, but it is an interesting question to ask, beyond individual words like them, how effectively language expresses the absence of tangible sensations. In this book, I attempt to address this question by focusing on auditory void, i.e., silence, as it is expressed in Japanese.

We find ways to speak of silence and similar scenes by simply using adjectives and phrasal expressions that straightforwardly denote (near) lack of sound. Included in this type of verbal descriptions are *It's quiet/silent around here*; *There is no sound*; *We don't hear anything/any sound*; *There is a total silence in the room*. But, soon enough we run out of words, exhausting all similarly possible expressions. Luckily, language offers richer resources for us to be far more creative and expressive with words. Across languages, ambient silence that seems to penetrate the atmosphere and its intensity are cleverly described by means of a variety of linguistic and rhetorical means including metaphors, similes, and the subjunctive mood. Through these means, we express the hypothetical or potential ability to hear a sound that is not normally audible to the human ear. Examples from English, German, and

Japanese are given in (1–3).¹ Comparable expressions are not hard to find in other languages either.

(1) a. It's so quiet that you could hear a mouse/rat piss on cotton.

(Hillbilly saying)

b. The airplane took off, and the first 20 minutes were silent. "You could hear a feather," Gonzalez said. (Sla 2014)

(2) a. Es ist so leise, dass man die Floehe husten hoert.

"It's so quiet that you can hear a flea cough."

b. Es ist so leise, dass man das Gras wachsen hoert.

"It's so quiet that you can hear the grass grow."

(3) a. Yoru-ga shinin-no-yō-ni shizumari-kaeru.

夜が死人のように静まりかえる。

"The night becomes totally silent like a dead person."

(*Kamisori* by Naoya Shiga; https://hyogen.info/content/353394667)

b. Koe-dake-ga sora-ni huwahuwa tadayotta-yō-na seijaku

声だけが空にふわふわ漂ったような静寂

"the kind of silence in which only voices float in the sky"

(*Ishikarigawa* by Mutsuo Honjo; https://hyogen.info/content/309744552)

Given that linguistic expressions like (1–3) are cross-linguistically common, a communication breakdown I describe below came as a surprise. On a sunny Sunday morning in late spring a few years ago, my husband and I were enjoying a leisurely breakfast in our backyard. Fully content with the absence of irksome noises, I said to him: "Wow, I can't believe how quiet it is. All I hear is the chirping of birds. Don't you think so?" I did not realize for a moment that my husband was hesitating to respond to me. To my second prompt "You know what I mean?," he finally said, "Not really." While the entire conversation was carried out in English, it occurred to us that the failure of communication between us may have to do with the way in which "quiet" and "chirping of birds" mean to each of us. My husband is a native speaker of English, growing up in the United States, with a minimal amount of exposure to Japanese language and culture; and I am a native speaker of Japanese who was born and raised in Japan. My reference to birds' singing is a very natural way of describing silence in our surroundings, common to many, if not all, Japanese people. In turn, my husband explained that the sound that birds make is dissonant vis-à-vis silence: How can it be silent when birds are chirping? Each of us was intrigued by the other's remark. At the same time, we were reminded that our sensory reactions and language apparatus that expresses them could be different depending on our cultural and linguistic backgrounds.[2] Our contrastive reactions show that the presence or absence of perceptible sound in the surroundings does not necessarily enter into core criteria of what silence means to speakers of human languages in a uniform fashion. This miscommunication is reminiscent of the "subtle but significant differences" in describing emotions across cultures that Childs (1999) speaks of, specifically regarding the nature of love as it is portrayed in premodern Japanese literature as opposed to in American society.

The dialogue on silence that I had with my spouse sowed the seeds to investigate ways in which we express ambient silence in Japanese. In exploring linguistic manifestations of auditory void in this book, I particularly single out two modes of depicting ambient silence: (i) by asserting sounds that are otherwise taken to be background or secondary sounds (as in my anecdotal story), and (ii) by way of mimetic words (onomatopoeia). They are paradoxical in that silence is represented through sound, and yet they are enormously common linguistic means for Japanese speakers to portray quiet atmospheres. Below I give a brief sketch of these two modes, which the next two chapters illustrate and discuss.

SECONDARY SOUNDS

Sounds that are generally considered secondary in a setting, or in the background, can be either from man-made sounds or from sounds in nature. For instance, a ticking clock, dripping water, a radiator, and humans' breathing, swallowing, and whispering are examples of man-made sounds; whereas sounds that exist in nature such as those that animals and insects make as well as the sounds of rain, ocean waves, and wind fall under that rubric of nature sounds. The examples below illustrate the use of secondary sounds to depict the absence or suppression of noise in surrounding areas, by man-made sounds in (4–5) and by nature sounds in (6–8). The word that denotes silence is given in bold, and the underlined expression indicates the secondary sound.

(4) Mata **chinmoku**-ga otozureta. Kabe-ni kakatte-iru tokei-no byōshin-ga susumu oto-dake-ga, yukkuri-to byōshitsu-ni hirogatte-iku.

また**沈黙**が訪れた。壁にかかっている時計の秒針が進む音だけが、ゆっくりと病室に広がっていく。

"**Silence** came back again. Only the ticking of the clock on the wall slowly spreads all over the hospital room." (*Kōshōnin* by Takahisa Igarashi, 370)

(5) Jijijit-to <u>tōshin-no moeru oto</u>-no hoka, nan-no oto-mo shinai. Kinpaku-shita **seijaku**-ga ita-no ma-o tsutsumi-konde-iru.

じじじっ、と<u>灯芯の燃える音</u>のほか、何の音もしない。緊迫した**静寂**が板の間を包み込んでいる。

"Other than the sound of <u>a burning lampwick</u>, 'jijiji,' there is no sound. Tense **silence** envelopes the wood-floored room."
(*Akinai Seiden Kin-to Gin* by Kaoru Takada, 178)

(6) Hontō-ni mawari-ga **shizuka**-na-node, <u>tori-no saezuri</u>-ga, yori **seijaku**-o kiwadat-asete-iru-no deshita.

ほんとうに周りが**静か**なので、<u>鳥のさえずり</u>が、より**静寂**を際立たせているのでした。

"It was so very **quiet** that <u>the birdsong</u> was making **the silence** stand out even more."
(Fukuhara 2002)

(7) <u>Ōame</u>-ga hutte-iru toki-no **seijaku**-no naka, atashi-wa katsute hashiru uma-o mita.

<u>大雨</u>が降っている時の**静寂**の中、あたしはかつて走る馬を見た。

"In the **silence** during <u>a heavy rain</u>, I once saw a horse running."
(*Mitsubachi-to Enrai* by Riku Onda, 401)

(8) Kono midori-no naka, **shizuka-na** umibe, ao-zora. **Oto-ga shinai**. Kasuka-na tsubuyaki-no-yō-na <u>shizen-no koe</u>-ga anmari ōsugite, **muon**-da.

この緑の中、**静かな海辺**、青空。**音がしない**。かすかなつぶやきのような<u>自然の声</u>があんまり多すぎて**無音**だ。

"In this green, a **quiet** seaside, a blue sky. No sound is made. There are so many <u>voices of nature</u>, like some faint muttering, that there is absolutely no sound."
(*Amurita* by Banana Yoshimoto; https://hyogen.info/scate/290192)

In the first two passages, silence penetrating the scene is asserted using the words *chinmoku* "[verbal] silence" in (4) and *seijaku* "silence" in (5). Although *chinmoku* usually means verbal silence resulting from the absence of words, the context of the narrative from which (4) is extracted confirms ambient silence in the room. The only audible sounds mentioned are the ticking sound of a clock in (4) and the sound coming from a burning lampwick in (5). These sounds are normally not noticeable, hidden by human voices and numerous kinds of other sounds of daily life, but the depth of silence in these settings makes them surface at a perceptible level. The shifting perspectives between man-made sounds and ambient silence in these soundscapes are linguistically explained in terms of the figure-ground relation. In investigating characterizations and typological patterns pertinent to lexicalization, Talmy (1985) sketches the way to dissect a verb's meaning in terms of a limited number of components including Figure, Path, Ground, and Manner. Of immediate relevance to our discussion are Figure and Ground, which are respectively defined as cognitive functions "performed by the concept that needs anchoring" and "performed by the concept that does the anchoring" (Talmy 2000, 311). In the English sentence *The pie is on the table*, the pie is figure while the table is ground. These terms are helpful in relating one object to another in space. Applying the figure-ground relational concept to the context of soundscape in our examples, the sounds that are otherwise rarely audible or noticeable like the ticking clock and the sound of a burning lampwick as described in the Japanese examples in (4–5) are foregrounded and perceived as figure while the silence in the scenes serves as ground.

The situation is robustly different in the examples of (6–8), where the sounds and the ambient silence are interpreted as being inseparable, either in time or in space. As such, the scenes represented in (6–8) cannot be given a comparable analysis in figure-ground terms, because the sounds and silence in these depictions are both simultaneously anchored and anchoring. Instead, sound and silence display a symbiotic relation. In (6) the sounds coming from birds make silence more striking. The apparent causal relation, that is, the idea that silence becomes more prominent by sounds in nature, does not mean that silence surfaces after the birds' sounds have ceased. Rather, silence is being increased because we hear the natural sounds. Sounds and silence here are not in a temporal sequence; they are simultaneous. In (7) silence and a heavy rain are referred to coextensively. The sound of a downpour is far from soft. We witness from a few sentences before (7) in the original text that the sound of the downpour has particular characteristics. The description reads as follows: トタン屋根に落ちる雨が不思議なリズムを刻み . . . "the rain falling on a galvanized sheet metal roof beats a mysterious rhythm . . ." (p. 401). Raindrops, especially during a heavy rain, make more than a subtle noise, and in this verbal sketch, sound and silence exist together, without the former disturbing or breaking the latter. The passage in (8) exhibits three expressions that correspond to ambient silence: *shizuka-na* "quiet," *oto-ga shinai* "no sound is made," and *muon* "no sound." The narrator repeatedly announces the quiet ambience of the scene with those three different ways of expressing the absence or suppression of sound. The critical point is the last part, where "so many voices of nature" are said to be the reason that the setting is conclusively considered to be *muon* 無音 (literally, "no sound": 無 "nothing, void" + 音 "sound"). That is, the abundance of natural sounds defines the silence in this depiction. Emerging from these samples is a symbiotic relation between nature sounds and ambient silence rather than a view of them as separate entities, each with its own, different quality. Nature sounds serve as the active agents for the silence in the described scenes, and because sound and silence are symbiotically related, sound participates in constructing the concept of silence.

It is my supposition that representations of silence by means of man-made sounds, as in (4–5), and those by nature sounds, as in (6–8), are also different in their range of psychological, sensual, affective, and spiritual undertones. In their reciprocal manifestation depicted in (6–8), nature sounds and silence convey a sense of serenity, comfort, calmness, peacefulness, tranquility, as well as reverence and veneration. Ample examples illustrating the nuances characteristic of the symbiotic sound-silence association are found in venues not limited to literary works but more broadly across contents and styles, suggesting its expansive familiarity to the language users. Similar orientations to the symbiotic relation of silence and sound in Japanese are particularly pervasive in travel advertisements and diaries on social media that speak of sites for retreats, spas, temples, shrines, and the like as locations for physical and mental relaxation. The sense of reverence and veneration is instantiated in (7) and elucidated in the context of the narrative. The passages before and after (7) in the original text indicate that the feeling the protagonist is experiencing in the setting described by (7) is *osore* "fear, reverence, veneration." The word *osore* is normally understood to mean "fear," corresponding to the Chinese character of 恐れ, but the character used in (7) is 畏れ with the same pronunciation. The latter character is polysemic, connoting something like awe, between fear and reverence/veneration. The narrator goes on to further describe *osore* as the emotion that she felt when "I was surprised how insignificant I am as soon as I have realized that the world is filled with unspeakably beautiful things that are not known to me or to anybody" (pp. 401–402; my translation, NT). This context precisely points to reverence and veneration toward sublime existence rather than fear—a feeling that connects to the silence associated with the sound of rainfall. The undertones that accompany the symbiotic relation of sound and silence—i.e., nuances related to serenity, comfort, calmness, peacefulness, tranquility, reverence, veneration—are not always explicated verbally (or through context), but they are yet dormant beneath the interdependence of sound and silence. They are distinct from the sound-silence relation that is discernible in figure-ground terms, namely, the type of relation demonstrated in (4–5).

I have thus far demonstrated that ambient silence expressed by Japanese words like *chinmoku*, *seijaku*, *shizuka*, and *muon* in the above examples can mean "the absence or suppression of sound" and "general stillness," and that the latter may further be associated with psychological connotations of hushed tranquility that leads to a peaceful state of mind. These nuances underlying the Japanese words embody psychological effects that sound, notably instantiated by a constellation of natural sounds, brings to Japanese people's minds. In the next chapter, I will argue that this sense of hushed tranquility serves as an important—and arguably default—mode of constructing silence in culturally specific terms. Examinations of the relationship between how silence is perceived and is expressed in linguistic forms as they are pursued in this book are not centered on a mechanical, narrow definition of silence, i.e., the complete absence of sounds. Instead, I explore less categorical situations of how Japanese expressions that refer to silent and quiet atmospheres are understood in Japanese society. To that end, our discussions will focus not so much on the linguistic (or cross-linguistic) meaning of the specific word *silence* and its cross-linguistic equivalents as on unpacking the nuanced undertones and their conceptual foundations.

MIMETIC WORDS

The second paradoxical way of expressing ambient silence in Japanese is the use of mimetic words. The mimetic vocabulary is sometimes referred to under other terms in languages of the world that show an extensive inventory of a similar word class. These include onomatopoeia, ideophones, and expressives. Mimetic expressions like onomatopoeia and ideophones (e.g., *meow*, *pitter-patter*, and *helter-skelter* in English) have been discussed to illustrate the iconic aspect of natural language because they represent "form miming meaning" par excellence.

Onomatopoeic words of the direct auditory nature in Japanese include *nyā* "meow," *gōn* "gong," *batan* "bang," *kasa-kasa* "the sound of dry leaves," and *jara-jara* "jingling sound," among many more. In this characterization of the vocabulary class, it seems highly contradictory or literally impossible to speak of mimetics that represent or symbolize silence. Particularly sound-based mimetics, or onomatopoeia, are perceived as a linguistic representation of mimicked sounds, and they presuppose the existence of perceptible auditory sources. In spite of such a potential incongruity, Japanese is remarkably rich in mimetics, and there are indeed mimetic words that make verbal depictions of silence not only possible but also tremendously effective. Questions that immediately arise are: What does it mean to "mimic" or simulate silence? That is, given the miming nature of the mimetic vocabulary, what is it that a mimetic word of silence mimics when there is little or no sound?

Mimetic words that depict ambient silence in Japanese include *shin*, *hissori*, and *shinshin*. The three examples in (9–11) provide brief contexts in which they appear in verbal renderings of silence in the surrounding environment. The mimetic word is in bold.

(9) Kono sabireta machi-no mayonaka-wa, **hissori**-to shizumari-kaette-iru.

この寂れた町の真夜中は、**ひっそり**と静まり返っている。

"The deep of night in this backwater town is **stony silent**."
(H. Ono 1984, 290)

(10) Hoshi-akari-no moto-ni, **shinshin**-to shite mono-oto hitotsu shinai.

星明りの下に、**しんしん**として物音一つしない。

"Under the starlight, it is **utterly silent** and not a single sound is heard."
(Wakayamaken Kikakubu Kikakuseisakukyoku Bunkageijutsuka, n.d.)

(11) **Shin**-to shita yamaoku-made shokurin-ga susumi, kaihatsu-no te-ga nobiru-yō-ni natta.

しんとした山奥まで植林が進み、開発の手がのびるようになった。

"Afforestation and the hand of development have advanced deep into the **utterly peaceful** mountains."
(H. Ono 1984, 156)

The mimetic words *hissori* in (9) and *shinshin* in (10) cooccur with non-mimetic (prosaic) expressions—*shizumari-kaette-iru* "it has fallen completely silent" and *mono-oto hitotsu shinai* "not a single sound is heard," respectively—that denote or suggest silent settings in the environment. While the mimetics serve as modifiers for the prosaic descriptions in (9–10), by adding further details, the mimetics could also stand by themselves while maintaining the meanings. For example, *hissori-to shite-iru* "be in the state of hissori" for (9) and *shinshin-to shite-ite* "being in the state of shinshin" for (10) in their predicative forms can replace those prosaic descriptions of ambient silence without significantly altering the sense of deep silence already conveyed in (9) and (10). That is, each of these mimetic words in its solely independent occurrences makes a linguistic contribution to the depiction of silence with an equal level of descriptive accuracy that the prosaic expressions demonstrate. (11) exhibits precisely the point: the mimetic *shin* is the sole word that refers to hushed stillness that is permeated deep into the mountains. Without *shin-to shita* "being in the state of shin" that modifies *yamaoku* "deep in the mountains," the rest of the sentence gives no information regarding auditory stimuli in the surroundings. Thus, a richly descriptive function is densely packed in a single linguistic form, mimetics. Furthermore, they capitalize on their ability to appeal to our senses and emotional reactions—a critical point that I will elaborate in chapter 3. Given that silence is inherently intangible, mimetic words help to transform that which is intangible into the tangible through associated images. In this way, they provide the means to *express* silence. Here, by image I mean to include those that are outside the optic domain. In this role, mimetics serve as a vehicle that leads us to subjective images that are engraved in our senses and emotions. The translations of the examples in (9) and (11) provided by H. Ono, "stony silent" for *hissori* and "utterly peaceful (mountain)" for *shin*, signify deeper reflections of what mimetic expressions can represent, since their interpretation is especially sensitive to contextually rich settings. It is in this sense that the mimetic vocabulary serves as staging tools that supplement what an individual word of the regular (prosaic) vocabulary would be insufficient to do.

On the one hand, these mimetics of silence obviously do not mimic auditory absence and suppression in a strict sense, and are thus unlike prototypical onomatopoeic words like *bow-wow* in English and *wan-wan* in Japanese that imitate dogs' barking. On the other hand, they evoke global multi-sensory images of silent scenes that immediately connect to our subjective experiences. The force of the mimetics in (9–11) typically evokes a vivid image of a tranquil scene for us. The image, in lieu of direct auditory stimuli, is enriched by other sensory reactions and emotional responses in association with whatever subjective experiences we have had. In (9), for instance, helped by the reference to a backwater town at night, *hissori* gives the sense of sadness or even coldness (both in feeling and in temperature). This likely prompted Ono to translate it as "stony silence." In contrast, Ono interprets the silent scene depicted by *shin* in (11) as "utterly peaceful" even though the rest of the sentence does not suggest it. It is of note that the difference in interpretation does not come from the two individual words of *hissori* vs. *shin* since as mimetics of silence, they are compatible with both phrasal environments in (9) and (11) (and also [10]). Rather, this points to what I mean by the subjectivity of mimetics. Since our experiences and memories of them are personal, our construction of images in response to cues like these mimetics depends on our individual sensual reactions and emotional landscape. So, Ono projects peacefulness into the particular silent scene referred to by *shin* in (11) but the same mimetic could evoke some other images like darkness, coldness, or fear, given the right contextual particulars. Importantly, mimetic words of silence present to us multi- and cross-modal images as they relate to the concept of silence. Thus, the personally evoked images embody sensual and affective reactions that we have in what we conceptualize as silence in or for the circumstances given. The bridge between the scene and the language users that the mimetic words create is immediate, unlike the process of rationalization characteristic of prosaic words.

The pervasive use of mimetics and the expressive power of the mimetic vocabulary are recurrently discussed in both public and academic forums at varying degrees of depth. One such arena is the world of tanka, traditional Japanese poetry, where the rhetorical efficacy of mimetics has been celebrated by poets, critics, and commentators alike. The characteristics of mimetics that we have discussed above are, in fact, summarized as the two functions that Fujishima (2007) points out: one as memory search and another as imagination arousal. The features to which we have referred with terms like sensual and affective reactions, subjective experiences, and evoked images, all coalesce into these memory-searching and imagination-arousing functions. Viewed in this manner, mimetics of silence simulate hushed environments not by paradoxically imposing silence-like sound, but instead by placing them in a larger setting, accessed in our individual memories, where our senses and emotions are (re-)activated. That is, by using the mimetic vocabulary, the absence or suppression of sounds is vividly depicted and viscerally interpreted through evoked multi-modal and affective images that lend their specifics to characterizing the auditory void.

* * *

This book intends to be a case study in Japanese language and culture. Its primary goal is to demonstrate how silence is conceptualized and linguistically expressed in Japanese. How silence is expressed and interpreted is deeply intertwined with how sound is expressed and interpreted. Motivated by intriguing relations between sound and silence, I will approach the subject by highlighting the two paradoxical situations in which ambient silence is represented by sounds in Japanese, along the lines that are briefly outlined above. Clearly, depictions of ambient silence encompass something far beyond the absence or suppression of sound. The seemingly paradoxical linguistic tools that I have described further suggest that extrinsic factors centering on psychological effects that sound arouses to language users pertain to understanding how silence is conceptualized in Japanese. I will deliberate on these conceptual issues in the chapters to follow while examining how ambient silence is linguistically manifested.

The conceptual matters that I will discuss in this book are tied to the question of what sound means to an individual and to the society in which s/he is embedded. It also seems—at least tangentially—relevant to ask whether the concept of silence is to be looked at as an absolute principle valid for both the individual and their society, or as a scalar phenomenon to be viewed in a continuum. Interestingly, the literature on American Sign Language (ASL) and Deaf culture foregrounds the weighty role culture plays in constructing the meaning of sound. One such piece of confirmation comes from Padden (1988, 93).

> The fact that different cultures organize sound in different ways shows that sound does not have an inherent meaning but can be given a myriad of interpretations and selections. . . . In any discussion of Deaf people's knowledge of sound, it is important to keep in mind that perception of sound is not automatic

or straightforward, but is shaped through learned, culturally defined practices. It is as important to know the specific and special meaning of a given sound as it is to hear sound.

Furthermore, the relevance of culture to sound and other human senses has been highlighted by Bahan (2014, 233), not only in relation to Deaf culture but more generally.

> As Edward Hall explains, "[p]eople of different cultures don't only speak different languages, but what is possibly more important inhabit different sensory worlds." Hall raises an interesting point. We are familiar with the five senses: sound, sight, taste, touch, and smell. However, each sense possibly has a different meaning or interpretation in different cultures. One such instance of this is how sound is controlled and what it means in different cultures.

As a hearing person, I am reminded that Deaf people are not totally dissociated from the conceptualization of sound but in fact they do have a concept of sound. Of course, the concept of sound is shaped differently for Deaf people and hearing people, but differences also exist within and across hearing culture(s). For instance, Padden explains that a cough as a sound can mean either a voluntary or involuntary bodily reaction in clearing the windpipe, an indication of approval, or a signal (of a sort that is to be understood by communicating participants). The intra- and inter-cultural variation, then, begs further questions regarding the role that culture and language mutually play in relating our experience of cognitive perceptions to the linguistic (broadly conceived) tools for expressing them.

With these questions in mind, this book engages in linguistic investigations into rhetorical modes, i.e., genres, discourses, and other frames, in which portraying and gauging ambient silence in Japanese are pertinent. By sampling and analyzing both the content and the context of representations of silence, I aim to demonstrate that the lack or dearth of sound indeed can be made as expressive as its presence by way of these linguistic means in Japanese. The topic of silence has been more frequently discussed in relation to verbal silence (e.g., Ephratt 2011; Nakane 2007), but there seems to be a notable dearth of linguistic investigations of the expression of silence in the surroundings or the environment.[3] It is hoped that the presentation, analysis, and discussion of data to follow will fill that significant gap and inspire further studies.

NOTES

1. I thank Dennis Preston for informing me about the expression in (1a) and Tracy Hall for providing the German examples in (2).

2. I should hasten to add, however, that there are indeed some American-English speakers who understand and even use the same type of expressions to describe silence in the atmosphere. Although I will later discuss some cultural grounding for conceptualizations of silence in Japanese, I do not intend to claim that the type of miscommunication I have described resulted from a concept of silence unique to Japanese culture.

3. Hiraga (2005) and Hiraga and Ross (2013) are notable exceptions to this. I will discuss their work in chapter 2.

Chapter Two

The Sound of Silence

Silence is experienced by all humans, including those in the Deaf community, and language provides us with linguistic means to express it. Japanese enables a construction of silence that includes sound, as the examples below illustrate.

(1) ... **seijaku**-no naka, kikoete-kuru-no-wa tada <u>tori-no koe</u>-dake.

...**静寂**の中、聞こえてくるのはただ<u>鳥の声</u>だけ。

"... in the **silence**, only <u>the birds' chirping</u> is heard." (Takayama 2021)

(2) Yoru-wa <u>nami-no oto</u>-dake-ga kikoeru **seijaku**-ga atari-o tsutsumi-komu.

夜は<u>波の音</u>だけが聞こえる**静寂**が辺りを包み込む。

"At night, the area is enveloped by a **silence** in which you hear only the <u>sounds of waves</u>." (Walkerplus 2018)

The birds' chirping in (1) and the sounds of the waves in (2) are not interpreted as agents of breaking the silence; instead, they not only describe silence, *seijaku* (静寂), but enhance its presence and intensity. Each of the examples in (1) and (2) asserts that the surrounding area is quiet by means of the very noun denoting that quality, *seijaku*. Such a noun alone suffices to inform us of the silence, but the reference to the sounds coming from birds and the shore's waves, in fact, enriches the descriptive depth of silence even more effectively. Furthermore, the juxtaposition of *seijaku* and the nature sounds in these verbal descriptions deliver an undertone of tranquility and peacefulness.

The reciprocal relationships of sound and silence as well as the additional nuance separate this kind of portrayal of silence from the type that is subject to analysis in figure-ground terms. The musician Brandon LaBelle made an interesting remark about the nature of sounds, as quoted by Toop (2004, 257): "'[s]ound is always present as a momentary force, a temporal form,' writes sound artist Brandon LaBelle, 'because it is always deflected and refracting against its surroundings—it is always interfered with by other stimuli, by bodies and space. In this way, sound is never isolated.'" This statement was presumably made from a professional and technical standpoint, specifically, in the context of music, and as such, it probably has particular meaning pertinent to trained specialists. Yet, in light of the last sentence—"sound is never isolated"—it does not seem too far-fetched to say that the samples to be examined in this chapter also suggest, in their way, that silence can hardly be isolated, at least in a nontechnical sense. In what will follow, I shall examine the construction of ambient silence as instantiated by examples like (1–2), which are common and embraced in describing silence in Japanese.

The aim of this chapter is twofold. The first, the descriptive of the two, is to give detailed discussions of the content and the context of various discourses in which sound and silence are described and talked about in Japanese. To give a broader view I will also include at the end of the chapter a brief illustration of linguistic means that are used to further elaborate on descriptions of ambient silence. Second, I will discuss the concept of silence as it is relevant to its linguistic manifestations in Japanese. The discussion is informed by the collection of examples that are particularly suggestive of what we may call the harmony of sound and silence, and what it means for and feels like to Japanese speakers. I shall further attempt to reflect on cultural grounding that may contribute to the linguistic pattern of representing silence in the language. These two goals will be pursued in a discursive, rather than sequential, order, so that descriptive and conceptual matters are presented and discussed in an interactive fashion.

It should be kept in mind throughout the discussion that the primary focus is on literal, rather than figurative, descriptions of silence by way of secondary sounds—literal in the sense that people actually hear the sounds in describing silence, as opposed to the hypothetical or imaginary sense of "as if" they could hear them. The sampling below is intended to demonstrate why depicting silence by noting the presence of sounds can achieve a rhetorically rich descriptive tool without internal contradictions. In presenting and discussing the selected samples, it is important to maintain neutrality of interpretation and analysis, especially since we will try to decipher delicate nuances and undertones. To that end, I have relied on and included here as many textual illustrations as possible to represent a wide variety of sources. Together, these illustrations will show members of the Japanese speech community, both specialists and laymen, voicing their own opinions and assessments from diverse professional and nonprofessional perspectives. Throughout this and the next chapter, I provide example sentences and texts both in Japanese script and their Romanized transliterations where particular words and linguistic expressions are singled out for examination. On the other hand, when the overall content of a text or a commentary is the focus for discussion, I provide just the Japanese originals and my own translations of them (unless indicated otherwise) without their transliterations.

1. WHAT DOES SILENCE MEAN? WHAT DOES SOUND MEAN?

1.1 The Range of Nature Sounds

There is a variety of secondary or background sounds that are included in depictions of ambient silence in Japanese, but they are united around those in nature as opposed to man-made noises. For expository purposes, examples to be discussed below are organized into three general groups: (i) small animals, (ii) insects, and (iii) water, leaves, and wind. In my data collection, I looked only for linguistic samples that include a term that literally denotes silence in the surroundings (e.g., *seijaku, shizukesa, shizuka*) AND secondary sounds cooccurring in describing the scene. That is, it is important to remember here and throughout the discussion in this chapter that these two kinds of seemingly contradictory expressions exist simultaneously in the scenes as described. In each example, the word that directly denotes ambient silence is presented in boldface, and the accompanying expressions of secondary sounds (i.e., sounds in nature) are underlined. Note also that the English translations of the Japanese samples may not necessarily seem natural. This is intentional, in the attempt to maintain what the original Japanese sentences correspond to in their direct (almost word-by-word) English translations, so that differences between the two languages in verbal portrayals of ambient silence can be noted. Examples are presented collectively first according to their types, (i–iii), followed by explanations; individual examples may be repeated for further elaboration.

(i) *Small animals (birds, frogs)*

(3) Hontō-ni mawari-ga **shizuka**-na-node, tori-no saezuri-ga, yori **seijaku**-o kiwadat-asete-iru-no deshita.

ほんとうに周りが**静か**なので、鳥のさえずりが、より**静寂**を際立たせているのでした。

"It was so very **quiet** that the birdsong was making **the silence** stand out even more." (Fukuhara 2002)

(4) Tori-ga hanatsu hitokoe-ga, yama-no **shizukesa**-o issō hukai mono-ni shite-iru-yō-ni omoimasu.

鳥が放つ一声が、山の**静けさ**を一層深いものにしているように思います。

"A voice from a bird seems to me to deepen **the silence** in the mountains all the more." (Matsuya 2014)

(5) Usu-gurai shin'yōju-no mori-no naka-kara ruribitaki-no mono-ganashii tanchō-na koe-ga kikoete-kuru-to, mori-no **shizukesa**-ga yori kyōchō-sarete-kuru-yō desu.

薄暗い針葉樹の森の中からルリビタキのもの悲しい短調な声が聞こえてくると、森の**静けさ**がより強調されてくるようです。

"When the Siberian bluechat's sound of a sad minor key is heard in a dusky coniferous forest, **the silence** in the woods seems to become more accented." (Nikko Kirihurikogen Kisugedairaenchi, n.d.)

(6) **Shizuka**-da. Ie-no mae-ni aru ōki-na ike-de-wa, kaeru-ga naite-iru.

静かだ。家の前にある大きな池では、カエルが鳴いている。

"It's **quiet**. A frog is making a sound at the big pond in front of the house." (Ehon-no Mori 2017)

(7) Asa yoji. Tsuwanoekisha-ni akari-ga tsuku-to, tsubame-ga jijiji-to sawaida. Menukidōri-ni hitokage-wa nai. Suiro-no nishikigoi-wa hitokatamari-ni natte jit-to shite-iru. Sekishūgawara-no hukareta akachaketa ienami-mo, tōku tsuranaru yamayama-mo, ima-wa mada aoku **shizuka-na kūki-no naka-ni** shizunde-ita.

朝4時。津和野駅舎に灯りがつくと、ツバメがジジジと騒いだ。目抜き通りに人影はない。水路の錦鯉はひとかたまりになってじっとしている。石州瓦の葺かれた赤茶けた家並みも、遠く連なる山々も、今はまだ青く**静かな空気のなかに**沈んでいた。

"It is 4:00am. As the lights came on at the Tsuwano Station, a swallow sang 'jijiji.' There is not a single soul on the main street. A school of Nishiki carp remain still in a waterway. Rows of houses with reddish-brown tiles on the roofs and a distant range of mountains were all sunk in the still blue and **quiet air**." (Watanabe 2014, 166)

(8) Machi-wa **shizuka**-desu. Baiku-ya kuruma-no enjin'on-mo, hito-no koe-mo shimasen. Kaeru-to tori-no nakigoe, inu-no tōboe, kaze-ni yureru kigi-no oto-nomi.

街は**静か**です。バイクや車のエンジン音も、人の声もしません。カエルと鶏の鳴き声、犬の遠吠え、かぜにゆれる木々の音のみ。

"The town is **quiet**. There is no noise from motorbikes and cars; nor is there is a human voice. There are only <u>sounds from frogs, chickens, barking dogs in a distance, and trees shook by the wind</u>." (Kaji 2015)

Birds' chirping leads the pack of small animal sounds that frequently appear in descriptions of silence, but sounds that frogs make are also regularly used, as demonstrated in (6) and (8). Although less common, chickens and dogs are referred to, especially when those sounds are heard from a far distance as in (8). Sounds made by small animals like birds, frogs, and the like, unless they are the central topic at issue, are generally perceived to be only part of the background. However, the sounds referred to in (3–8) play a more active role as agency in representing ambient silence. As such, they are no longer simply background sounds; instead, they enter into the realm that is conceptualized as silence. This may seem a bit peculiar given that some of these nature sounds could be perceived as noisy. For example, there are quite a few different types of sounds mentioned in (8) that together strike us as being loud. Sounds from frogs, chickens, dogs (in the distance), and rustling leaves in this example represent quite diverse types of sound in nature. Yet, these sounds in nature are clearly distinguished from man-made mechanical sounds of motorbikes, engines, and humans.

(7) describes a street scene at 4:00 in the morning before most people wake up.

(7) Asa yoji. Tsuwanoekisha-ni akari-ga tsuku-to, <u>tsubame-ga jijiji-to sawaida</u>. Menukidōri-ni hitokage-wa nai. Suiro-no nishikigoi-wa hitokatamari-ni natte jitto shite-iru. Sekishūgawara-no hukareta akachaketa ienami-mo, tōku tsuranaru yamayama-mo, ima-wa mada aoku **shizuka-na kūki-no naka-ni** shizunde-ita.

朝4時。津和野駅舎に灯りがつくと、<u>ツバメがジジジと騒いだ</u>。目抜き通りに人影はない。水路の錦鯉はひとかたまりになってじっとしている。石州瓦の葺かれた赤茶けた家並みも、遠く連なる山々も、今はまだ青く**静かな空気のなかに**沈んでいた。

"It is 4:00am. As the lights came on at the Tsuwano Station, <u>a swallow sang 'jijiji.'</u> There is not a single soul on the main street. A school of Nishiki carp remain still in a waterway. Rows of houses with reddish-brown tiles on the roofs and a distant range of mountains were all sunk in the still blue and **quiet air**." (Watanabe 2014, 166)

Here, silence is staged by motionless carp and the tranquil air as well as the synesthetic effect of the morning darkness. The swallow's singing is described by an onomatopoeic word, *jijiji*. From the perspective of sound-symbolism, we may be led to expect that the onomatopoeia consisting of all voiced sounds (i.e., a sequence of the voiced consonant [ʝ] and the vowel [i]) would yield an effect opposite of quietude. Moreover, the verb *sawaida* collocating with the onomatopoeic word means to make a noise, generally suggesting a negative impression of a loud sound. Despite all these, nothing prevents *jijiji* from sounding dissonant in the "quiet air" before dawn in a small town. Thus, the single source of sound from a swallow is portrayed as more than gentle, yet perfectly serves the purpose of embodying silence in this setting. In fact, it does not seem implausible to think that the swallow is unreservedly making a racket as it should be in the natural environment to which it belongs. And, it is in such a scene with its uninhibited sounds of nature that the Japanese concept of silence finds a home.

Even a more active involvement that sound exhibits in descriptions of silence is illustrated particularly in (3), (4), and (5). In each of these examples, not only are birdsongs in unison with the silence in the setting, but they also add a dynamic force to enhance and deepen it. Take (5), for example.

(5) Usu-gurai shin'yōju-no mori-no naka-kara <u>ruribitaki-no mono-ganashii tanchō-na koe</u>-ga kikoete-kuru-to, mori-no **shizukesa**-ga yori kyōchō-sarete-kuru-yō desu.

薄暗い針葉樹の森の中から<u>ルリビタキのもの悲しい短調な声</u>が聞こえてくると、森の**静けさ**がより強調されてくるようです。

"When <u>the Siberian bluechat's sound of a sad minor key</u> is heard in a dusky coniferous forest, **the silence** in the woods seems to become more accented."   (Nikko Kirihurikogen Kisugedairaenchi, n.d.)

The naming of an exact bird species (i.e., Siberian bluechat) along with the detailed quality of the sound it makes (i.e., a sad minor key) transforms a generic description of ambient silence into a specific sound portrait that invites the reader into the experiential, "felt" perspective. Note that the adjective *mono-ganashii* "sad, melancholic" further details the sound of the bird that mirrors an emotional reaction that the writer felt upon hearing it. Since the bird sound is described to accentuate the tranquility permeating in the woods, the feeling of sadness and melancholy denoted by the adjective also captures the more nuanced nature of the ambient silence in this scene.

(ii) Insects

(9) **Shizukesa**-ga kiwadatsu mushi-no ne-to suiro-no seseragi.

静けさが際立つ虫の音と水路のせせらぎ。

"The sounds of insects and the murmur of the waterway in which the **silence** stands out." (Inagaki 2017)

(10) . . . kaeru-no gasshō-ya suzumushi-no oto-wa **shizukesa**-o saegiru oto-de-wa naku, **shizukesa**-ni toke-iru oto

. . . カエルの合唱や鈴虫の音は**静けさ**を遮る音ではなく、**静けさ**に溶け入る音

". . . the chorus of frogs, the sounds of bell crickets, and the like are the kind of sounds that do not interrupt the **silence** but melt into it [silence]" (Haruki 2007)

(11) Shizen-ni-wa ironna **seijaku**-ga aru. Hiru-sagari-no semi-shigure, yonaga-no mushi-no ne, sarasara-to nagareru mizuoto, kaze-no soyogi, tōi shiosai . . . sō iu **shizukesa**-wa kokoro-o ochitsuk-ase, sum-asete-kureru.

自然にはいろんな**静寂**がある。昼下がりの蝉しぐれ、夜長の虫の音、サラサラと流れる水音、風のそよぎ、遠い潮騒......そういう**静けさ**は心を落ち着かせ、澄ませてくれる。

"There are various sorts of **silence** in nature. The chorus of cicadas in early afternoons, the insects' sounds in the long night, the water ripples, the rustling of wind, the sound of the sea from the distance. . . . These sorts of **silence** calm and clarify our minds." (Kosugi 2018)

(12) **Shizuka**-na den'en-no naka-ni tatazumu 'Suzumushi-sō'-de-wa, . . . suzumushi-tachi-ga . . . suzu-no neiro-no yō-na yasashiku kokochi-yoi 'kyūai-no shi'-o kanadete, watashi-tachi-no kokoro-o iyashite-kuremasu.

静かな田園の中に佇む「すずむし荘」では、．．．鈴虫たちが．．．鈴の音色のような優しく心地よい「求愛の詩」を奏でて、私たちの心を癒してくれます。

"At Suzumushiso in the **quiet** rural area, . . . bell crickets . . . restore serenity by playing for us a gentle and pleasant 'poem of courtship' like the tones of a bell." (Suzumushi-no Sato, n.d.)

(13) Mushi-no neiro-ga tsukuri-dasu shinshin-to shita yoru-no **seijaku**-ga anata-o kokochi yoi iyashi-e sasoimasu.

虫の音色が創り出すシンシンとした夜の**静寂**があなたを心地よい癒しへ誘います。

"The deep **silence** at night created by the tones of insects invites you into pleasant serenity." (music.usen.com, n.d.)

(14) Tōi <u>higurashi-no koe</u>-ga chikai <u>higurashi-no koe</u>-o yobi, tōi rinshō-ni chikaku-no <u>higurashi</u>-ga kuwawari, enkin kyōjaku-ni tonda rinshō-to naru hibiki-ni-wa, sunda **seijaku**-sae kanjimasu.

遠い<u>ヒグラシの声</u>が近い<u>ヒグラシの声</u>を呼び、遠い輪唱に近くの<u>ヒグラシ</u>が加わり、遠近強弱に富んだ輪唱となる響きには、澄んだ**静寂**さえ感じます。

"Voices of <u>evening cicadas</u> in the distance invite those of nearby <u>cicadas</u>; the nearby <u>cicadas</u> join the trolling of the distant; we find even the crystal tone of **silence** in the sound of the trolling rich with a variety of sound qualities."
(Sugawara Jinja 2019)

(15) <u>Matsumushi</u>-ya <u>suzumishi</u>-wa, sunda takai koe-de mijikaku nakimasu. <u>Kirigirisu</u>-mo <u>umaoi</u>-mo, shizuka-ni himeru-yō-ni nakimasu. Aki-no yoru-no **shizukesa**-o migoto-ni enshutsu-shimasu.

<u>松虫</u>や<u>鈴虫</u>は、澄んだ高い声で短く鳴きます。<u>きりぎりす</u>も<u>馬おい</u>も、静かに秘めるように鳴きます。秋の夜の**静けさ**を見事に演出します。

"<u>Matsumushi</u> [xenogryllus marmoratus] and <u>bell crickets</u> make short, pure, and high-pitch sounds. <u>Kirigirisu</u> [long-horned grasshopper] and <u>umaoi</u> [katydid] sing quietly and almost secretly. They brilliantly orchestrate **the silence** in the fall evening."
(Kuwana City Medical Center 2017)

(16) **Shizukasa**-ya / iwa-ni shimi'iru / <u>semi-no koe</u>

閑さや岩にしみ入る<u>蝉の声</u>

"**tranquility** / penetrating into rocks / <u>cicada's voice</u>"   (Ogura 1977, 2)

Appreciation of insect sounds by Japanese people is anecdotally known to members of other cultures as a cultural phenomenon, perhaps more so than other sounds discussed here. Especially those that strongly correlate with, and thus identify, seasons (for summer and autumn, in particular) are considered to add an aesthetic sense to auditory perceptions. Not surprisingly, reference to insects—mainly seasonal insects—in depictions of silence is extremely prevalent and, in many instances, increases the level of rhetorical depth. Typically, cicadas (*semi, higurashi*) in summer as well as crickets (e.g., *matsumushi, suzumushi*) and grasshoppers of various kinds in autumn (e.g., *kutsuwamushi, umaoi, kirigirisu*) appear in close association with portrayal of a quiet and often soothing atmosphere. The sound of *suzumushi* "bell cricket" as mentioned in (10), (12), and (15) is habitually likened to beautiful musical tunes that are perceived as a harmonious part of outdoor silence and tranquility, especially in the evening.

Just as the previous set of examples with small animals demonstrates, the juxtaposition of sound and silence in (9–16) does not merely indicate their appositional presence in a given scene but signifies more active roles that individual insect sounds—coupled with additional sounds in some cases—play in capturing ambient silence. In (9–11), for instance, the sounds of insects (e.g., *semi*, *suzumushi*) as well as the sounds of the water, the wind, and frogs participate in identifying that sort of silence.

(9) **Shizukesa**-ga kiwadatsu mushi-no ne-to suiro-no seseragi.

静けさが際立つ虫の音と水路のせせらぎ。

"The sounds of insects and the murmur of the waterway in which the **silence** stands out." (Inagaki 2017)

(10) . . . kaeru-no gasshō-ya suzumushi-no oto-wa **shizukesa**-o saegiru oto-de-wa naku, **shizukesa**-ni toke-iru oto

…カエルの合唱や鈴虫の音は**静けさ**を遮る音ではなく、**静けさ**に溶け入る音

". . . the chorus of frogs, the sounds of bell crickets, and the like are the kind of sounds that do not interrupt the **silence** but melt into **it [silence]**" (Haruki 2007)

(11) Shizen-ni-wa ironna **seijaku**-ga aru. Hiru-sagari-no semi-shigure, yonaga-no mushi-no ne, sarasara-to nagareru mizuoto, kaze-no soyogi, tōi shiosai . . . sō iu **shizukesa**-wa kokoro-o ochitsuk-ase, sum-asete-kureru.

自然にはいろんな**静寂**がある。昼下がりの蝉しぐれ、夜長の虫の音、サラサラと流れる水音、風のそよぎ、遠い潮騒 … そういう**静けさ**は心を落ち着かせ、澄ませてくれる。

"There are various sorts of **silence** in nature. The chorus of cicadas in early afternoons, the insects' sounds in the long night, the water ripples, the rustling of wind, the sound of the sea from the distance. . . . These sorts of **silence** calm and clarify our minds." (Kosugi 2018)

In (9) the sounds from insects and from the waterway enhance the silence felt in the surroundings. The unity of sound and silence is even more directly addressed in (10). It describes that the "chorus" of multiple frogs, joined by bell crickets' singing, does not disturb or break the silence. Instead, those nature sounds effortlessly interflow into stillness. (11) mentions a variety of sounds in nature, originating from cicadas and other insects, from brooks and the sea, and from the wind. Each of these sounds is viewed not only as a type of silence but as a relaxing and purifying agent for the soul.

The agency of ambient silence that the insect sounds demonstrate is more directly displayed in (12–13). In these examples, the reciprocal relationship of sound and silence is manifested in terms of the healing effect that their coexistence brings out.

(12) **Shizuka**-na den'en-no naka-ni tatazumu 'Suzumushi-sō'-de-wa, . . . <u>suzumushi</u>-tachi-ga . . . suzu-no neiro-no yō-na yasashiku kokochi-yoi 'kyūai-no shi'-o kanadete, watashi-tachi-no kokoro-o iyashite-kuremasu.

静かな田園の中に佇む「すずむし荘」では、．．．鈴虫たちが．．．鈴の音色のような優しく心地よい「求愛の詩」を奏でて、私たちの心を癒してくれます。

"At Suzumushiso in the **quiet** rural area, . . . <u>bell crickets</u> . . . restore serenity by playing for us a gentle and pleasant 'poem of courtship' like the tones of a bell." (Suzumushi-no Sato, n.d.)

(13) <u>Mushi-no neiro</u>-ga tsukuri-dasu shinshin-to shita yoru-no **seijaku**-ga anata-o kokochi yoi iyashi-e sasoimasu.

<u>虫の音色</u>が創り出すシンシンとした夜の**静寂**があなたを心地よい癒しへ誘います。

"The deep **silence** at night created by <u>the tones of insects</u> invites you into pleasant serenity." (music.usen.com, n.d.)

The sounds of the insects mentioned in these examples are entrenched in the silence in the surroundings, and the whole unified soundscape serves as a spiritual antidote. The verbal root *iyas*- "heal, cure" of *iyashite-kuremasu* in (12) and its noun form *iyashi* "healing, therapy" in (13) are repeated in these examples. More generally, however, these words also collocate frequently with similar discourse that captures ambient silence by way of nature sounds. It is indicative that the concept of silence as it is represented in these Japanese expressions extends beyond lack of noise.

The sounds from insects can be equated to musical tones that create a pleasant, serene atmosphere. It is suggested by music-related terms like *kaeru-no gasshō* "the chorus of frogs" in (10), *'kyūai-no shi'-o kanadete* "play (in the sense of music) 'a poem of courtship'" in (12), and *rinshō* "a round (in music); trolling" in (14). In addition, (14–15) illustrate that a collection of insect sounds amounts to a musical performance of silence.

(14) Tōi <u>higurashi-no koe</u>-ga chikai <u>higurashi-no koe</u>-o yobi, tōi rinshō-ni chikaku-no <u>higurashi</u>-ga kuwawari, enkin kyōjaku-ni tonda rinshō-to naru hibiki-ni-wa, sunda **seijaku**-sae kanjimasu.

遠いヒグラシの声が近いヒグラシの声を呼び、遠い輪唱に近くのヒグラシが加わり、遠近強弱に富んだ輪唱となる響きには、澄んだ静寂さえ感じます。

"Voices of evening cicadas in the distance invite those of nearby cicadas; the nearby cicadas join the trolling of the distant; we find even the crystal tone of **silence** in the sound of the trolling rich with a variety of sound qualities." (Sugawara Jinja 2019)

(15) Matsumushi-ya suzumishi-wa, sunda takai koe-de mijikaku nakimasu. Kirigirisu-mo umaoi-mo, shizuka-ni himeru-yō-ni nakimasu. Aki-no yoru-no **shizukesa**-o migoto-ni enshutsu-shimasu.

松虫や鈴虫は、澄んだ高い声で短く鳴きます。きりぎりすも馬おいも、静かに秘めるように鳴きます。秋の夜の静けさを見事に演出します。

"*Matsumushi* [xenogryllus marmoratus] and bell crickets make short, pure, and high-pitch sounds. *Kirigirisu* [long-horned grasshopper] and *umaoi* [katydid] sing quietly and almost secretly. They brilliantly orchestrate **the silence** in the fall evening."
(Kuwana City Medical Center 2017)

In (14) the sounds of evening cicadas, located near and far, are heard as a musical round, *rinshō*, full of modulation, where one would find purified silence. On the surface, the sounds of multiple cicadas do not seem consistent with ambient silence, but this is an aesthetically rich description that emerges from an understanding of the relationship of sound and silence. Insects belonging to the families of crickets and grasshoppers are individually identified in (15), describing each unique singing manner and voice quality. The verb of the last sentence, *enshutsu-shimasu* "to produce, direct," emphasizes the insects' active and direct participation in creating, in their performance, the silence that fills a fall evening. It is as if the insects were a conductor in charge of an orchestra. The unity of the sounds and the silence created by them further gives rise to a serene feeling, as expressed implicitly as an undertone in (14–15). The frequent collocation of sounds of insects and hushed tranquility along with the comforting, peaceful frame of mind that their fusion brings out is repeated throughout the examples we have discussed thus far.

(16) is a famous haiku of Matsuo Basho (1644–1694).

(16) **Shizukasa**-ya / iwa-ni shimi'iru / semi-no koe

閑さや岩にしみ入る蝉の声

"**tranquility** / penetrating into rocks / cicada's voice" (Ogura 1977, 2)

The sound from a cicada (or multiple cicadas) during the summer season, as is captured in this poem, varies widely depending on the type. For instance, the following types are included in a list of cicadas that have Japanese names (although I have not been able to find English translations for all): *nīnī-zemi* "kaempher cicada," *higurashi* "clear-toned cicada," *abura-zemi* "large brown cicada," *ezo-zemi* [lit. Ezo-cicada], *kuma-zemi* [lit. bear-cicada], *minmin-zemi* "robust cicada,' and *tsukutsukubōshi*. Sounds from these cicadas do not seem to be perceived uniformly in terms of the degree of loudness, and some are considered to emit a relatively loud noise even to native Japanese. In fact, scholars and non-professionals have debated that certain cicada types cannot be the topic of the haiku in (16) because they are too loud for the poet Basho to compose a haiku poem about stillness of the surroundings. Notwithstanding precise sound qualities inherent to specific types of cicadas, key to our discussion is that a clearly perceptible level of sound coexisting with the noted silence and stillness is undeniable in this poem. That is, sound and silence are not mutually exclusive, but instead, they are viewed as perfectly counter-balancing agents in the same space and time.

(iii) Water, leaves, wind

(17) Yoru-wa <u>nami-no oto</u>-dake-ga kikoeru **seijaku**-ga atari-o tsutsumi-komu.

夜は<u>波の音</u>だけが聞こえる**静寂**が辺りを包み込む。

"At night, the area is enveloped by **silence** in which you can hear only <u>sounds of waves</u>."
(Walkerplus 2018)

(18) Hanashi-ga togireta. **Shizuka**-datta. **Shin**-to shite, <u>konoha-ga kasakasa-to yureru oto</u>-shika shinai. Amari-no **shizukesa**-ni uttori-shite-shimau.

話が途切れた。**静か**だった。**しん**として、<u>木の葉がかさかさと揺れる音</u>しかしない。あまりの**静けさ**にうっとりしてしまう。

"The conversation broke. It was **quiet**. It's **silent** and <u>rustling leaves</u> are all we can hear. I get mesmerized by **the sheer silence**."
(*Ōdubon-no Inori* by Kotaro Isaka;
https://hyogen.info/content/242575515)

(19) <u>Ōame</u>-ga hutte-iru toki-no **seijaku**-no naka, atashi-wa katsute hashiru uma-o mita.

<u>大雨</u>が降っている時の**静寂**の中、あたしはかつて走る馬を見た。

"In **the silence** during <u>a heavy rain</u>, I once saw a horse running."
(*Mitsubachi-to Enrai* by Riku Onda, 401)

(20) Chorochoro-to sasayaka-na <u>mizu-no oto</u>-ga **shizukesa**-o kiwadatete-imasu.

チョロチョロとささやかな水の音が静けさを際立てています。

"The gentle trickling sound of water is making the silence more striking."
(Japan Federation of Landscape Contractors, n.d.)

(21) Dokoka-de uguisu-ga naite-iru, mimi-o sumasu-to iroiro-na toritachi-no koe-ga kikoete-kuru. Kono hūkei-no naka-de-wa, sono koe-mo, seseragi-no oto-mo, seijaku-o iya-masu-dake-no mono-to naru.

どこかで鶯が鳴いている、耳を澄ますと色々な鳥たちの声が聞こえて来る。この風景の中では、その声も、せせらぎの音も、静寂を弥増すだけのものとなる。

"A bush warbler is singing somewhere; upon listening intently, sounds of various birds reach our ears. In this scenery, the sounds of those birds and of the stream simply increase the silence." (Nozarashi, n.d.)

(22) Yama-ni mukau-to kikoete-kuru kaze-no oto, kawa-no seseragi-ya amaoto, mushi-no ne-ni tori-no koe. Sono seijaku-to iu oto-o motomete, yama-ya shizen-ni mukau hito-mo sukunaku-nai-darō.

山に向かうと聞こえてくる風の音、川のせせらぎや雨音、虫の音に鳥の声。その静寂という音を求めて、山や自然に向かう人も少なくないだろう。

"Upon embarking for the mountain, I hear the sound of the wind, the murmuring of the brook and the sound of rain, the insect's singing and the bird's chirping. Not a few seem to be headed toward the mountain and nature in search of the very sound called silence."
(Yamap Editorial Department 2018)

(23) Koko-ni aru-no-wa daishizen-to shizukesa-dake—hoka-ni-wa nanimo arimasen

Midori hukaki sankan-ni tatazumu hoshigaokasansō-ni kaze-to tomo-ni todoku-no-wa, oto-naki oto.

Shiki oriori-no iro-ni somaru keshiki-no naka, kawa-no seseragi, mushi-no koe, tori-no saezuri-ni, kigi-no zawameki.

ここにあるのは大自然と静けさだけ—他には何もありません

緑深き山間に佇む星ヶ岡山荘に風と共に届くのは、音なき音。

四季折々の色に染まる景色の中、川のせせらぎ、虫の声、鳥のさえずりに、木々のざわめき。

"There exist only Mother Nature and silence—there is nothing else //
It is soundless sound that reaches Hoshigaoka Inn, which stands in the green mountains.
The murmuring of a river, voices of insects, birdsongs, and the rustling of trees in the scenery that tinges with seasonal colors."
(Hoshigaoka Sanso, n.d.)

(24) Ame-ga suki-desu. Hudan kikoeru zatsuon, seikatsuon-nado-ga kakikes-areru-node. Amaoto-to **seijaku**-ga kokochi ii-desu.

雨が好きです。普段聴こえる雑音、生活音などが欠き消されるので。雨音と静寂が心地いいです。

"I like rain. Because it erases noises and other sounds in our daily life. The sound of rain and **the silence** are pleasant." (mle*****san 2010)

(25) Ōmisoka-no onsen'yado-ga kōmo **shizuka-na** mono-da-to-wa. Hubuki-no gōgō-to iu oto-ga nanimokamo nomi-konde-iru sei-darō-ka. Tokiori kaze-ga tsuyoku mado-garasu-o uchi, buruburu-to huruw-asete-ita.

大晦日の温泉宿が、こうも静かなものだとは。吹雪のごうごうという音が何もかも飲み込んでいるせいだろうか。時折風が強く窓ガラスを打ち、ブルブルと震わせていた。

"(I never imagined that) an Onsen spa on the New Year's Eve could be this **quiet**! I wonder if it is because the howling sound of the blizzard has swallowed everything. Occasionally the wind pounded the glass windows, making them shudder noisily."

(*Amakara Karutetto* by Asako Yuzuki, 212)

Water of various sorts—river, creek, ocean, rainfall—and rustling leaves as well as the wind in these examples indeed emit a degree of sound that is audible to the human ear with very little effort. These are sounds that can signify the presence of, and sometimes actively create, silence in the atmosphere. As is the case with the previous two categories, their sound levels (i.e., the loudness) vary, but even sounds on the loud side maintain a perfectly symbiotic, rather than opposing, relation with silence in the portrayals of a variety of scenes.

The description of silence in (17) is reminiscent of (13) in that what precedes *seijaku* "silence" specifies it by way of a relative clause.

(17) Yoru-wa nami-no oto-dake-ga kikoeru **seijaku**-ga atari-o tsutsumi-komu.

夜は波の音だけが聞こえる静寂が辺りを包み込む。

"At night, the area is enveloped by **silence** in which you can hear only sounds of waves." (Walkerplus 2018)

Of many ambient scenes that can be referred to as *seijaku*, the exact "strain" of silence that is detailed here is one in which no other sounds than ocean waves are heard at night. The sole sound mentioned in this depiction is a necessary and important facet in characterizing the exact type of silence. (18) informs us that the setting is utterly quiet by repeatedly using different words:

the adjective *shizuka* "quiet," the noun *shizukesa* "quietness," which is additionally modified by the intensifier *amari-no* "overly, excessively," and the mimetic word of silence, *shin-to*.

(18) Hanashi-ga togireta. **Shizuka**-datta. **Shin**-to shite, <u>konoha-ga kasakasa-to yureru oto</u>-shika shinai. Amari-no **shizukesa**-ni uttori-shite-shimau.

話が途切れた。**静か**だった。**しん**として、<u>木の葉がかさかさと揺れる音</u>しかしない。あまりの**静けさ**にうっとりしてしまう。

"The conversation broke. It was **quiet**. It's **silent** and <u>rustling leaves</u> are all we can hear. I get mesmerized by **the sheer silence**."

(*Ōdubon-no Inori* by Kotaro Isaka;
https://hyogen.info/content/242575515)

The reference to the rustling sounds from leaves cooccurs with the onomatopoeic word *kasakasa-to* to mimic them, and yet the sounds are in perfect unity with all the words that describe the silent scene. The rustling sounds are treated not as an exemption to but as part of what is perceived as silence. In addition, the sheer silent setting that immerses the sounds of rustling leaves is the source of a mesmerizing feeling. It is the common undertone that recurs with descriptions of ambient silence that coexists with nature sounds. Recall that included in similar undertones are reverence and veneration, as is exemplified in (19).

(19) <u>Ōame</u>-ga hutte-iru toki-no **seijaku**-no naka, atashi-wa katsute hashiru uma-o mita.

<u>大雨</u>が降っている時の**静寂**の中、あたしはかつて走る馬を見た。

"In **the silence** during <u>a heavy rain</u>, I once saw a horse running."
(*Mitsubachi-to Enrai* by Riku Onda, 401)

As I explained in chapter 1, the context of this sentence identifies as awe the emotional reaction to an image of a horse running in the silence during the heavy rain: "I was surprised how insignificant I am as soon as I have realized that the world is filled with unspeakably beautiful things that are not known to me or to anybody" (pp. 401–402; my translation, NT). A heavy rain indisputably produces more than a gentle noise, but the silence described in (19) is perceived internal to the rainfall and is far deeper than the sort of silence determined by auditory measures. Such an internal feeling corresponds to the range of undertones beneath various depictions of silence by nature sounds, and the discourse around (19) helps to magnify the sense of awe or reverence toward beauty that fills a larger universe.

The examples in (20–21) are similar to some of the earlier examples in which insect sounds serve as active agents of silence.

(20) Chorochoro-to sasayaka-na <u>mizu-no oto</u>-ga **shizukesa**-o kiwadatete-imasu.

チョロチョロとささやかな<u>水の音</u>が**静けさ**を際立てています。

"The gentle <u>trickling sound of water</u> is making **the silence** more striking."
(Japan Federation of Landscape Contractors, n.d.)

(21) Dokoka-de <u>uguisu</u>-ga naite-iru, mimi-o sumasu-to <u>iroiro-na toritachi-no koe</u>-ga kikoete-kuru. Kono hūkei-no naka-de-wa, <u>sono koe</u>-mo, <u>seseragi-no oto</u>-mo, **seijaku**-o iya-masu-dake-no mono-to naru.

どこかで<u>鶯</u>が鳴いている、耳を澄ますと<u>色々な鳥たちの声</u>が聞こえて来る。この風景の中では、<u>その声</u>も、<u>せせらぎの音</u>も、**静寂**を弥増すだけのものとなる。

"<u>A bush warbler</u> is singing somewhere; upon listening intently, <u>sounds of various birds</u> reach our ears. In this scenery, <u>the sounds of those birds and of the stream</u> simply increase **the silence**." (Nozarashi, n.d.)

Like previous examples, the gently trickling water (in a garden) in (20), the stream, and the sounds from many species of birds in (21) are not simply foregrounded in quiet settings. In addition, they are in force in their role as dynamically painting a soundscape called silence. The description in (20) has appeared in a website that promotes gardening. As the last line of the narrative asserts, quoted in (26) below, sound in a garden and silence in a garden are parallel and interdependent. Pleasure resides in the equation of the two. It confirms that calming natural sounds are quintessential symbols for silence.

(26) Niwa-no oto-o tanoshimu-to iu koto-wa, niwa-no shizukesa-o tanoshimu koto-na-no desu.

庭の音を楽しむということは、庭の静けさを楽しむことなのです。

"Enjoying the sounds in a garden means enjoying the silence in a garden."
(Japan Federation of Landscape Contractors, n.d.)

Equations of nature sounds and silence are more robustly espoused in (22–23). The depictions in (22–23) refer not only to water (e.g., brooks and rain) but to a laundry list of nature sounds that have been discussed thus far.

(22) Yama-ni mukau-to kikoete-kuru <u>kaze-no oto</u>, <u>kawa-no seseragi</u>-ya <u>amaoto</u>, <u>mushi-no ne</u>-ni <u>tori-no koe</u>. Sono **seijaku**-to iu oto-o motomete, yama-ya shizen-ni mukau hito-mo sukunaku-nai-darō.

山に向かうと聞こえてくる<u>風の音</u>、<u>川のせせらぎ</u>や<u>雨音</u>、<u>虫の音</u>に<u>鳥の声</u>。その**静寂**という音を求めて、山や自然に向かう人も少なくないだろう。

"Upon embarking for the mountain, I hear <u>the sound of the wind</u>, <u>the murmuring of the brook</u> and <u>the sound of rain</u>, <u>the insect's singing</u> and <u>the bird's chirping</u>. Not a few seem to be headed toward the mountain and nature in search of the very sound called **silence**."

(Yamap Editorial Department 2018)

(23) Koko-ni aru-no-wa daishizen-to **shizukesa**-dake—hoka-ni-wa nanimo arimasen

Midori hukaki sankan-ni tatazumu hoshigaokasansō-ni kaze-to tomo-ni todoku-no-wa, oto-naki oto.

Shiki oriori-no iro-ni somaru keshiki-no naka, <u>kawa-no seseragi</u>, <u>mushi-no koe</u>, <u>tori-no saezuri</u>-ni, <u>kigi-no zawameki</u>.

ここにあるのは大自然と**静け**さだけ—他には何もありません

緑深き山間に佇む星ヶ岡山荘に風と共に届くのは、音なき音。

四季折々の色に染まる景色の中、<u>川のせせらぎ</u>、<u>虫の声</u>、<u>鳥のさえずり</u>に、<u>木々のざわめき</u>。

"There exist only Mother Nature and **silence**—there is nothing else //

It is soundless sound that reaches Hoshigaoka Inn, which stands in the green mountains.

<u>The murmuring of a river</u>, <u>voices of insects</u>, <u>birdsongs</u>, and <u>the rustling of trees</u> in the scenery that tinges with seasonal colors."

(Hoshigaoka Sanso, n.d.)

Strikingly, both passages call the collection of these sounds in nature under the rubric of *seijaku-to iu oto* "the sound called silence" in (22) and *oto-naki-oto* "soundless sound" at the end of the second line in (23). The demonstrative *sono* "that/those" that modifies *seijaku-to iu oto* in (22) refers back to all the sounds listed in the sentence immediately preceding it, making clear the treatment of those nature sounds as active existence in the silent setting. The first line in (23) asserts Mother Nature and silence as unique presence, even further emphasizing it by repeating "there is nothing else." The phrase at the end of the second line, *oto-naki oto* "soundless sound," points to all the nature sounds listed in the last sentence. These nature sounds are audible but relationally silent; conversely, silence consists of tangible sounds in nature. It all appears completely paradoxical and yet perfectly consistent with the recurring pattern of illustrating ambient silence. The codependent descriptions of sound and silence in (22–23) eloquently convey the symbiosis of the two. A sense of relaxation and restoration of serenity that the mutual relation of sound and silence brings out is made clear by the contexts in which these passages appear. (22) is an excerpt from a trailer of an English-language documentary film, *In Pursuit of Silence* (2015, directed by Patrick Shen), which has been translated into Japanese with an added sub-title: *seijaku-o motomete: iyashi-no sairensu* "in pursuit of silence: silence as antidote."[1] The publicity for the film further inserts an advertising phrase, *noizu-ni kakomareta gendai-o ikiru watashitati-e-no "seijaku"-to iu shohōsen* "a prescription called 'silence' for those of us who live the modern noise-filled time." So, *seijaku-to iu oto* "the sound called silence" in (22) is entrenched with a cluster of sounds in nature and stands for a source of the healing agent that people yearn for. (23) is an advertisement of a local hot-springs spot, Hoshigaoka Inn. Focusing on the natural environment around the Inn, its marketing strategy is to commoditize the therapeutic calmness that nature sounds, namely, *oto-naki oto* "soundless sound," are expected to induce in our mind.

Finally in (24–25) the sounds of rain and of a blizzard generate the sense of tranquility by overriding other kinds of sound.

(24) Ame-ga suki-desu. Hudan kikoeru zatsuon, seikatsuon-nado-ga kakikesareru-node. <u>Amaoto</u>-to **seijaku**-ga kokochi ii-desu.

雨が好きです。普段聴こえる雑音、生活音などが欠き消されるので。<u>雨音</u>と**静寂**が心地いいです。

"I like rain. Because it erases noises and other sounds in our daily life. <u>The sound of rain</u> and **the silence** are pleasant."　　　　(mle*****san 2010)

(25) Ōmisoka-no onsen'yado-ga kōmo **shizuka-na** mono-da-to-wa. <u>Hubuki</u>-no gōgō-to iu oto-ga nanimokamo nomi-konde-iru sei-darō-ka. Tokiori <u>kaze</u>-ga tsuyoku mado-garasu-o uchi, buruburu-to huruw-asete-ita.

大晦日の温泉宿が、こうも**静かな**ものだとは。<u>吹雪</u>のごうごうという音が何もかも飲み込んでいるせいだろうか。時折<u>風</u>が強く窓ガラスを打ち、ブルブルと震わせていた。

"(I never imagined that) an Onsen spa on the New Year's Eve could be this **quiet**! I wonder if it is because <u>the howling sound of the blizzard</u> has swallowed everything. Occasionally <u>the wind</u> pounded the glass windows, making them shudder noisily."

(*Amakara Karutetto* by Asako Yuzuki, 212)

It is stated in (24) that the sound of a rainfall drowns out various—especially man-made—noises that surround us in our daily life. The word *seijaku* "silence" in the last sentence of (24) refers to the calmness arising from the masking force that the sound of rain elicits. It is concluded that the sound of a rainfall and silence are treated as coexistent and together bring a pleasant and comfortable feeling to the writer. A similar expression of the overriding effect is observed in (25): the writer wonders if the exceedingly quiet atmosphere in a hot springs inn has been caused by the blizzard that swallows and erases other sounds. Of apparent contradiction is the use of onomatopoeia, *gōgō*, to depict the howling sound made by the snowstorm. In addition to the howling of the blizzard, furthermore, the sound of a strong wind hitting glass windows is heard along with their visible tremors, which are also depicted by the mimetic *buruburu*. Altogether, the actual auditory level of the scene must not be subtle, and yet these sounds originating from nature are perceived not as disturbing noises but as a source of a peaceful mind and tranquility under the term of *shizuka* "quiet." By comparison, a passage in Isabel Allende's novel *In the Midst of Winter*—translated from Spanish to English—paints a blizzard scene very similar to that in (25), with a sharply contrastive rhetorical manner and associated nuances: "[t]he wind blew in gusts, rising and falling as if weary with the effort, then moments later stirring up swirls of loose snow. When it died down, complete silence reigned, a threatening stillness" (p. 117). In this portrayal, silence and stillness arrive subsequently after the snow accompanied by the gusty wind has tapered down, rather than concomitantly.

Before leaving this subsection, I wish to include the example in (27) as an illustration of silence portrayed by what appears to be a strongly incompatible reference to sound and silence.

(27) Kono midori-no naka, **shizuka-na** umibe, ao-zora. **Oto-ga shinai**. Kasuka-na tsubuyaki-no yō-na <u>shizen-no koe</u>-ga anmari ōsugite, **muon**-da.

この緑の中、**静かな**海辺、青空。**音がしない**。かすかなつぶやきのような<u>自然の声</u>があんまり多すぎて**無音**だ。

"In this green, **quiet** seaside, blue sky. There is **no sound**. There are so many <u>nature voices</u> like faint muttering that there is absolutely **no sound**."

(*Amurita* by Banana Yoshimoto; https://hyogen.info/content/321628545)

Close attention should be paid to three expressions that describe silence here, indicated by boldface: *shizuka-na* "quiet," *oto-ga shinai* "there is no sound," and *muon* "no sound" (無音 "void-sound"). Of these, the second declares no sound, literally saying there is no sound; and the third, *muon-da* "there is no sound," is said to be a consequence of too many nature sounds. Nature sounds are not individually named in (27), but collectively they are considered outside of *oto* "sound," as *muon* 無音 "void-sound" indicates. The silence in (27) is verbally referred to as "no sound, sound void," and nature sounds are described to be completely encircled in that void. A relevant boundary seems to be drawn between man-made sounds and nature sounds: the one outside of silence, the other embedded in it. This dichotomy seems to strongly remind us that the concept of silence cannot be effectively constructed without considering how sound is understood.

1.2 Conceptualization of Silence in Japanese

To deepen our understanding of the instrumental role that nature sounds play in descriptions of ambient silence, I shall take a closer look at the concept of silence underlying the linguistic representations. Japanese words and phrases that can be considered rough equivalents of "silence" include *seijaku*, *shizukesa*, *muon*, and *oto-ga shinai*, among others. They exhibit connotative ranges just as English words like *silent*, *quiet*, *hushed*, *tranquil*, *still*, and *noiseless* manifest. These Japanese vocabulary items mean the absence, dearth, or suppression of sound, and this clearly forms a conceptual basis of what we generally recognize as silence. But at the same time, the recurring pattern observed with the samples we have seen in (1–27) somewhat diverges from it and is better characterized as hushed tranquility in the surroundings. As the examples illustrate, hushed tranquility admits certain types of sound, a variety of sounds existing in nature and crucially in contrast with man-made sounds. Of further import is that hushed tranquility gives rise to a critical psychological impact on us as emotional antidote. It is my conjecture that ambient hushed tranquility, instantiated in (1–27), is a well-acknowledged and valued concept that appeals to the Japanese people for verbal descriptions of silent scenes.

Ambient hushed tranquility created or enhanced by nature sounds in our examples accompanies undertones like serenity, calmness, and reverence, uniformly generating the contexts in which Japanese-speaking listeners and readers are to be brought into a comforting, meditative state of peacefulness. All our samples are at least implicit in this respect, while some are explicit about the tranquil state of mind that results from the symbiotic relation between silence and nature sounds. For example, in (11), the silence in which nature sounds participate is described to help us calm down and restore a clear mind; and (12–13) uniformly use the language related to (spiritual) healing, *iyasu*, in explaining the type of impact the tranquility has on people. The line in (13), repeated below, is used in an online service for music of diverse genres including insects' sounds that are considered to be pleasant to the listeners' ears.

(13) Mushi-no neiro-ga tsukuri-dasu shinshin-to shita yoru-no **seijaku**-ga anata-o kokochi yoi iyashi-e sasoimasu.

虫の音色が創り出すシンシンとした夜の**静寂**があなたを心地よい癒しへ誘います。

"The deep **silence** at night created by the tones of insects invites you into pleasant serenity." (music.usen.com, n.d.)

The sounds of insects immersed in silent surroundings are likened to musical tunes that invite the listeners to the world of "pleasant serenity." It is additionally commented in the website that the insects' sounds referred to in (13) are suggested background music to induce sleep. (18) is an excerpt from a novel.

(18) Hanashi-ga togireta. **Shizuka**-datta. **Shin**-to shite, konoha-ga kasakasa-to yureru oto-shika shinai. Amari-no **shizukesa**-ni uttori-shite-shimau.

話が途切れた。**静か**だった。**しん**として、木の葉がかさかさと揺れる音しかしない。あまりの**静けさ**にうっとりしてしまう。

"The conversation broke. It was **quiet**. It's **silent** and rustling leaves are all we can hear. I get mesmerized by **the sheer silence**."
(*Ōdubon-no Inori* by Kotaro Isaka; https://hyogen.info/content/242575515)

Expressions of quietness, *shizuka* "silent, quiet" and *shizukesa* "silence, quietness," are repeated in the text, and the tranquil atmosphere is orchestrated by the sole sound made by rustling leaves. It is important to recognize that the sound of rustling leaves totally partakes in the mesmerizing silence, rather than being treated as a separate entity. As mentioned earlier, (20) and (26) appear in the same website for a gardening organization.

(20) Chorochoro-to sasayaka-na mizu-no oto-ga **shizukesa**-o kiwadatete-imasu.

チョロチョロとささやかな水の音が**静けさ**を際立てています。

"The gentle trickling sound of water is making **the silence** more striking."
(Japan Federation of Landscape Contractors, n.d.)

(26) Niwa-no oto-o tanoshimu-to iu koto-wa, niwa-no shizukesa-o tanoshimu koto-na-no desu.

庭の音を楽しむということは、庭の静けさを楽しむことなのです。

"Enjoying the sounds in a garden means enjoying the silence in a garden."
(Ibid.)

(20) is the first sentence and (26) appears at the end of the narrative that speaks to the pleasure and beauty of a general scenery that features a traditional garden. Thus, the nature sounds instantiated in (1–27) serve as agency of emanating serenity in people's minds. It should be reminded, furthermore, that the affective range that nature sounds evoke with silent settings is not

limited to a refreshing, energizing, or even "sunny" kind of comfort. Instead, it includes a calm but sorrowful or melancholic frame of mind, as is demonstrated by the sentiment articulated in (5).

(5) Usu-gurai shin'yōju-no mori-no naka-kara <u>ruribitaki-no mono-ganashii tanchō-na koe</u>-ga kikoete-kuru-to, mori-no **shizukesa**-ga yori kyōchō-sarete-kuru-yō desu.

薄暗い針葉樹の森の中から<u>ルリビタキのもの悲しい短調な声</u>が聞こえてくると、森の**静けさ**がより強調されてくるようです。

"When <u>the Siberian bluechat's sound of a sad minor key</u> is heard in a dusky coniferous forest, **the silence** in the woods seems to become more accented."　　　　　　　　(Nikko Kirihurikogen Kisugedairaenchi, n.d.)

The sound of a Siberian bluechat in (5) is described as *mono-ganashii* "sad, melancholic" and *tanchō-na* "of a minor key (in music)" and viewed to accent the silence in the woods, while inducing, say, an introverted and introspective sort of calmness. Similarly, as I have explained earlier, the undertone in (19) may be likened to reverential and awed feelings toward nature or a space that transcends our imagination. The nuances underlying (25) and (27) fall under the same affective range.

(19) <u>Ōame</u>-ga hutte-iru toki-no **seijaku**-no naka, atashi-wa katsute hashiru uma-o mita.

<u>大雨</u>が降っている時の**静寂**の中、あたしはかつて走る馬を見た。

"In **the silence** during <u>a heavy rain</u>, I once saw a horse running."
(*Mitsubachi-to Enrai* by Riku Onda, 401)

(25) Ōmisoka-no onsen'yado-ga kōmo **shizuka-na** mono-da-to-wa. <u>Hubuki</u>-no gōgō-to iu oto-ga nanimokamo nomi-konde-iru sei-darō-ka. Tokiori <u>kaze</u>-ga tsuyoku mado-garasu-o uchi, buruburu-to huruw-asete-ita.

大晦日の温泉宿が、こうも**静かな**ものだとは。<u>吹雪のごうごうという音</u>が何もかも飲み込んでいるせいだろうか。時折<u>風</u>が強く窓ガラスを打ち、ブルブルと震わせていた。

"(I never imagined that) an Onsen spa on the New Year's Eve could be this **quiet**! I wonder if it is because <u>the howling sound of the blizzard</u> has swallowed everything. Occasionally <u>the wind</u> pounded the glass windows, making them shudder noisily."
(*Amakara Karutetto* by Asako Yuzuki, 212)

(27) Kono midori-no naka, **shizuka-na** umibe, ao-zora. **Oto-ga shinai**. Kasuka-na tsubuyaki-no yō-na <u>shizen-no koe</u>-ga anmari ōsugite, **muon**-da.

この緑の中、**静かな**海辺、青空。**音がしない**。かすかなつぶやきのような<u>自然の声</u>があんまり多すぎて**無音**だ。

"In this green, **quiet** seaside, blue sky. There is **no sound**. There are so many <u>nature voices</u> like faint muttering that there is absolutely **no sound**."
(*Amurita* by Banana Yoshimoto; https://hyogen.info/content/321628545)

A constellation of nature sounds generates ambient hushed tranquility, and crucially the coexistence of sound and silence leaves a narrow but focused array of psychological impressions on us. In the Japanese sample depictions of ambient silence, the causal chain is explicitly articulated in some and implicitly in others. Beyond those verbal portrayals of silent scenes, we also find comparable conceptualizing paths elucidated in insightful cultural commentaries in Japanese that allude to the pivotal relationship between silence and sound. Let us now turn our focus to them. Textual analyses of such observations and reflections by native speakers are helpful not just for a better understanding of the conceptualizing process germane to silence. As we shall investigate later in this chapter (section 1.3), they also confirm the broader extent to which similar paths are shared in evaluating the notion of silence embodied in cultural artifacts like music and paintings. Forming a mutual thread, they attest to individuations of common conceptual practices. In the discussions of the numbered examples below, I refrain from providing their Romanized transliterations because the focus will be placed more on what each text says (i.e., the content) than on how it is said (i.e., linguistic and rhetorical means). Translations are mine.

To begin, the range of nuances that sounds in nature express might be looked at in terms of the figure-ground frame, i.e., the circumstances under which we hear certain sounds that are only in the background. It is widely understood that we usually take very little or no notice of the type of sounds in nature we have been discussing. In most parts of our daily lives, they often do not reach a perceptible level in our consciousness. They only obliquely exist in the background. However, it could also be viewed that when our mind gains utmost tranquility, while leaving all worldly things behind, we come to be instinctively aware of secondary sounds that are otherwise not at a tangible level. That is, having a peaceful mind can predispose us to be sensitive to nature sounds and the like. Once our mind is at such a serene state, the sounds that were formerly secondary are now foregrounded by the force of silence. The interdependence of our auditory sensitivity to subtle sounds and the state of mind receptive to them is noted by Takahashi (2004, 273–74) from a viewpoint of a musician (pianist).

(28) 見えにくいものに眼をこらし、ききとりにくい音に耳を澄ますとき、心が澄んでいるのに気づく。

"When we fix our eyes on something hard to see or listen intently to something hard to hear, we notice that our mind is clear."

Interestingly, Takahashi's remark on the state of mind being relevant to our hearing extends to its interaction with vision. Then, we may view more generally that a sense of calmness or purity in mind can be a concept that serves as an integral force for capturing an essence of a void in our senses. Whether or not peacefulness in the human mind is interpreted as a cause or a consequence of the perceptive level of background sounds in nature, the very presence of such sounds is indispensable to appraising the process in which silence is conceptualized. We may perhaps even say that those nature sounds play a significant role as sounds of silence in illuminating the essential nature of the relationship between the two seemingly contradictory notions.

Japanese people's interpretation of the relationship between nature sounds and silence is further articulated by the Web advertisement for a record player in (29). It should be remembered that sounds in nature are often likened to music in our earlier examples. (29) presents another instance of that analogy, as is reflected by the word *ongaku* (音楽) "music."

(29) 物音1つしない静けさの中から耳を澄ませば、やがて気づき始める小鳥のさえずりや風になびく木々のざわめき。鈴虫やコオロギ、オケラの鳴き声すら日本人は音楽として捉えていると言われています。

"When we strain our ears in soundless silence, we soon start to notice birdsongs and sounds of trees rustling in the wind. Japanese people are known to perceive as music even the sounds of *suzumushi* [bell crickets], *kōrogi* [crickets; grylloidea], and *okera* [mole crickets]."

(Yoshino Trading, n.d.)

The important role that nature sounds play in our conception of silence is additionally reinforced by a commentary from Muneo Sato in relation to the tea ceremony.[2] In it he notes that various nature sounds that we have been discussing thus far guide us to a keener awareness of silence, which ultimately has the healing effect on us. Such an experience we have reminds us that silence shapes deeply revered concepts within Japanese culture. These characterizations of silence clearly separate silence as ambient hushed tranquility from silence as absence, dearth, or suppression of sound in the surroundings. Auditory void alone does not make us come to the realization or the awareness of silence, but rather, the absence of sounds is brought to consciousness almost in tandem with small auditory stimuli. Importantly, those small sounds in nature must intrinsically evoke pivotal images—broadly conceived rather than limited to vision-related—that are connected to serenity and peacefulness. As noted above and also in the previous section, the evoked images are frequently associated with musical tunes, melodies, and harmonies that are pleasant and soothing to our ears and soul. In this sense, what seem to be minor and insignificant sounds in nature serve as an internal factor critical to conceptualizing silence. The absence of man-made sounds as an external factor and the presence of small audible stimuli as an internal agency coalesce into a sense of tranquility necessary for generating peace of mind. This is why the two elements are complementary and indispensable to each other.

The range of nature sounds that silence welcomes are contrastive with man-made sounds or auditory void that is synthetically created by humans. An essay on a personal blog articulates that difference, reiterating the role of nature sounds in leading to a serene mind.[3] In comparison with man-made sounds and artificially created silence (i.e., presumably the kind produced in a sound-proof room), the writer explains, nature sounds exist without an effort to be heard, and it is such a departure from artificial intentions that gives them a significant advantage. It is also notable that silence here refers not only to ambient silence but to silence inside ourselves, i.e., abstract silent space with a deeper, spiritual meaning. The blog writer goes so far as to affirm that the way of viewing, interpreting, and appreciating nature sounds, silent atmosphere, and calmness in mind as an interwoven conceptual sequence is part of cultural practices that have been lodged and fostered as a Japanese tradition.

This last point, i.e., that natural sounds' relevance to conceptualizing silence in the Japanese context mirrors spiritual and aesthetic values that are appreciated in the society, should lead us to consider what sound means to the society in which we are embedded. The following quotation from Padden (1988, 93) that was mentioned in chapter 1 reminds us of the point of departure that motivated me to pursue this question.

> The fact that different cultures organize sound in different ways shows that sound does not have an inherent meaning but can be given a myriad of interpretations and selections. . . . In any discussion of Deaf people's knowledge of sound, *it is important to keep in mind that perception of sound is not automatic or straightforward, but is shaped through learned, culturally defined practices.* It is as important to know the specific and special meaning of a given sound as it is to hear sound. (emphasis added, NT)

Indeed, nuanced meanings of silence that nature sounds define in Japanese are not uniformly transparent to members of different cultures. Remarks on cultural differences concerning how nature sounds are interpreted in the context of ambient silence are commonly made and anecdotally acknowledged. My personal story introduced in chapter 1 is part of such discourse. A blogger also speaks of the Japanese people's sensitivity to insects' sounds, which seems foreign to many people from other cultures.[4] The stance underlying the blogger's observation is that the same insect sounds could be understood in one culture as a nuisance that breaks silence, whereas it could convey a contrastively positive spiritual meaning to the members of another culture. The root of the distinct contrast signified by these remarks resides in potentially diverse paths that each culture takes in tailoring presumed concepts like silence into more nuanced interpretations.

Our understanding of the susceptibility to sound and its harmonious relationship with silence in the Japanese language and culture may be deepened by further considering the place of nature in the conceptualizing process. The above-mentioned remarks as well as our examples describing ambient silence explicitly and implicitly point to the interdependence of sound, silence, and nature. The significance of nature as a component integral to grasping the conceptualization process of silence in the Japanese context is touched on by Horikiri's (2006) commentary on Matsuo Basho's famous haiku in (16). I will return to it again in the next subsection, but I cite Horikiri's thought here as a starting point since it provides a general insight that introduces the relevance of nature to the concept of silence.

(30) In the Zen master Dogen's teachings there is the phrase "body and mind drop off" (*shinjin datsuraku*), which means breaking through the shell of body, mind, and ego, and achieving a state of mind that accepts things just as they are. This is what the verse "silence" (*shizukasa ya*) is all about; it is not simply a depiction of silence per se. I believe that it is an expression of a state of mind in which nature and the mind become one. (Horikiri 2006, 164)

In Horikiri's assessment the concept of silence, which is linguistically represented by the word *shizukasa/shizukesa* "silence," carries a deeper meaning of spiritual importance: silence, instantiated by Basho's haiku piece, depicts a state of mind rid of worldly things that enables one to appreciate "things just as they are." Horikiri's account puts substantial weight on nature and on the ways to achieve unity with it. A similar line of reasoning is recurrent that gives credence to the importance and high value of nature. Yamaori (2004), for one, attempts to elucidate the cultural underpinnings of the reciprocity among sound, silence, and nature in a broader and more general context like those illustrated in (31–34).

(31) 風がさっと吹いて梢を揺らす音に、「ああ、秋だ」と感じる。小鳥の鳴き声に、「ああ、春が来た」と思う。日本人は自然山野の音に敏感な文化を育んできた民族であるのは確かでしょう。そして、この日本人の音に関していえば、重要なのは、きっと自然です。

"Upon hearing the sound of the wind shaking the treetop we feel 'Oh, it's autumn.' Birdsongs lead us to think 'Oh, the spring has come.' Japan is certainly a nation that has fostered the sensitivity to the sounds of nature and wilderness. And, it must be nature that is critical to the Japanese sense of sound." (Yamaori 2004, 19)

(32) 日本人の音の敏感さには、あくまでその基本に自然がある。

"Nature is the absolute foundation of Japanese people's sensitivity to sound." (Ibid., 24)

(33) もしかすると大切なのは音ではなく静寂なのかもしれない。

"Perhaps, it may be silence rather than sound that is important." (Ibid.)

(34) そう、音に敏感であるためには、沈黙や静けさが大切だったんですよ。静かなる自然、物言わぬ自然だからこそ、人々はそこに音を聞こうとした。対話しようとした。対話が成立しない自然だったからこそ、豊かな自然が発する多様な音に敏感になった。

"Yes, silence and stillness were important in order to be sensitive to sound. People tried to listen to sounds in nature simply because nature is silent and does not speak. They tried to have a conversation [with nature]. They could not communicate with nature; this is how they have come to be sensitive to various sounds that rich nature produces." (Ibid.)

While another essay by Yamaori—not quoted here—bears religious (Buddhist) undertones, his thoughts expressed above are neutrally understood that nature is personified as a spiritual agent whose messages are sought out by the people. The habitual practice of observing and appreciating the static and the dynamic under nature's control is carried out and enriched through the medium of numerous sounds that belong to nature.

Some sounds in the environment are confined to regional areas that accordingly have even more specific meanings to the local people. One such case is illustrated by the passage in (35), where Torigoe (2004) insightfully articulates the profound interdependence that sound and silence hold; and the people's predisposition to it acts as a cultural practice, however unconscious it may be.

(35) 反対している人たちが求めているのは、静けさです。静けさというのは、ただ音がないのではありません。静かだからこそ、その土地の生きた環境の音がいろいろと聞こえてくる。静けさが支え

ているそれぞれの土地の気配があり、そこにいろいろな文化が発生してくる。高尾山も、そういう豊かな静けさがあるからこそ修験の地、信仰の地になったのだろうと思います。

> "It is silence that the opponents are seeking. Silence is not simply the absence of sound. Living sounds of the environment in the region reach our senses exactly because it is quiet. There are signs in each individual region that are maintained by silence, where various cultures emerge. I think it is for such enriched silence that Mt. Takao has come to be a place of mountaineering asceticism and a place of faith."   (Torigoe 2004, 30)

The background of (35) is Mt. Takao, located on the outskirts of Tokyo, where a plan for an underground expressway has met with opposition. Torigoe's characterization of the resistance mentioned in this passage underscores the cultural underpinning of what is conceived of as silence. A variety of natural sounds living in the quiet and tranquil environment reflects distinctive features that shape a unique local culture. Underlying the silence in this context, then, is not only the sense of serenity that is evoked by familiar sounds in nature but additional appreciation for new narrowly identified cultural manifestations that those sounds represent.

The sensitivity and sensibility to the scope of these sounds and the silence identified with and by them does not simply mirror the linguistic pattern that we have observed. It also reflects a cultural pattern that looks at sound and silence coextensively and finds deep meaning that their synchronization generates. The sentiments underlying the observations and statements cited above speak uniformly to the tight-knitted relationship among sound, silence, and nature; and together, they ultimately have significant bearings to non-material values. Their relationship sheds light on the way in which each of the three (i.e., sound, silence, and nature) participates in the conceptualizing process of the other(s). And, without a full comprehension of the conceptual workings, the linguistic and rhetorical expressions of our sample will remain anomalous and beg for reasonable explanations as to why sound and silence can be expressed simultaneously and so coherently.

Audible sounds are viewed as incompatible with silence in many cultures. As previously noted, sounds that disrupt silence are typically human voices and man-made objects that have direct connections with people. The passages in (36–38) below, for instance, draw a clear line between sounds that exist in nature and man-made sounds in their relation to the concept of silence.

(36) Kyūni <u>bannin-tachi-no dosei-ga shizukesa-o yaburi</u>, ikuninka-no danjo-ga, rōmon-kara uchiniwa-ni oitate-rareru ranzatsu-na ashioto-ga kikoeta-kara-de aru.

急に番人たちの怒声が静けさを破り、幾人かの男女が、牢門から内庭に追い立てられる乱雑な足音が聞こえたからである。

"Suddenly the silence was broken by the angry barking voices of the guards, and he could hear the confused scuffling of several men and women being dragged out from the prison gate into the courtyard.
(*Chinmoku* by Shusaku Endo, 162; translated by William Johnston, 171)

In (36) the human voices, especially loaded with angry emotions, break silence. Additionally, *ranzatsu-na ashioto*, here professionally translated as "the confused scuffling of men and women," literally means "disorderly footsteps," which suggests that the disturbing noise emerges from a human commotion. Obviously, neither angry yelling nor disharmonious footsteps would create a sense of comfort or peacefulness. The distinction in sound sources is unmistakably made in (37).

(37) Tokidoki, yane-no ue-ni ki-no mi-ga ochi-tari, shōdōbutsu-ga kake-mawaru oto igai-ni terebi-nado-no zatsuon-wa issai naku, mattaku shizuka-na mori-no naka-no bessō-ni-wa, ōkina danro-ga arimasita.

時々、屋根の上に木の実が落ちたり、小動物が駆け回る音以外にテレビなどの雑音は一切なく、全く静かな森の中の別荘には、大きな暖炉がありました。

"There was a big fireplace at the villa in the utterly quiet woods; there was absolutely no noise like the sounds from the TV except for those made by the nuts occasionally falling on the roof and by small animals running around." (Hosoya 2015, 99)

The nature-oriented noises coming from falling nuts and small playful animals do not break silence but are spontaneously absorbed in it. What does break silence, in contrast, are sounds and voices originating from the TV and similar man-made objects that symbolize people or are a surrogate for people. In this passage (37), *zatsuon* (雑音) "noise" in the phrase *terebi-nado-no zatsuon* "noise like the sounds from TV (and the like)" is a Sino-Japanese compound that literally means rough-sound. When they are in the background, the sounds from the TV are perceived only as "rough" and disturbing. In the description of the quiet atmosphere in (37), not only is the absence of disruptors like TV sounds affirmed, but the presence of small nature sounds additionally confirms the hushed state that leads to calmness in the environment and in one's mind. It is also notable that the scene surrounding the woods is described not simply as *shizuka-na* "quiet" but its degree is further intensified by the adverb *mattaku (shizuka-na)* "utterly, absolutely (quiet)." It seems that all these auditory depictions maximizing the silent and hence undisturbed state skillfully provide a rhetorically rich setting for a warm and pleasant portrayal of a villa with a large fireplace. A similar distinction is made in (38) between what is welcomed to silence and what is not.

> (38) Machi-wa shizuka-desu. <u>Baiku-ya kuruma-no enjin'on-mo, hito-no koe-mo shimasen.</u>
>
> Kaeru-to tori-no nakigoe, inu-no tōboe, kaze-ni yureru kigi-no oto-nomi.
>
> 街は静かです。バイクや車のエンジン音も、人の声もしません。カエルと鶏の鳴き声、犬の遠吠え、かぜにゆれる木々の音のみ。
>
> "The town is quiet. <u>There is no noise from motorbikes and cars; there is no human voice.</u> There are only sounds from frogs, chickens, barking dogs in a distance, and trees shook by the wind." (Kaji 2015)

Sounds made by frogs, chickens, dogs, and trees are smoothly blended in silence, while mechanical sounds and human voices disturb and override it. Particularly in these two examples, the sharp separation of the two types of sounds vis-à-vis silence, one as agency that leads to an affective sense of calmness and the other as a silence-breaker, perfectly illuminates their contrastive meanings relevant to constructing the concept of silence. At the same time, it is adeptly used to achieve descriptive efficacy.

I will later discuss some variability in the manner that nature sounds are perceived in relation to ambient silence. But, here I briefly touch on the role that cicada sounds—sounds that could be considered a silence-breaker—play in the haiku piece in (16). The example is repeated below.

> (16) Shizukasa-ya / iwa-ni shimi'iru / semi-no koe
>
> 閑さや岩にしみ入る蝉の声
>
> "**tranquility** / penetrating into rocks / <u>cicada's voice</u>" (Ogura 1977, 2)

As I briefly mentioned earlier, the cicada referred to in this well-known poem by Matsuo Basho has been rigorously debated in the literary forum, for example, by the poet Mokichi Saito and the literary critic Toyotaka Komiya in the 1920s. According to Toyama (1997), the debates revolved around, though not limited to, the specific species and the number of cicadas as well as the interpretation of the word *shizukasa* "stillness" at the beginning of the poem. First, it has been argued as to which species of cicadas Basho heard in writing the poem in (16). This question is motived by the consideration that some species of cicada would be too loud to be included in the poem that portrays the superbly quiet air surrounding a temple in the mountains. Specifically, central to the debate is the choice between the louder *aburazemi* "large brown cicadas," especially in the case of a plural number, and the quieter *nīnīzemi* "kaempfer cicadas." Despite rigorous exchanges on this issue, it appears to be a majority opinion that the type of cicadas in Basho's poem is the quieter one, consistent with the interpretation of the nature sound in the poem that cicada sounds are not a nuisance that would disturb the peacefulness in the surrounding.

Second, the word *shizukasa* for silence or stillness at the beginning of the poem can be written with either of the two Chinese characters: 閑 or 静. In the modern use of the word *shizuka* as is confirmed by contemporary dictionaries, either character can be used for the meaning although the latter seems more common. Basho's choice of the former character, 閑, for *shizukasa* has been interpreted to mean "quiet, peaceful," which seems to be a dominant position among scholars according to the summary Toyama provides. On the other hand, Toyama himself gives a slightly different interpretation that the selection of 閑 in (16) rather than 静 indicates that Basho tried to express a sense of *kanka* 閑暇 "leisure" (the first character is identical with *shizukasa* 閑さ "stillness" in the poem) that the poet experienced in the temple site while listening to loud cicada sounds. Toyama further gives his own interpretation of Basho's haiku in (16) as follows.

(39) Nanto-iu shizukasa-de arō. Sanagara iwa-ni shimi'iru-ka-no yō-na semi-no koe-wa, watashi-o setsunai-hodo-no seichō-na shinkyō-ni hiki-irete iku.

何という閑さであろう。さながら岩にしみ入るかのような蝉の声は、私を切ないほどの清澄な心境に引き入れて行く。

"What stillness! Like seeping into rocks, the cicada's voice takes me to a painfully clear/pure frame of mind."

(Toyama 1997, 8; my translation, NT)

While maintaining the loudness of the cicada sound, Toyama simultaneously asserts that the cicada's voice never disturbs the serenity of the poet's mind. He goes on to elaborate that just as the cicada's voice seems to seep into rocks, the quiet and still atmosphere around the temple permeates into the poet's inner self to create a sense of tranquility and solitude. Finally, Toyama emphasizes that the poem is not about describing the breathtaking milieu but about painting the poet's mental image. Toyama's commentary on Basho's haiku suggests that what is really at issue is not necessarily whether a certain sound is physically perceived as loud enough to disturb a quiet ambiance or soft enough to maintain it. The focus of attention should rather be on the role that the sound plays in shaping an individual's state of mind in a given time and space. Deep meaning that a sound can bring to our senses may well vary depending on the individual, generating different interpretations, but variability in individual sensibility is not only expected but also respected as part of aesthetic values. Especially in the traditional poetry forms like haiku and tanka, where a poet has to express himself within a very limited number of syllables, how a poem is interpreted and the way it is appreciated overall are largely left up to the reader. Although it is still possible even for a Japanese reader to view the poem in (16) to be incongruous, the mutual dependence between the cicada sound and the stillness of the temple scene is rhetorically well motivated for the poet's preferred way in expressing his state of enlightenment. And this is entirely coherent within the concept of silence. It is not the physical auditory quality of a cicada sound as such but instead the sound's affective impact on the poet that is of direct import to what is meant by silence. To that extent, the meaning of sound and the meaning of silence can be subjectively constructed even among the people embedded in the same culture. I will come back to this discussion in section 2 of this chapter.

An interesting consequence of the conceptualization of silence in the Japanese context that we have laid out thus far is that the representation of silence by way of the presence of nature-oriented sounds can extend even to imaginary sounds that do not exist in reality. This has been observed in poetry, especially in Basho's poems. According to Horikiri (1998, 301), Basho wrote several haiku poems that refer to sounds made by spiders and bagworms even though those insects are known to make no sound.[5] It is important to note, however, that these imaginary sounds by insects in Basho's poems are staged to create a silent and tranquil scene. Given the way in which silence is conceptualized, the symbolism established between the imaginary sounds and the serene atmosphere is straightforwardly interpreted and appreciated without additional rhetorically forced aids. Basho's ingenious use of fictional insect sounds indeed follows the same pattern of linguistic and rhetorical practices that is demonstrated in our samples under the analogous concept of silence.

Conflicts stemming from cultural preferences and differences in interpreting sounds vis-à-vis ambient silence have already been noted and illustrated (e.g., my personal anecdote, the commentary on cultural differences in interpreting insect sounds). Another example of the challenges that may arise from non-uniform concepts of silence is found in literary translations especially when the concept of silence has overlapping but non-identical meanings in target and source languages. Simultaneous juxtaposition of silence and sound as the Japanese samples represent may not readily be sustained in English, for instance. The comparison between the original Japanese and its English translation by a professional translator elucidates the difference. (40) is one such example.

(40) Hayashi-no hō-de semi-ga kareta koe-de naite-imashita. Atari-wa shizuka-deshita.

林のほうで蝉が嗄れた声で鳴いていました。あたりは静かでした。

"In the woods a cicada was singing hoarsely. <u>Everywhere else</u> was silent." (emphasis added, NT)

(*Chinmoku* by Shusaku Endo, 103; translated by William Johnston, 116)

The cicada's singing described by the first sentence of the Japanese original serves as an ambient sound that becomes part of the silence penetrating the surroundings. The silence is further confirmed by the second sentence, *Atari-wa shizuka-deshita* "It was quiet in the surrounding area." Of special note is that the area referred to as *atari* in the Japanese passage is understood to include "the woods" where the cicada is singing. That is, this passage in Japanese depicts only one whole area. For English speakers, the cicada's singing constitutes a full-fledged sound that is perceived to break silence, and it would lead to a contradiction to assert the presence of the cicada's singing in an environment that is described as silent. The English translation, thus, cannot identify the surroundings as being silent and simultaneously as being occupied by the insects' noise. This is why the second Japanese sentence in the original is necessarily translated into English as "Everywhere else was silent," separating one place with the insects' noise from another that lacks any type of audible sound. In the Japanese original, the woods and the location referred to as silent are captured within the identical range of sound perception; and importantly, a depiction of a scene that subsumes the cicada's singing uniquely as silent does not result in a paradox. This is why there is no sense of "everywhere else" in the Japanese original. In contrast, a word-by-word translation of the Japanese original into English would not make much sense: it would only lead to a contradictory statement because conceptualization patterns concerning silence may not fully coincide in the two cultures.

Thus far, the emotional landscape has been considered important to the concept of silence in the Japanese context. I want to take a final moment to think further about sensual and affective responses that the interactions of sound, silence, and nature bring about in our mind. In particular, a question that I wish to contemplate is whether there are any conceivable cultural foundations for the concept—ideological guides to a concept of silence associated with a defined emotional landscape. Reflection on this issue is motivated by Padden's (1988) remark I cited earlier, namely, that what sound means is "shaped through learned, culturally defined practice." Recall, for instance, our earlier discussion of a remark that considers the sensibility to silence in nature to be a cultural practice that is part of a long-standing cultural tradition. Furthermore, the recurring conceptual and linguistic pattern shown in depicting ambient silence has been recognized widely enough to deem its connection to a role that culture might play.

In delving into cultural bases that might be of relevance to the question, I find it helpful to look at the meanings of *wabi* and *sabi*. These terms constitute fundamental principles of the tea-ceremony and traditional poetry (tanka and haiku), and ultimately are in close connection to Zen Buddhism. It may be heard in the context of imperfection or lack of asymmetry as is embodied in Japanese pottery because ceramic pieces play a significant role in the tea ceremony. Examining the semantic scope of these nouns and their verbal forms, *wabiru* and *sabiru*, seems to provide an insight into constructing the meaning of nature sounds in the way our Japanese example sentences represent. Below I list the exact Japanese definitions of the terms along with the relevant meaning entries of the verbs from which they derived. They are taken from several well-recognized Japanese-language dictionaries for comparison. The translations are mine.[6]

(41) wabi
Nihon Kokugo Daijiten 2006[7]

a. Kanjaku-o tanoshimu koto. Mata, sono tokoro.

閑寂を楽しむこと。また、その所。

"to enjoy the quiet and tranquil; or a quiet and tranquil place"

b. Chadō, haikai-nado-de iu kanjaku-na hūshu. Kanso-no naka-ni aru ochitsuita sabishii kanji.

茶道、俳諧などでいう閑寂な風趣。簡素の中にある落ち着いたさびしい感じ。

"quiet and tranquil atmosphere, sensibility, as in the tea ceremony and (haiku) poetry; the calm and lonesome sense that one feels in simplicity"

Meikyo Kokugo Jiten 2008

a. Chadō, haikai-nado-no biteki-rinen-de, kanjaku, shisso-no naka-ni mi'idas-areru kotan-no omomuki.

茶道・俳諧などの美的理念で、閑寂・質素の中に見いだされる枯淡の趣。

"an aesthetic doctrine in the tea ceremony and (haiku) poetry; a subdued and refined sensibility found in tranquility and simplicity"

b. Sezoku-o hanarete kanjaku-na seikatsu-o tanoshimu koto.

世俗を離れて閑寂な生活を楽しむこと。

"to enjoy a quiet and tranquil life away from the (ordinary) world"

(42) wabiru
Nihon Kokugo Daijiten 2006

Sezoku-kara tōzakatte, toboshii naka-de kansei-na kurashi-ni shitashimu. Kanjaku-o tanoshimu.

世俗から遠ざかって、とぼしい中で閑静な暮らしに親しむ。閑寂を楽しむ。

"to be comfortable with a life that is quiet and peaceful although destitute, away from the (ordinary) world; to enjoy the quiet and tranquil"

Kojien 2008

Kanjaku-na chi-de seikatsu suru. Zokuji-kara tōzakaru.

閑静な地で生活する。俗事から遠ざかる。

"to live in a quiet and tranquil place; to move away from the (ordinary) world"

Meikyo Kokugo Jiten 2008

Shisso-de ochitsuita omomuki-ga aru.

質素で落ち着いた趣きがある。

"to have a modest and subdued elegance"

(43) sabi
Nihon Kokugo Daijiten 2006

Hurubite kareta ajiwai-no aru koto. Kanjaku-na omomuki-no aru koto. Jimi-de omomuki-no aru koto. Sabishimi. Seijakumi.

古びて枯れた味わいのある事。閑寂な趣のある事。地味で趣のある事。淋しみ。静寂味。

"with an old and withered appeal; with a quiet and tranquil elegance; with a reserved taste; lonesomeness; a touch of stillness"

Kojien 2008

a. Hurubite omomuki-no aru koto. Kanjaku-na omomuki.

古びて趣のあること。閑寂なおもむき。

"with a (cultivated) sensibility resulting from maturing; a quiet and tranquil elegance"

b. Bashō-haikai-no konpon-rinen-no hitotsu. Kanjakumi-no senren sarete jun-geijutsuka sareta mono. Ku-ni sonawaru kanjaku-na jōchō.

蕉風俳諧の根本理念の一つ。閑寂味の洗練されて純芸術化されたもの。句に備わる閑寂な情調。

"one of the fundamental doctrines in the Basho-style poetry; the quiet and tranquil that is refined into pure art; a quiet and peaceful tone in a haiku"

Meikyo Kokugo Jiten 2008

   a. Hurubite-ite mono-shizuka-na omomuki-ga aru koto.

   古びていて物静かな趣きがある事。

   "matured with a calm elegance"

   b. Bashō-haikai-no kihon-rinen-no hitotsu. Chūsei-no wabi, yūgen-no bi'ishiki-ga hatten shita mono-de, geijutsuteki-na bi-to shite senren sare, ku-kara shizen-ni nijimi-deru yō-na kotan, kanjaku-no jōchō-o iu.

   蕉風俳諧の基本理念の一つ。中世のわび・幽玄の美意識が発展したもので、芸術的な美として洗練され、句から自然ににじみ出るような枯淡・閑寂の情調をいう。

   "one of the fundamental doctrines in the Basho-style poetry; a simple, quiet, and peaceful tone that naturally reveals itself in a haiku; developed from the aesthetics of *wabi-yugen* in the medieval, and refined into artistic beauty"

(44) sabiru

Nihon Kokugo Daijiten 2006

Hurubite omomuki-ga aru. Rōjuku shite ajiwai-o shōjiru. Kanjakumi-ga aru.

古びて趣がある。老熟して味わいを生じる。閑寂味がある。

"to have an elegance resulting from maturing; to yield an appeal after having matured; to have a quiet and tranquil flavor"

Kojien 2008

Hurubite omomuki-ga aru. Kotan-no omomuki-o motsu.

古びて趣がある。枯淡の趣を持つ。

"to have an elegance resulting from maturing; to have an elegance of simplicity"

Meikyo Kokugo Jiten 2008

   a. Huruku natte mono-shizuka-na omomuki-ga deru. Kanga-no omomuki-ga aru. Mono-sabiru.

   古くなって物静かな趣が出る。閑雅の趣がある。物さびる。

   "to become old and yield a calm charm; to have a refined elegance; to become desolate"

   b. Zokuke-no nai kiyoraka-na kokoro-ni naru.

   俗気のない清らかな心になる。

   "to attain a pure mind without worldliness"

In perusing these dictionary definitions of the verb and noun forms of *wabi* and *sabi*, we notice repeated references to sets of adjectives corresponding to quiet, peaceful, tranquil, calm; elegant, refined, mature; simple, subdued; lonesome, desolate. Note that the first set of these adjectives—quiet, peaceful, tranquil, and calm—overlaps with the characterizations of the emotional landscape that is painted by verbal depictions of silence that embed nature sounds (e.g., [11], [13], [18]).[8] The sense of departure from the ordinary world and abandonment of worldliness that generates the feeling of closeness to nature and oneness with nature reminds us of what underlies the symbiotic relation of sound and silence. This connection is implicit in (22–23), for instance. In addition, the rejection of, and departure from, worldliness, when understood with religious or spiritual overtones, may further be united with the sense of reverence and veneration, as (25) and (27) illustrate.

It suggests that the state of mind represented by *wabi* and *sabi* resembles, in concept, what nature sounds mean and in effect what silence means in the Japanese discourse. The common thread between what *wabi* and *sabi* mean and the concept of silence relevant to our discussion (i.e., ambient hushed tranquility) is an ultimate appreciation of harmony with nature and spiritual closeness to the universe. Furthermore, a broader implication of *wabi* as an aesthetic view that is factored into the fabric of Japanese culture is noted, for instance, by Mizuo (1971, 8): "[t]here does not seem to be anybody who does not admit that *wabi* is an aesthetic concept unique to Japan, even though there may be differences in the depth at which the people comprehend its substance and the degree to which they evaluate its value" (my translation, NT). To put it in a historical context, *wabi* and *sabi* emerged as part of an aesthetic ideology stemming from Zen Buddhism. It follows and contrasts with the luxurious and gaudy view of beauty and its representations during the Heian period (794–1185).[9] At the turn of the twentieth century, notable writers including Yasunari Kawabata (1899–1972), Junichiro Tanizaki (1886–1965), and Yukio Mishima (1925–1970) used their literary works to present Japan "in its most aestheticized manner" (Marra 1999, 264). The view in which these writers painted "aestheticized Japan" is very much in line with what *wabi* and *sabi* stand for, as Tanizaki's 1933 essay 陰翳礼讚 "In Praise of Shadows" and Kawabata's 1968 Nobel Prize acceptance speech 美しい日本の私 "Japan, the Beautiful and Myself" fervently aspire to portray.[10] For example, in interpreting Kawabata's 1968 speech, Fujimura (2016) comments on the beauty in nature and its healing and enlightening power to which it exposes humans: "Kawabata insists on connecting the beauty of the senses ('beauty of the full moon' or 'beauty of the cherries in bloom') and the inner experience of the beauty inherent in relationships. . . . He sees in beauty an integrative power that can awaken, heal and restore. In Kawabata's mind, culture is deeply, harmoniously connected with nature" (p. 59). It is implied that an assessment of beauty relies on an intuitive, immediate feeling that results from deployment of all senses and affects.[11] Thus, these prominent Japanese writers and those who were inspired by them at the time, for instance, harbored an aesthetic that might be reduced to *wabi* and *sabi*; and they rendered this privileged aesthetic view as a cultural practice that represents Japan. A similar line of thought that addresses what *wabi* and *sabi* represent for Japanese people today is found in Iwai (2006): ". . . today, 'wabi' and 'sabi' form the spirit of the tea ceremony and share the meaning of 'peaceful and calm beauty'" (p. 291; my translation, NT). In addition, Hirai (2019) analyzes that *wabi-sabi* thoughts in the tea ceremony have a latent philosophy that is "unique to Japanese people" and is "beneficial to Japanese people today." He further goes on to say, "[t]he most important is the impact that *wabi-sabi* ideology has on Japanese people's views of human beings and lifestyles, without our realizing it" (Hirai 2019, 32; my translation, NT). These observations seem to suggest that aesthetic values centering around *wabi* and *sabi* notions are recognized as a recurring belief that has a significant weight in Japanese culture beyond the tea ceremony.

Obviously, we cannot maintain that the principle coalescing *wabi* and *sabi* uniquely characterizes Japanese aesthetics across cultural representations throughout the history of Japan, since aesthetic values are often accepted with ideological motivation, and measures for values could transform over time. Nor is it within the scope of my investigation here to unpack aesthetic values in their historical complexities and diversity. Nevertheless, I conjecture that an aesthetic view around *wabi* and *sabi* can be "recycled" as a principle that is relevant to understanding the cultural context for how silence is conceptualized and linguistically represented.[12] That is, I presume it is through recycling an aesthetic value as a reference point that the meaning of sound and silence is constructed and linguistically expressed accordingly. I take such a conceptual re-application of aesthetic ideology to correspond, at least in part, to an instance of what Padden (1988) refers to as "learned, culturally defined practice."

1.3 Conceptualization of Silence in Space

If the concept of silence underlying and manifest in our Japanese samples is guided and culturally contextualized by an aesthetic view that relates to *wabi* and *sabi*, it seems to follow that similar instances of conceptual patterns may be detected by the language in which contemporary cultural artifacts such as music and paintings are described and commented on. The presence of recurring rhetorical practices in distinct spaces would provide reasonable validation that the conceptualization of silence as we view it here is not randomly constructed but reflects a cohesive, broader manifestation of a cultural ideology fostered and cultivated on similar conceptual and aesthetic grounds.

Among contemporary cultural areas, I will start with an examination of the language used in the music field because it is obviously a well-defined disciplinary area that deals with sound and our auditory perception. Particularly relevant to this exploration is the manner in which traditional Japanese music is dissected and assessed, where traditional Japanese music in our examples of commentaries below refers to *hōgaku* (邦楽) or *wagaku* (和楽) rather than the contemporary music in modern popular culture. On the one hand, aesthetic appreciation pertinent to silence—broadly conceived—is widely noted beyond Japanese culture. American composer John Cage, for one, composed *4'33,"* which consists of no sounds of musical notes for a duration of 4 minutes and 33 seconds. His composition is considered avant-garde especially in the field that assumes sequences of musical notes are systematically arranged into a form of music art. His intention, of course, is to recognize and respond to a beauty found in the context of a musical—and auditory—void. So, the aspect of aesthetic values focusing on the absence of expected musical notes is acknowledged by some experts although it does not seem customary in Western music.

On the other hand, professional commentaries written in Japanese remark that sensitivity to auditory absence or pause has been captured as a distinctive feature that separates Japanese music from its Western counterpart. In particular, the contrast of sound and silence that is articulated and elaborated on from the music specialists' points of view speaks to the extensive weight placed on silence in Japanese music. For instance, Ro Ogura's (1977) *Nihon-no Mimi* [Japanese Ears], here interpreted by Nakagawa (1995), asserts the differences. A line of thought that illuminates the symbiotic existence of apparent opposites, i.e., sound and silence, is evident in the excerpts in (45–47). Translations are mine.

(45) ヨーロッパの音楽とは、静かな時よりもむしろ、音が鳴っている時に重点を置いているのであると。だが、東洋-日本の芸術は、むしろ「静寂」を際立たせるために音を鳴らすのであり、「静」が主「動（音）」が副の芸術世界であると読み解いている。

"[Ogura says that] European music focuses more on the moments of sounds than on the moments of silence. But, in Eastern or Japanese arts, sounds are made in order to highlight 'silence'; it is a world of arts in which 'stillness' is primary while 'motion (sound)' is secondary."
(Nakagawa 1995, 28)

(46) すなわち、「静寂」の中に容易に溶け込める音楽-それが日本音楽であり．．．

"In other words, the music that can be effortlessly unified with 'silence'—that is Japanese music . . ." (Ibid.)

(47) 動の中に静を求めて充足する耳

"ears that are satisfied in finding the unmoving in the midst of motion."
(Ogura 1977, 4)

It is not our goal to essentialize the East vs. West contrast, as in (45). Relevant to our discussion, instead, is the way in which purpose and process of constructing music as art is elucidated in the Japanese context, particularly as it concerns the relationship of silence and sound on which we have been focusing. An audible sequence of sounds in Japanese music has the appearance of belying a silent sphere, and yet the listeners are naturally drawn to the silent space. So, when Japanese ears perceive musical notes, they listen not only to the presence of sounds that are delivered by way of musical notes but at the same time to the absence of sounds—or the absent part of a sequence of sounds. The presence and absence of sounds together partake in creating music as art that is worthy of aesthetic evaluations and appreciation. Throughout the three excerpts above, sound is equated to constant movement and a sequence of motions, while silence is associated with the stillness that occurs between motions or after a motion. Japanese music is characterized as a silence-centered music, in which both sound and silence are indispensable to each other. Their intricate weaving targets stillness as the primary goal. (46) also points to the notable characteristic of Japanese music that sound and silence are merged together, creating a harmony rather than a discord. This, at least, is the manner in which Japanese music is listened to and is appreciated for its artistic value, as suggested by the view expressed in (47).[13] Note that a similar observation is made by Horikiri (1998), who discusses "the world of no sound" in his extensive investigation of Basho's poetry. Horikiri surmises that in Asia, including Japan, silence is positively valued in its own right and appreciated independently, rather than contrastively with sound. This concept of silence, which Horikiri considers typical of the East, including Japan, makes it possible and natural to recognize nature sounds as a sign of silence. It seems most appropriate of Horikiri to characterize it as "the soundless world with sounds in it" (Horikiri 1998, 76).

As expressed in (48), Ogura goes on to elaborate on an apparent boundary between sound and silence in Western music as opposed to the fluid relation between the two in traditional Japanese music. In so doing, he views the difference in terms of the dichotomy of subjectivity vs. objectivity with which the tonality of each music is constructed and interpreted.

(48) 日本の音楽は知的作用を隔絶した世界である。ヨーロッパの音楽は、記譜法を確立するとともに、理論的体系を積み重ねながら調的な力を追求してきた。．．．すなわち、ヨーロッパの音楽は調的な力の把握に知的作用の援けを借りたが、日本の音楽は、調性をひたすら体験的なものとして感じ、伝承してきたのである。．．．いいかえれば、ヨーロッパの音楽は客観的、日本の音楽は主観的性格を持つということになる。

"Japanese music is a world far from intellectual effects. Music in Europe established musical notation and has sought tonal force while acquiring theoretical systems. . . . That is, in the music of Europe the interpretation of tonal force has been aided by intellectual effects, whereas in the [traditional] music of Japan, tonality has been perceived as solely experiential and handed down from generation to generation. . . . In other words, European music can be characterized for its objectivity while Japanese music for its subjectivity."   (Ogura 1977, 9–10; my translation, NT)

Independent of the technical analyses of Japanese and Western music, the subjective and experiential response to Japanese music and its heritage that Ogura explicates in (48) is reminiscent of the emphasis on intuitive, immediate feeling (直観) over reason and argument (理論) that is embraced in Kawabata's aesthetic view discussed earlier.[14] Such an instinctive, experiential trait that Ogura considers Japanese music to exhibit seems to follow the same pattern of thought that underlies the conceptualization path from sound to silence and ultimately to spiritual harmony, as attained through subjective reactions through our individual senses and affects (the specifics of which are, again, formed in interaction with our cultures).

Recurrent patterns of coexistence of sound and silence, of movements and stillness have also been used in the language introducing and evaluating paintings. The apparently opposing notions of sound and silence are not considered paradoxical or incompatible in the language of art appreciation. In the November 2008 issue of the monthly art journal *Gekkan Bijutsu*, which introduces artists and reports on art shows, the editorial department features the painter Juri Furukawa's one-woman exhibition. Highlighted are the three of her paintings under the title "A Lotus Pond," shown in figures 2.1, 2.2, and 2.3.[15]

Figure 2.1.   A lotus pond ~刻 II~ 15F by Juri Furukawa, Gekkan Bijutsu 34 (11): 185.
Source: Housed in the National Diet Library. Reprinted by permission of Juri Furukawa.

Figure 2.2.   A lotus pond ~玉響~ 15F by Juri Furukawa, Gekkan Bijutsu 34 (11): 186.
Source: Housed in the National Diet Library. Reprinted by permission of Juri Furukawa.

Figure 2.3. A lotus pond ~揺蕩うI~ 10F by Juri Furukawa, Gekkan Bijutsu 34 (11): 186.
Source: Housed in the National Diet Library. Reprinted by permission of Juri Furukawa.

The commentator notes in (49) that the underlying thematic concept around which Furukawa's paintings coalesce is *seijaku* 静寂 "silence, tranquility, stillness." In (50), it is more concretely elaborated that the silent and tranquil theme is represented by the contrastive and yet contemporaneous existence of dead lotus leaves as the motionless, and ripples as the moving.

(49) ...すべてが作家の追求するテーマ、「静寂」を孕む作品であるということに気が付く。

"... we notice that all (of her pieces) are filled with 'silence (tranquility),' the theme that the artist pursues."
(*Gekkan Bijutsu* 2008, 184; my translation, NT)

(50) ... 古河作品に流れるのは静かな空気。枯れた蓮に波紋という「静」と「動」、...

"... a quiet air flows throughout Furukawa's paintings. 'Stillness' and 'motion' are depicted by dead lotus leaves and ripples ..."　(Ibid.)

The synchronicity of two opposites appeals to our vision, similar to the effect on our hearing in the aural domain, as in (45). It is intended that the silence and stillness of the landscape portrayed in Furukawa's paintings is created by the juxtaposition of dead lotus leaves and ripples made by the duck. The "a quiet air" referred to in (50) is the important holistic goal that the artist attempts to capture and express in the paintings. Interpreting and appreciating the thematic concept of these paintings as *seijaku* "silence, tranquility, stillness" is enabled by a pair of eyes, just as with the ears in the aural domain in (47), "that are satisfied in finding the unmoving in the midst of motion." This is where we see a parallelism between the auditory and visual senses in our subjective reaction to a seeming void.

A similar conceptual grounding that resides in appreciating paintings appears in Kuwako's (1999) reference to the famous screen painting, *Shōrinzu*, by Hasegawa Tohaku (1539–1610).[16] Painted in black-and-white ink, *Shōrinzu* portrays the landscape of pine trees blanketed in part by fog. Kuwako (1999) articulates his cross-modal, synesthetic impressions, as in (51), that speak of the perception of silence along the lines similar to those argued above.[17]

(51) 『松林図』の前では、わたしたちは霧の冷気さえ感じてしまう。触覚を刺激する絵画というべきか。さらに、この絵を支配するのは、えもいわれぬ静寂である。音を知覚するのは聴覚であるが、聴覚は音の不在をも知覚する。静寂とは音がしないことである。その静寂がこの絵から聞こえてくる。しかし静寂といってもまったくの音がしないのではなく、耳元には霧の流れる音が聞こえる。

"Facing 'Shōrinzu' we even feel a chilly air from the fog. Should we call it a painting that stimulates our tactile sensation? Furthermore, what dominates this painting is indescribable silence. The auditory sense perceives not only sounds but their absence. Silence means lack of sounds. Such silence is audible in this painting. However, in this silence it is not that we hear absolutely no sound; rather, the sound of fog setting in enters into our ears."   (Kuwako 1999, 55; my translation, NT)

Of note is Kuwako's remark that we hear silence in the painting and that the audible silence comes from the flowing fog. The cross-modal reference, i.e., the audible silence (hearing) in the painting (vision), encapsulates the meaning of silence in the Japanese context that transcends the auditory sense, defining silence to be experienced by vision. And, the way in which such a cross-modal perception of silence is made possible is closely connected to viewing something in motion—namely, the fog—as an agent to elevate what is still. This resembles the dichotomy of the static vs. the dynamic where the presence of the latter signifies the former, just as traditional Japanese music is interpreted as in (45). It is also parallel to how Furukawa's paintings are evaluated in (49–50) as well. So, in the cross-modal depiction of (51), the blanketing fog in motion is explained to create a silent soundscape in a visual landscape. While the manner in which "silence" is evoked may not be exactly identical as it is reflected by the language of the commentaries on the two sets of paintings, the presence or absence of motion that appeals to the vision sense corresponds reasonably to the presence or absence of sound. Important to the discussion of conceptualization of silence is that the two seemingly opposite concepts—presence and absence of a sensory stimulus—need to be coextensive in understanding what it means by silence in a context of Japanese culture, and that the presence of a stimulus is critical to making its absence discernable enough to be a target of attention.

In this subsection, we have observed parallel views of silence expressed in various writings available in the fields of music and paintings. In these hearing- and vision-centered areas, it is shown that the concept of silence as it is expressed in the language of commentaries that evaluate and appreciate art forms comports with the conceptual and linguistic patterns observed in our earlier data set. The ultimate and utmost relevance of silence across these fields has to do with spiritual serenity and peace in mind that it brings about. The recurring notion of embracing the harmonious coexistence of sound-silence and the dynamic-static pairings, I believe, lends support to its underlying aesthetic grounding. Sound, to the extent that it is admitted to coexist in unison, is an indispensable element to elucidate the effect of what silence means in the Japanese cultural context.

1.4 A View from Metaphor

One of the central premises in explaining the conceptualization of silence is that the process of structuring the concept does not rely on or involve metaphor (e.g., Lakoff and Johnson's [1980] conceptual metaphor). I have emphasized that the meaning of silence that unites all the samples culled from numerous sources provided in section 1.1 is interpreted literally rather than figuratively. That is, it is important for our analysis to distinguish between conceptualization and metaphorization. Using Fromkin and Rodman's (1993) example, the sentence *Walls have ears* is anomalous when it is taken literally but is perfectly acceptable as a metaphor. They give the following definition of metaphor in less technical terms: "... the literal meaning is so unlikely that listeners stretch their imagination for another interpretation. That 'stretching' is based on semantic properties that are inferred or that provide some kind of resemblance. Such nonliteral interpretations are called **metaphor**" (Fromkin and Rodman 1993, 151; emphasis original). We have argued that a variety of examples that describe silence and its intensity in Japanese is not considered anomalous, nor does it need any "stretching" of the imagination to understand what is depicted. Rather than through metaphor, our samples are individual reflections of what silence means based on how it is conceptualized and contextualized within the Japanese culture and language. That is, those silent scenes that are described in Japanese language directly and literally mirror the way in which each of sound, silence, and their coexistence means in cultural contexts. I close this section with a brief discussion of a metaphor-based analysis of ambient silence since such an approach may be thought to explain a similar underlying concept of silence argued here.

Hiraga (1987, 2005) and Hiraga and Ross (2013) provide intriguing intertextual analyses of Matsuo Basho's haiku poems, focusing on their overall rhetorical structure. They select two of Basho's celebrated poems to dissect a metaphorical thread that runs through them in effectively showcasing silence in the literary form. Hiraga and Ross (2013) claim that the "global metaphor"[18] of SILENCE IS SOUND is central to these two poems.

(52) Shizukasa-ya iwa-ni shimi'iru semi-no koe

閑さや岩にしみ入る蝉の声

"stillness—ah! / seeps into rocks / cicada's voice"
(translation in Hiraga and Ross 2013, 26)

(53) Huruike-ya kawazu tobikomu mizu-no oto

古池や蛙飛び込む水の音

"old pond; a frog jumps in / sound of water"
(translation in Horikiri 2006, 164)

Concentrating on the relationship between the sound of a cicada and silence in (52), Hiraga and Ross analyze: "[i]n short, the whole text can be interpreted as a global metaphor for the fusion of voice and silence. . . . Thus, silence is metaphorically equated with the cicada's voice seeping into the rocks: SILENCE IS SOUND" (p. 28). As for the effect of the frog on silence in (53), they comment: "[h]ence, we could say that the text can be read as a global metaphor; and that silence embodied by the old pond is metaphorically equated with the sound of water produced by the frog's jump: SILENCE IS SOUND" (p. 27). They further summarize the parallelism between the two sets of rhetorical structure, as quoted in (54–55).

(54) In our view, these haiku essentially arise out of the profound stillness prevailing in nature. Basho lets us feel the immensity of nature's silence by letting it be broken through the actions of two small creatures—the

joining of frog and water, the shrill drilling of the cicada's cry.... The sound of water caused by the frog and the shrilling of the cicada's voice may at first seem to disturb the moment, but then, after the interruption, they serve to produce a deepened mood of quietness in the poet's mind. It is an overwhelming silence that is resonant with the tranquility of the pond and the rocks, and with the eternal loneliness of the poet. (p. 26)

(55) In sum, both the frog poem and the cicada poem grow out of very similar themes: the profound stillness of nature, activated or made manifest by spikes of vivid action of the frog and the cicada, though they are typically taken to be mere noisemakers, thanks to the Chinese proverb. In both poems, a surprising new meaning is assigned to the frog and the cicada: a radical change from being prototypically noisy creatures to becoming activators of, or guides to, silence. In both, SILENCE is achieved metaphorically by the absorption of SOUND by a container of LIQUID (i.e., pond and rocks). (p. 30)

The metaphor-based analysis that Hiraga and Ross present shares two points with the view subscribed to in the current work: first, silence and stillness in nature are the center of rhetorical descriptions; and second, the silence in the depiction has a deeper meaning of spiritual appeal. However, while recognizing the shared insights and relevance to the view advanced here, I discuss how different the central theme of this book is from the metaphor analysis of silence as is demonstrated in Hiraga and Ross (2013) and Hiraga (1987, 2005).

First, the sources of sounds in nature referred to in depictions of silence are not always inherently noisy, despite their characterization as such in (55). Throughout the texts sampled in section 1.1, the cries of small animals and insects, other sounds in nature, and the like are not characterized as noisy but rather as soothing. For instance, frog-associated sounds are referred to in (8) and (10); and although less frequently used, the sound of a cicada appears in (11) and (14). As we have commented on them, these sounds do not represent agents that break or violate the silence in nature; instead, they are heard directly as sources of comfort that lead to a state of peaceful mind. In contrast, Hiraga and Ross in their analysis of Basho's haiku poems in (52) and (53) view the sounds of the cicada and the frog as noisy, attributing to a Chinese idiom *wa-ming-chan-zao* "frog.cry.cicada.noise" (p. 29), which Basho is presumed to have known.[19]

Second, following up on my first point, Hiraga and Ross analyze that these noisy sounds ultimately gain "a new meaning of silence" and express "a more profound kind of stillness." They further explain this new meaning of silence: "one which arises after the motion through the air of a jumping frog or the motion in the air of the sound waves produced by the shrill cry of the cicada.

The frog and cicada's new function is to paradoxically cancel their proverbial connotation as the producers of meaningless noises, and instead to both serve as guides into the deepest silence" (p. 29). The silence to which they refer is the quiet moment right after the sound of splashing water ceases or presumably the imperceptible sound waves coming from the cicada. This view can be interpreted to imply temporal (in the frog case) or spatial (in the cicada case) dissociation between sound sources and created silence. That is, they seem to suggest that silence follows the tangible sounds produced by living beings in nature, and furthermore that the process of this creation of silence is mediated by conceptual metaphors like VOICE IS LIQUID and SILENCE IS ROCK. As I have demonstrated throughout this chapter, silence and nature sounds do not appear in the scene sequentially but instead always exist in an identical temporal and spatial extension. At the same time, descriptions of a variety of sound environments that I have illustrated in connection with the conceptualization of silence are made *literally* and not figuratively. Unlike the metaphorical way of describing silence, ambient sounds in our illustration are acoustically tangible, perceived by humans, and the presence of silence is confirmed because those sounds are tangible. Neither silence nor tangible ambient sounds can be affirmed or acknowledged without making reference to the other for the range of samples that we have discussed. Recall, moreover, that nature sounds are an indispensable element in order for a relevant concept of silence to be constructed around the sense of ambient hushed tranquility. I have amply argued above that our sample discourses describing silence in nature relate sound and silence as coexistence in both time and space and are directly expressed in literal speech.

Third, there seem to be three crucial elements in order for a metaphorical relation to hold in their analysis, as it is indicated in (52): SOUND, SILENCE, and LIQUID. SOUND refers to the cicada's noise and the sound the frog makes when it jumps into the pond; SILENCE is a scene to be described and ultimately is a state to be arrived at with a deeper meaning; and LIQUID is "a container" that (metaphorically) absorbs the sounds. The transformation of the sounds to silence is bridged by metaphor, and the presence of rocks and a pond is critical to establishing the metaphorical relation between the sounds and silence.[20] Their goal is to analyze the rhetorical structure of the poems, with a focus being on intertextual similarities, and the metaphor analysis may well be insightful and on the right track. Setting aside evaluations of their claim as a rhetorical analysis, from which I shy away here, the discourse of our samples we have examined earlier do not rely on intermediate agents such as rocks and a pond that serve as crucial ingredients for metaphors to illustrate the way in which sounds are absorbed in order to create silence both in the atmosphere and finally in an individual's mind. One may consider that the kind of metaphorical reasoning along the lines of Hiraga and Ross's argument could be underlying the conceptualization of silence vis-à-vis sounds in nature. This consideration is well taken, and I do not entirely disagree particularly as far as the two poems are concerned. But, given the sheer number of examples that depict silence by way of nature sounds without referring to what counts as elements that correspond to LIQUID in the metaphorical equation, the range of sounds listed in section 1.1 is expressed and interpreted more directly and literally as an integral part of silence in conceptualizing silence in the cultural context.

Parenthetically, one might consider an alternative analysis based on metonymy. Such an approach would view nature sounds as a metonym of ambient silence, similar to the example *Table 2 wants more coffee*: *Table 2* in this example is a metonym for "a customer sitting at Table 2." Metonymy is figurative speech in that the literal interpretation of *Table 2 wants more coffee* leads to an anomaly. In contrast, the examples in section 1.1 are not anomalous under the literal interpretation. It is important to recognize that those Japanese samples are not considered odd because the association of nature sounds and ambient silence directly embodies the concept of silence in the Japanese context (i.e., hushed tranquility), not because they are interpreted figuratively, whether by metaphor or by metonymy.

Metaphor undeniably provides an excellent rhetorical tool in our depictions of silence. Yet, the point I wish to underscore is that at the same time, the Japanese language is fully enabled for a more direct way of achieving the same goal equally effectively. The role that nature sounds play in linguistic depictions of ambient silence has sufficiently been demonstrated beyond their instantiations in poetry forms, fiction, nonfiction, journalistic and professional writings, and webpages and blogs. The phenomenon under examination, thus, is observed across genres of writing. Furthermore, the evaluative language used in distinct fields like music and paintings replicates a similar pattern of viewing sound and silence. Individually and collectively, our examples point to a sustained pattern of linguistic representations that seems to be culturally pervasive in a diverse range of discourse types.

2. INTRA- AND INTER-CULTURAL CONSIDERATION

Ways of depicting silence that a language affords cannot be fully unearthed without figuring out what silence means to the speakers; and conversely, what silence means cannot be assayed without addressing the question of what sound means to the speakers. We are constantly surrounded by a wide gamut of sounds, both in type and in intensity, and these sounds could carry to each individual a specific meaning. At the same time, a single sound could also take different meanings depending on the individual, time, space, and the society, among many more potential factors. One of the clearest examples of the diversity of this variability is the sounds that pedestrians hear at traffic lights in Japan. Repetitions of a mechanical sound imitating a chick or a cuckoo last for some seconds when the lights for pedestrians turn green. Originally created to guide people with visual impairment, these sounds at traffic lights have a specific functional meaning to them. Similarly, as the following example of contemporary Japanese tanka poetry (Endo 2013) reminds us, even ordinary sounds in a society can be interpreted uniquely to specific circumstances.

(56) Kyūkyūsha-no // chūya-o towazu // hibiku oto // kinchōkan-naku // byōshitsu-ni kiku.
救急車の // 昼夜を問はず // ひびく音 // 緊張感なく // 病室に聞く

"In my hospital room, I hear the sound of the ambulance, running day and night, without a sense of urgency."

The sound of a siren from an ambulance is intentionally loud, and naturally bears a sense of urgency; it is associated with a perception of emergency and urgency. But, when the poet listens to the same sound repeatedly day and night in a room where she seems to be a patient herself, the loud siren loses its urgent meaning. It is interesting to note that this tanka is included in a poetry collection entitled *Seijaku* "silence." Let me give yet another example of variation in the meaning of a sound. Senba et al. (2015) explain that the sounds of machines may strike many people as loud noise and thus a nuisance, but they are key to mechanics who operate them daily. That is, a sound that gives crucial information to some people can simply be an annoying noise to others. So, this functional factor is sometimes applicable to only a group of people in a society, and the meaning of a single sound can thus carry different and even contrastive messages. An interesting aspect that these instances demonstrate is that while sounds can have their culturally grounded meanings, they can also pick up unexpected meanings or affective values, depending on the time and circumstance in which the sounds and their perceivers are placed. Given regular recurrence, these values can become conventionally associated with those sounds, or they can remain unique to a particular occasion.

In this section, I will begin by looking at variability in the extent to which nature sounds are admitted to linguistically depicted silent scenes. Intra-cultural variability indicates that speakers within a larger Japanese cultural context can set different thresholds for what does and does not contribute to constructing the meaning of silence in such scenes. It follows that the concept of silence in a community should be viewed on a continuum rather than strictly compartmentalized, so that it allows room for individual variation in the manner of perception and its linguistic expressions. I will also look into inter-cultural correspondences which indicate that linguistic means and their underlying concepts common in Japanese are instantiated also in other languages and cultures. It should be noted that the term "culture" is to be interpreted broadly, inclusive of communities other than those defined by the standard criteria like geographical and ethnic factors.

2.1 Intra-Cultural Variability

A constellation of sounds in nature (e.g., sounds emanating from small animals, insects, trees, water) can evoke silence, and linguistic descriptions of the interdependent sound-silence harmony appear regardless of the genre and form of communication. However, it is not the case that every instance of these sounds that are tangible in nature is equally embedded in silence. The same ambient sound can be perceived to evoke comforting silence or an annoying noise by the same individuals at different occasions, or by different individuals at a concurrent time. As the poem in (56) above shows us, an identical sound can be interpreted as a silence promoter or a silence breaker depending on the particular person and circumstances. For instance, as many of our earlier samples demonstrate, quiet evenings in the late summer and in the fall can be described and evoked by referring to the sounds made by a family of crickets including *kōrogi*, *suzumushi*, and *matsumushi*, as well as a species of grasshopper called *umaoi*. Their sounds are regarded as pleasant enough to make them visible agents of silence, as was amply evidenced by our examples in section 1.1. In contrast, another kind of grasshopper, *kutsuwamushi*, makes a loud noise that disturbs sleep, and as such is unlikely to be part of the evocation of silence in any plausible sense. Furthermore, we have above seen many examples of frogs, cicadas, and crickets, among others, admitted to silence, but we also find statements that decry how their tangible sounds break silence. These contrastive reactions are readily confirmed with a quick online perusal. For example, frog sounds are collocated with descriptive terms like *iyashi* "healing," *rirakkusu* "relax(ation)," and *yasuragi* "calmness," and are sometimes marketed as sound effects for sleeping aids. On the other hand, there are also complaints about frog sounds as an unwanted noise that prevents people from falling asleep. Concrete instantiations of sound in nature are thus subject to situation-specific meanings, and individuals react to them vis-à-vis their relation to silence.

In addition to the association of a sense of serenity that nature sounds create in us, we may need to consider another criterion for constructing the meaning of nature sounds as it relates to the concept of silence. Dr. Hideko Abe (personal communication, July 2016) shared with me her insight that prompts the further consideration. To her, cicadas are a natural agent of silence while frogs are not. She explains that the sounds of cicadas are perennially expected to be heard, especially as a marker of the summertime, while those of frogs are not anticipated to recur regularly as part of a seasonal cycle. Frog sounds are often considered to indicate a precursor for, or a consequence of, rain, but perhaps they are not in the natural course of our life in the same sense as cicadas are. Underlying her perceptive distinction seems to be the extent to which a given sound is embedded in people's sensual experiences in their life environments. We may customarily view that these sounds are assumed to exist and remain to be implanted in the natural background, but at least to Dr. Abe, frog sounds are not quite entrenched enough in her perception to partake in conceptualizing silence. The degree of entrenchment in natural life as a criterion for the embodiment of silence, if further justified, seems to be properly situated within the sense of harmony with nature. Viewed that way, Dr. Abe's insight, based on her own subjective sensory responses, still follows the cultural pattern of perceiving sound and silence in a larger frame, while revealing some leeway in personal assessment.

Following up on the point regarding the degree of entrenchment in life, I discuss the narrative in (57–58), in which Torigoe (2004) reports on her expedition trip to Monbetsu City in Hokkaido, the northern island of Japan. It is about the soundscape with ice floes in her pursuit of the "crying/calling" sound that they are known to make in the Sea of Okhotsk; and the sounds of ice floes have been considered to symbolize silence in the local community. I refer to these excerpts to illustrate shifting views of an identical sound that have transformed over time.

(57) 流氷の鳴く音は聞こえず、ただ寒くて風の音が聞こえるだけ。その場を支配していたのは静けさでした。．．．流氷が来ると海面が蓋をされるので、いつもは聞こえている潮騒の音が聞こえなくなる。つまり、生活実感としての流氷の音は、静けさだというのです。静かだからこそ、ときどき流氷が軋んだり、こすれ合ったりするときの「鳴くような音」が聞こえることもあるのだと言われました。

"I did not hear the sound that ice floes make [lit. cry]; I only heard the sound of wind in the bitter coldness. It was silence that dominated the scene. . . . When ice floes approach, they cover the surface of the sea and erase the sound of the waves that are otherwise audible. That is, according to them [=local people], the sound of ice floes in daily life means silence. They told me that simply because it is quiet, they sometimes hear the sound of ice floes' squeaking and abrading each other 'as if they were crying/calling.'"   (Torigoe 2004, 26; my translation, NT)

(58) 昔、流氷は「白い悪魔」と言われて嫌われ、その音に耳を傾ける人はいなかったそうです。．．．ところが今、流氷は地域の人たちに大事にされています。．．．同じ流氷の音でも、昔は聞きたくもなかったものが、それを大切に思うようになったからこそ聞き取る耳もでき、遂には「二十一世紀に残したい音」とまで思うようになった。流氷の音そのものは物理的にはまったく変わっていないかもしれないけれど、それが「いい音」「好きな音」かどうかは、そうした文化的・社会的な要因にも左右されているわけです。

"In the past, people disliked ice floes as 'white devil' and never listened to their sound.... However, the local people value them now.... They opted for not listening to the sound before, but now considering it valuable, they have developed the sensitivity to perceive it and finally regard it as 'the sound that should be kept for the twenty-first century.' There is probably no physical change in the sound of ice floes itself, but whether it strikes us as 'good sound' or 'affable sound' depends on such cultural and social factors."   (Ibid., 27–28; my translation, NT)

Torigoe explains in (57) that ice floes create silence by shutting up the sound of the waves but as a consequence, the silence in turn magnifies the sound that floes produce. This cycle of natural phenomena leads the local people to equate the sound of ice floes with the concept of silence. The sound of ice floes in the Sea of Okhotsk embodies silence and has a meaning specific and significant to the residents of Monbetsu City. Moreover, floe sounds in the sea that represent silence are firmly lodged in the daily life of the local people. Just as the surrounding landscape, the sound of ice floes constitutes an integral part of the soundscape and the cultural climate of the remote city. In contrast, the commentary in (58) highlights that exactly the same sound has not been consistently perceived and interpreted. Torigoe explains that the negative association, as the name "white devil" suggests, came from the inconvenient reality that ice floes prevented local fishermen from fishing, subsequently resulting in less business and an inevitably reduced income. The floe sound thus forecasted a year of poor catch. However, the report continues that around the 1950s as a turning point, scallop culture turned out to be successful due to rich plankton that ice floes bring along. Scientific studies have also shown that the floes in the Sea of Okhotsk prevent sea salt from spreading to the land because they cover the surface of the sea. Accordingly, forests on the land have been protected from the damage that salt-ridden air causes. So, the sound of ice floes has been carrying the history pertinent to the local fishery and ecology. Depending on when people lived in relation to this history, the interpretation of the sound and the concept of silence that it has constructed take different forms. What the sound of ice floes means to the local people has shifted over time for socio-economic reasons in the local culture of the Sea of Okhotsk. The sounds that they make have inevitably come to be a crucial, perennial part of the local society and culture, and the residents have been associating themselves with them. Even within the same region, local communities at different times can experience shifting perceptions and express their reactions to them differently. Admittedly, these episodic narratives may not directly speak to variability in time regarding the concept of silence per se. Nevertheless, I would surmise that the local people's reckoning of those sounds in the sea as a representation of silence in the present day and the contrastive interpretation of the exact sound held in the past suggest that both meaning of sound and meaning of silence undergo historical transitions that cannot be explained without reference to the local culture and concepts that are shaped around it.

2.2 Inter-Cultural Correspondences

The concept of silence as it is argued within the cultural context seems to be shared, in part, by Korean culture and language. According to Dr. Seongha Rhee (personal communication, July 2016), the manner in which a variety of sounds in nature is perceived as defining silence and linguistically described as such is commonly attested to among Korean speakers. The type of expressions sampled in section 1.1 sounds very natural to the ears of many Koreans rather than giving them a sense of oddity. This suggests a wider applicability of the conceptualization process to another culture. However, he believes that of the nature sounds we have discussed, cicadas are more likely considered noisy and are less likely to be included in the range of sounds that would form a symbiotic relation with silence. Recall that a similar opinion has been expressed in the literature of Basho's poem on cicadas, and we also see literary debates over the type of cicadas in Basho's poem.[21] It has been argued that certain species of cicadas (e.g., *aburazemi* "large brown cicadas" contrastive with *nīnīzemi* "kaempfer cicadas") produce less than comforting sounds and thus people would feel annoyed rather than soothed. Again, the exact nature of a given sound as well as the specific circumstance under which a sound is heard greatly influence the readiness to discern peacefulness and serenity as its deep meaning.

Some lines from traditional Chinese poetry also suggest that a similar concept of silence is operative in appreciating ambient silence. The poet Wang Ji of the Southern Dynasties (420–589) wrote a poem, "Entering Ruoye Stream," which includes: 蟬噪林逾靜, 鳥鳴山更幽 "Cicadas chirp, the grove turns quieter still / Birds sing, the mountain grows more remote." According to Qian Zhongshu (1910–1998), *Family Instructions of Master Yan*, written by Yan Zhitui (531–591), talks about this line of Wang Ji's poem in relation to "noise without clamor"; and Qian further notes: "[t]he chirping of insects and singing of birds actually add to the stillness." Commenting on the relationship between silence and nature sounds, Qian goes on to say: "[b]irds, beasts, wind, waves, and all the other pipings of Heaven can peacefully coexist with silence, as the ancient poets who appreciated the true nature of things realized long ago" (Qian 2011, 64). It follows from this ancient Chinese poem and commentaries on it made at different time periods that the view of silence through sounds existing in nature echoes a very similar conceptual and aesthetic standpoint in regard to silence, at least in the world of Chinese poetry. Another poet of the Tang Dynastity (618–907), Chang Jian, has the following poem, 題破山寺後禪院 "Inscribed on the Meditation Hall Behind Poshan Monastry," in a very quiet and lonesome temple scene.[22]

(59) 清晨入古寺
初日照高林
竹徑通幽處
禪房花木深
山光悅鳥性
潭影空人心
萬籟此俱寂
但餘鐘磬音

As clear dawn I entered an ancient temple,
An early sun was shining on the high forest.
Through winding paths I reached this solitary place,
Its meditation cell hidden behind blossoming trees.
In the mountains the sunrays please the birds to song;
Floating shadows in the pool empty the hearts of men.
All sounds are hushed in this place,
Except the lingering peal of a bell.

(Smits 1995, 95)

In the desolate atmosphere of the temple, the only sounds heard are birdsongs and reverberation of a bell; other sounds are "hushed"; and the men's hearts become clear for reflection, "tak[ing] refuge from a hectic world" (Smits 1995, 95). The lonesome but calm sentiment aired in this poem is very much reminiscent of the *wabi-sabi* principle. The depicted sounds are in absolute harmony with the emotional landscape portrayed in this poem, creating a silent space in the men's mind. Notably, Smits remarks that (59) is one of the poems that were known to Japanese poets in the Heian period (794–1185), which may suggest a likely influence on Japanese poetic literature concerning the rhetorical use of ambient sounds for descriptions of silence and the concept underlining the relation between sound and silence.[23] Additionally, although an extensive textual analysis would be needed to confirm that the concept of silence originated from the Chinese literary practice and was sustained over time in the Japanese tradition, Cao (2001) observes that Basho's rhetorical technique of evoking silence by sound seems to be influenced by the literary work of the Chinese poet, Du Fu (712–770), who regularly depicted silence by way of nature sounds and voices.

The similar matching situations found in the Korean and Chinese culture and language indicate that the way in which sound and silence are viewed in the Japanese context is not a conceptual or linguistic outlier in a relevant sense. The question of whether an equivalent of the *wabi-sabi* principle of Zen Buddhism is the source of a likely conceptualization process relevant to the Korean and Chinese cultures is left to be pursued elsewhere although the religious and philosophical influence of Zen Buddhism seems to be a reasonable and logical source of the conceptualization pattern.

Beyond the Korean and Chinese cultures and languages, the Deaf culture sheds an interesting light on the conceptualization of silence. Especially regarding our five senses, the ways in which sensory experiences are interpreted exhibit cultural differences, as a quotation from Bahan (2014) suggests. Recalling an African Deaf man speaking of "smelling danger" in the jungle coming from smells of urine, corpses, and the like, Bahan, also a Deaf person, comments that while fully able to smell the same range of scents, he "was from a culture that didn't incorporate this awareness" (p. 233). As we have been discussing regarding sounds, not only the ability of the members of the culture to react to sensory stimuli but what sensory reactions mean to a specific culture can give rise to variability. In that light, as I have noted above, it is important to understand that "culture" has broader references than the one that is classified by factors like geographic area, ethnicity, and language.

On that note, it provides an interesting perspective to investigate a view of cross-modal conceptualization of silence in the Deaf culture. I continue to focus on ambient silence. Dr. Janis Cole, who is a Deaf speaker of American Sign Language (ASL), has been instrumental in offering a view of silence in the Deaf culture.[24] For Dr. Cole, silence is a visual experience, and its perception and conceptualization relies on the visual sense. So, the type and degree of physical movements count as a primary basis for the concept of silence. For instance, movements of the hectic kind, even the constant movement of the waves in the ocean, do not represent silence. Contrastive with this, the subtle movement of trees and the like in nature as well as slow movements in the outdoors symbolize silence. The concept of silence that she constructs is also based on the tactile sense, more specifically, things that are soft. Importantly, Dr. Cole regards silence as what gives her a sense of calmness and peace, and she even mentions Zen-like feelings that accompany the concept of silence. A similar insight is shared by a deaf father, Peter Artinian, in the documentary film *Sound and Fury* (2000). In it, Peter signs, "I really AM happy being deaf. It's very peaceful. Who'd wanna change that?"[25] Although his overall view of being deaf is made in response to a debate about cochlear implants, it is evident that his reference to "peaceful" is about a silent world connected to being deaf.[26] Although coming from a culture that is different in multiple ways, these views from the Deaf culture have much to share with the Japanese pattern of constructing the meaning of silence: it regards the spiritual impact of stimuli in the vision modality on people's mind as an essential ingredient for an interpretation of silence that seems to be shared and embraced in the Deaf community. Dr. Cole's mention of "Zen-like feelings" is of additional interest concerning *wabi* and *sabi* as forming an important principle underlying the Japanese conceptualization of silence. Whether or not it is the *wabi-sabi* principle itself that is a basis for Dr. Cole's view of silence, there seems to be a similar conceptual thread that ties her line of thinking to the concept of silence tailored to the Japanese cultural context.

It is noteworthy, moreover, that the linguistic expression for "silent" in ASL has more concrete manifestation of the "calmness" component in the concept.[27] The sign for "silent" in ASL consists of two sequential motions: first, an index finger is placed vertically at the lips, just like the gesture made by a hearing person upon saying *shhh* . . . in English, and then slowly lowering both hands (slightly outward), palms down, with the elbows about 90 degrees bent along the torso at the end of the motion. Significantly, the second hand movement is identical with the ASL sign for "calm." The visual ASL signs supplemented by verbal annotations distinctly suggest that the concept of silence in the Deaf culture is constructed with physical and affective (or spiritual) implications, and that both aspects of the concept are explicitly lexicalized by the sign consisting of the two successive hand movements, which resembles a compound in verbal languages used in the hearing culture. The soundscape perceived through the visual and tactile senses and the emotional landscape that it paints in the ASL context are compatible with how silence is conceptualized and linguistically represented in Japanese. Thus, the Deaf culture in the United States, as it is represented by ASL, and the Japanese cultural context in which the range of samples in section 1.1 is interpreted seem to show a mutually intelligible conceptualization pattern.

Before leaving this section, I would like to touch briefly on crickets again, although under a different cultural interpretation this time. Crickets or crickets' chirping in English-speaking culture are not considered to represent silence in the way our Japanese data exhibit. However, in a more contemporary context of popular culture, they symbolize silence with a specific and unique meaning of verbal silence or lack of communication rather than quiet atmosphere. Japanese lacks such a use of referring to (the sounds of) crickets. Relevant examples are in (60–61).

(60) Unfortunately, it's a common frustration and complaint from job seekers who generally speaking invest quality time and effort to apply for a new role only to hear nothing, silence—cricket(s)! (Beauchamp 2017)

(61) He gave a surprised grunt but didn't respond, instead letting the crickets fill the silence. (*Bento Box in the Heartland* by Linda Furiya, 12)

As these examples illustrate, crickets in US popular culture are used to signal awkward verbal silence accompanying the lack of an anticipated response. These instances are particularly interesting in that the silent situation described by the insect name has a specific pragmatic function attached to it for humorous effects in casual speech settings. Crickets here are a metaphor for verbal silence, as a sign of an awkward and negative response. Never can the expression be used to describe the type of ambient silence as demonstrated by Japanese samples in section 1.1.[28] Furthermore, no insects other than crickets can serve the same rhetorical purpose in English. All these points clearly separate the meaning that crickets or crickets' chirping bear in an American (or English-speaking) society vs. in a Japanese society, as it pertains to the concept of silence. It further confirms that an apparently uniform concept can branch out along disparate paths of conceptualization as these emerge from culturally fitted ways of viewing things.

3. SPECIFYING SILENCE

Verbal descriptions of silence are enriched by expressions that specify and intensify silence. In order to give a broader view of how silence is delineated beyond the single vocabulary items that denote "silence" and its equivalents, I will extend the scope of the examinations by including the way in which descriptions of silence are further modified. This comprises instances that are analyzed in the ground-figure terms, as in these examples discussed in chapter 1, renumbered here as (62–63).

(62) Mata **chinmoku**-ga otozureta. Kabe-ni kakatte-iru <u>tokei-no byōshin-ga susumu oto</u>-dake-ga, yukkuri-to byōshitsu-ni hirogatte-iku.

また**沈黙**が訪れた。壁にかかっている<u>時計の秒針が進む音</u>だけが、ゆっくりと病室に広がっていく。

"**Silence** came back again. Only <u>the ticking of the clock</u> on the wall slowly spreads all over the hospital room."

(*Kōshōnin* by Takahisa Igarashi, 370)

(63) Jijijit-to <u>tōshin-no moeru oto</u>-no hoka, nan-no oto-mo shinai. Kinpaku-shita **seijaku**-ga ita-no ma-o tsutsumi-konde-iru.

じじじっ、と<u>灯芯の燃える音</u>のほか、何の音もしない。緊迫した**静寂**が板の間を包み込んでいる。

"Other than the sound of <u>a burning lampwick</u>, 'jijiji,' there is no sound. Tense **silence** envelopes the wood-floored room."

(*Akinai Seiden Kin-to Gin* by Kaoru Takada, 178)

Following Talmy's (1985) analytical frame of lexicalization patterns and applying it to the soundscape sphere, man-made sounds like the ticking of a clock and the sound of a burning lampwick in (62–63) have been presented so as to instantiate the auditory figures in these scenes while the silence that permeates the rooms serves as their ground. Building upon our previous discussion on concepts of silence and their linguistic manifestations but looking at verbal portrayals of silence more broadly, this section will survey the range of rhetorical patterns that the Japanese language incorporates in detailing silent scenes.

3.1 Intensification by Auditory Expressions

It has already been mentioned that in many languages counterfactual expressions and nonliteral expressions, such as metaphors, are available to describe inaudible things as if they were audible. Still within the realm of literal expression but beyond ambient sounds of the type under consideration here, some sounds that come from humans and man-made artifacts become amplified in quiet surroundings, thus serving as excellent symbols for silence. For instance, a ticking clock, dripping water, the water in the cooling system, and people's breathing, among others, are frequent rhetorical devices, especially in literary works, in describing silence without directly asserting lack of other sounds of significance. The Japanese samples in (62–63) illustrate such a strategy. Additional examples in (64–66) demonstrate the prevalent pattern.

(64) Boku-wa nodo-no kawaki-o iyasu tame-ni <u>tsuba</u>-o nomi-konda-ga, yoru-no **seijaku**-no naka-de sono oto-wa hidoku ōkiku hibiita.

僕は喉の乾きを癒すために唾をのみこんだが、夜の**静寂**の中でその音はひどく大きく響いた。

"I <u>swallowed</u> in hopes of easing my thirst, but in **the stillness** of the night, the sound I made was huge."

(*Noruwē-no Mori* by Haruki Murakami, 269; translated by Jay Rubin, 130)

(65) Jit-to shite-iru-to mimi-ga itaku-naru-yō-na **seijaku**-no naka, kasuka-ni <u>okidokei</u>-ga toki-o kizamu oto-dake-ga kikoete-kuru . . .

じっとしていると耳が痛くなるような**静寂**の中、かすかに<u>置き時計</u>がときを刻む音だけが聞こえてくる...。

"When I don't move, **silence** hurts my ears—in that sort of **silence**, I only hear <u>the clock</u> ticking. . . ."　　　　(*Koi* by Mariko Koike, 88)

(66) Byōshitsu-no soto-no rōka-wa hissori-to shite-ori, mado-no soto-kara kasuka-ni kikoete-kuru <u>kuruma-no oto</u>-ga, kaette shitsunai-no **seijaku**-o kyōchō-shita.

病室の外の廊下はひっそりとしており、窓の外からかすかに聞こえてくる<u>車の音</u>が、かえって室内の**静寂**を強調した。

"The hallway outside the hospital room was quiet, and <u>the sounds of cars</u> vaguely heard from outside the window emphasized **the silence** in the room all the more."　　　　(*Koi* by Mariko Koike, 42)

All these passages stage silent scenes, unambiguously announcing that the depicted spaces are very quiet. The degree of silence referred to by the words *seijaku* "silence" is so intense that the sole sound that is audible in (64) is the sound of the protagonist swallowing his saliva; in (65) it is the ticking of a clock; and in (66) the distant sounds of cars. These sounds do not cancel or deny the presence of silence but are foregrounded in the verbal descriptions, so that the intensity of the silence is magnified. From the perspective of the figure-ground relation, the sounds referred to are the anchored, and the silence in the scenes plays the anchoring role. These sounds do not usually reach perceptible levels, typically remaining backstage, but it is their role as the figure in the linguistic perspective that produces the central effect of accentuating the depth of the silence.

The example in (67) presents an interesting interpretation of the man-made sound of a ticking clock.

(67) **Seijaku**-ni tsutsum-areta kono heya-o, boku-wa kekkō ki-ni itte-ita. Iki-o hisomeru-dake-de dokomademo **shizuka**-ni natte-kureru. Sono tsumetaku-mo odayaka-na kūkan-ga, yui'itsu anshin dekiru ibasho. <u>Ka-chikochi</u>, to ano toki-wa—sō, ano koro-wa, <u>toki-o kizamu oto</u>-dake-ga

seijaku-o yori kisoku tadashiku-si, nanimono-ni-mo obiyakas-are-nai annei-no kūkan-o tsukuri-agete-ita.

静寂に包まれたこの部屋を、僕は結構気に入っていた。息を潜めるだけでどこまでも静かになってくれる。その冷たくも穏やかな空間が、唯一安心できる居場所。カチコチ、とあのときは―そう、あの頃は、時を刻む音だけが静寂をより規則正しくし、何者にも脅かされない安寧の空間を作り上げていた。

"I quite liked this room covered with **silence**. The room falls eternally **silent** with my bated breath. The chilly yet calm space is the only place that gives me peace of mind. <u>Tick-tock</u>, then—yes, before, only <u>the ticking sound</u> made **silence** more regular, creating a peace and safe place that will not be threatened by anybody." (Kiyu, n.d.)

The room is described by the words *seijaku* "silent" and *shizuka* "silent, quiet." The only sound in the passage originates from a clock whose ticking sound is further depicted by the mimetic word *kachikochi* "tick-tock." Although the sole sound in the room intensifying the depth of the silence is of the man-made kind rather than of nature sounds, the narrator finds calmness and peace of mind in the silence of the room: *odayaka* "calm, tranquil," *anshin* "peace of mind," and *annei* "peace, tranquility" are descriptors for the space filled with the silent air. The narrator's liking of his silence-infused room and the underlying appreciation for comforting, hushed tranquil ambience is pervasive through the passage and overtly expressed. Note that the link between silence and peace of mind is reminiscent of the meaning of nature sounds that is constructed in a culturally tailored concept of silence. What is particularly intriguing in (67) is that the ticking sound of a clock, even though it is man-made, is identified as a critical link to both suppression of sound and hushed tranquility associated with the perception of silence. The mechanical sound of the clock, typical of man-made sounds, is favorably remarked on here to make the silence regular and orderly, contributing to the creation of peace of mind. In other words, the sound of the clock is admitted to the silence in the room just as nature sounds are embedded in ambient silence. In this example, then, the depiction of the silent scene highlighted by the man-made sound and the emotional landscape that emerges from that scene seem to cross the boundary between nature's sounds and man-made sounds to a rhetorical advantage.

A final example of intensifying silence by sound references is demonstrated by a passage from a novel where a poem is introduced, in (68).

(68) Ima, Masahiko-no tsukue-no ue-ni hirak-areta pēji-ni-wa, sakihodo, hi-o kesu mae-ni kaita mono-ga tsuzur-arete-ita.
Seijaku-nari banbutsu-ga shizumari-kaeri nemureru

>   Shinkai-no gotoku **seijaku**-nari shikashi yagate
>   Sono **seijaku**-to iu <u>sōon</u>-ni mimi-o hikisak-areru
>
>   今、雅彦の机の上に開かれた頁には、先程、灯を消す前に書いた
>   物が綴られていた。
>   **静寂**なり 万物が静まり返り 眠れる
>   深海の如く**静寂**なり しかし やがて
>   その**静寂**と云う<u>騒音</u>に耳を引き裂かれる
>
>   "Now, on the opened page on top of Masahiko's desk was found what he
>   had written before he turned off the light awhile back.
>   It is **silent**. Everything has fallen silent and asleep
>   It is **silent** like deep in the sea, but soon
>   The <u>noise</u> called **silence** will shred my ears [=deafen]"
>   (*Seijaku-to Iu Sōon* by Yoichi Yamano, 9)

The poem that the character in the novel, Masahiko, wrote is filled with descriptions of silence and its intensity: every line contains the word *seijaku* "silence," which is further qualified for its depth. Special attention should be paid to the last line of the poem since it exhibits an interesting use of polar opposites, *seijaku* "silence" and *sōon* "noise," the latter being the name for the former—"the noise called silence." The negative nuance of *sōon* "noise," to which silence is analogized here, has the effect of expressing an overwhelming degree of forceful silence.[29]

3.2 Intensification by Synesthetic Expressions

Ambient silence can be modified by referring to senses other than the auditory one. I will examine this by focusing on synesthetic metaphors. According to *Webster's New World College Dictionary* (4th ed., 1999), "synesthesia" is a psychology term that is defined as "a process in which one type of stimulus produces a secondary, subjective sensation, as when some color evokes a specific smell." In linguistics, the synesthetic phenomenon has been applied to metaphors in expressing one of our five senses—sight, hearing, taste, smell, and touch—by evoking another. Ullmann (1962, 216), for example, describes synesthetic metaphors as being "based on transpositions from one sense to another: from sound to sight, from touch to sound, etc." Examples of synesthetic metaphors in English include *sweet voice* (taste to hearing), *loud color* (hearing to sight), and *sharp odor* (touch to smell); and for Japanese *atatakai iro* "warm color" (touch to sight), *shizuka-na aji* "quiet taste" (hearing to taste), and *amai kaori* "sweet fragrance" (taste to smell). Synesthetic modifications to be demonstrated here play an effective descriptive role in heightening the intensity of silence. The examples below are grouped together according to individual senses that are crossed to modify the intense void in the auditory domain. Of synesthetic, or cross-modal, expressions detailing the nature and extent of silence that I came across, the touch and sight dimensions are more robustly represented as modifiers for the type and intensity of silence, but we do find synesthetic references to other senses as well as combinations of two separate modals. Following Williams (1976), terms describing visually perceived dimension like height, width, and depth are subsumed under sight. Synesthetic modifications are underlined, and the words denoting silence (including verbal silence in this set of examples) are double-underlined.

synesthetic expressions involving touch

(69) a. Tsumetai seijaku-no naka-ni hibiku sonāparusu-no kinzokuon

冷たい静寂の中に響くソナーパルスの金属音

"the metal sound of a sonar pulse that echoes in the cold silence."
(Reservoir, n.d.)

b. Kōri-no tsumatta heya-no yō-ni hiyayaka-ni shizumari-kaeru

氷の詰まった部屋のように冷ややかに静まり返る

"It falls frigidly silent as if the room were filled with ice."
(*Namida* by Michitsuna Takahashi; https://hyogen.info/content/950480196)

c. Kutsurogi-e-to sasou, atatakai seijaku-to hukai yasuragi.

くつろぎへと誘う、温かい静寂と深いやすらぎ。

"warm silence and deep serenity that lead to relaxation"
(Kurashiki Kokusai Hoteru, n.d.)

d. Shīn-to mimi-ga shimu, mimi-ga itamu yō-na seijaku

シーンと耳が沁む、耳が痛むような静寂

"silence that would sting my ears, that would hurt my ears"

(*Kaimu* by Otsuhiko Kaga; https://hyogen.info/content/106174224)

e. Mimi-no oku-ga jin-to hurueru mitai-ni shizuka

耳の奥がじんと震えるみたいに静か

"silent, as if the inner ear would quiver"
(*Ninshin Karendā* by Yoko Ogawa, 25)

f. <u>Komaku-ga hen-ni naru</u> yō-na <u>shizukesa</u>

鼓膜が変になるような静けさ

"<u>deafening</u> <u>silence</u>" (lit: "silence that would <u>make the ear-drum lose control</u>")

(Shukkotōki by Toshio Shimao;
https://hyogen.info/content/451535202)

In the touch domain exemplified by the expressions in (69), the cold temperature and tactile sensations pertinent to ears, including pain, are effective tools that are customarily used to intensify the degree of silence. Because synesthetic expressions directly appeal to our senses, they immediately lead us to visceral, and thus subjective, experiences of the intended sensations, connecting those experiences to the depth of silence. Furthermore, the majority of the above silent scenes, with the exception of (69a) and (69c), are interpreted with an ominous and unwelcoming tone. (69a) is an advertisement for a high-end watch that has been made using advanced technology. The cooccurrence of *tsumetai* "cold" and *seijaku* "silence" in this context underscores the highly accurate mechanical working of the product. In (69b), *hiyayaka* literally conveys a frigid temperature, but it is frequently used as a metaphor for a lack of personal warmth, sympathy, or empathy. These literal and metaphorical meanings collocate well with *kōri* "ice" to represent an oppressive environment which one normally wishes to avoid. (69d), (69e), and (69f) each analogize intense silence to physical sensations in the inner ear—to the level of pain in the case of (69d), and a numbing or unpleasant stimulus in (69e) and (69f). The heightened degree of silence that these metaphors delineate is an unsolicited kind associated with negative images, particularly fear and death. On the other hand, there are indeed examples like (69c) in which ambient silence is portrayed in connection with a calming and pleasant sense.

synesthetic expressions involving sight

(70) a. Kūki-wa hat-to-suru-hodo shinsen-de, atari-ni-wa <u>seijaku</u>-ga michite-ita. Sore-ni awasete chōkaku-o chōseisinaos-anakute-wa naranai-hodo <u>hukai</u> <u>seijaku</u> datta.

空気ははっとするほど新鮮で、あたりには静寂が満ちていた。それにあわせて聴覚を調整しなおさなくてはならないほど深い静寂だった。

"The air was surprisingly fresh and filled with <u>silence</u>. It was such <u>deep silence</u> that I almost had to adjust my sense of hearing."

(1Q84 by Haruki Murakami;
https://hyogen.info/content/185538321)

b. Subete-no kōsai-o keshita yō-na kanjaku-na hūkei

総ての光彩を消したような閑寂な風景

"quiet scenery as if all luster were erased"

(*Ikada* by Shigeru Tonomura;
https://hyogen.info/content/999120524)

c. Atama-o huri, tashikame, mimi-o sumashita-ga, yahari yamabato-no koe-shika kikoenakatta. Yami-wa hukaku, kokatta.

頭をふり、たしかめ、耳をすましましたが、やはり山鳩の声しか聞こえなかった。闇はふかく、濃かった。

"Bowing his head he strained his ears for the sound of that voice again; but the only thing he could hear was the singing of the turtle-dove. The darkness was thick and black."

(*Chinmoku* by Shusaku Endo, 166;
translated by William Johnston, 174)

There are exact words that precisely denote ambient silence in the passages of (70a) and (70b), *seijaku* and *kanjaku*, while the turtle-dove's faint voice as the sole sound audible in (70c) points to the ambient silence. Just as the word "deep" is used as a metaphorical descriptor for silence in English, so too is *hukai* "deep" in Japanese, as is demonstrated in (70a). The adjective *hukai* is probably one of the most common (and somewhat mundane for that reason) modifiers for silence. In (70b) the word *kanjaku* means silence in the surroundings but further implies tranquility and sadness pervading the scene—the kind of inner feelings valued in the *wabi-sabi* aesthetic. So, a portrayal of such an atmosphere by appealing to the visual—little or no luster—evokes a calm image. The description of the silence in (70c) embodied by the sole sound of a turtle-dove is juxtaposed with the thick and black darkness of the night. In the absence of the second sentence, the exclusive sound of the turtle-dove, more likely than not, would be interpreted to represent the kind of silence that leads one to peace of mind. However, as a few more similar examples below reinforce the same effect, the night, especially with the emphasized darkness of the night, intensifies silence while at the same time overriding the comforting undertone. Note that *yami* "darkness (of the night)" is described as *hukaku kokatta* "was deep and thick," which connotes extreme darkness that disables the sense of vision. Then, the dual void in hearing and vision generates uneasy, helpless, ominous images, undermining the effect of the reverse nuance that the birdsong would otherwise put forth. This example reveals a curious and tactful interaction of linguistic mechanisms demonstrated in a depiction of silence.

synesthetic expressions involving sight (colors)

(71) a. Hukai <u>kuro</u>-no <u>seijaku</u>

深い<u>黒</u>の<u>静寂</u>

"Deep <u>black</u> <u>silence</u>" (Iisn 2015)

b. Okyakusan-to mori, mizūmi, yama soshite dōbutsu-tachi-ni kansha-shite, <u>gunjō</u>-no <u>seijaku</u>-o ato-ni shita.

お客さんと森、湖、山そして動物たちに感謝して、<u>群青</u>の<u>静寂</u>をあとにした。

"Thanking my guests, the forest, the lake, the mountains, and the animals, I left the <u>ultramarine</u> <u>silence</u>." (Ando 2010)

On rare occasions we come across distinct color terms serving as modifiers for words that denote silence. We have seen that the adjective *kurai* "dark," which falls under the sight class, is a frequent synesthetic descriptor for silence. Related to it but more clearly as a color term, *kuro* "black" is added to a list of words that intensify silence, as in (71a). Far less common is a modification by the color term *gunjō* "ultramarine" in (71b). Reliance on concrete color terms in descriptions and intensifications of silence is usually supplemented by pictorial impressions that directly provide visual embodiments. The website that contains (71a) posts several photos of an inkstone maker surrounded by ink, inkstones, and his workplace, all of which are pitch black. Likewise, (71b) appears in a blog in which the author chronicles his trip to Hokkaido. The travel blog is accompanied by spectacular photos of Lake Akan that are tinted in blue. Especially mediated by visual representations, the verbal references to "black silence" and "ultramarine silence" bring together the visual and auditory responses synesthetically, whereby an intense sensual experience is generated for direct reactions.

synesthetic expressions involving touch~sight

(72) a. . . . <u>koi</u> <u>seijaku</u>-to tōmei-na kurayami-no shitsukan-o migoto-ni hyōgen-shite-miseta.

. . .<u>濃い静寂</u>と透明な暗闇の質感を見事に表現してみせた。

". . . [music performance] beautifully expressed the texture of <u>dense silence</u> and clear darkness." ("Shinshōhūkei," n.d.)

b. Shisai-wa inotta-ga, umi-wa <u>tsumetaku</u>, <u>yami</u>-wa katakuna-ni <u>chinmoku</u>-o mamori-tsuzukete-ita.

司祭は祈ったが、海は<u>冷たく</u>、<u>闇</u>は頑なに<u>沈黙</u>を守りつづけていた。

"So he prayed. But the sea remained <u>cold</u>, and the <u>darkness</u> maintained its stubborn <u>silence</u>."
(*Chinmoku* by Shusaku Endo, 152; translation by William Johnston, 159)

c. Denwa-no beru-wa jūgo-kai natte, soshite kireta. Beru-ga shinde-shimau-to, marude jūryoku-ga kinkō-o ushinatte-shimatta-yō-na <u>hu-kai</u> <u>chinmoku</u>-ga atari-ni michita. Hyōga-ni tojikomer-arete-shimatta goman-nen-mae-no ishi-no yō-na <u>hukaku</u> <u>tsumetai</u> <u>chinmoku</u>-datta. Jūgo-kai-no denwa-no beru-ga boku-no mawari-no kūki-no shitsu-o sukkari kaete-shimatta-no-da.

電話のベルは十五回鳴って、そして切れた。ベルが死んでしまうと、まるで重力が均衡を失ってしまったような<u>深い沈黙</u>があたりに充ちた。氷河にとじこめられてしまった五万年前の石のような<u>深く冷たい沈黙</u>だった。十五回の電話のベルが僕のまわりの空気の質をすっかり変えてしまったのだ。

"After ringing 15 times, the phone stopped. Once the bell tone died, <u>deep</u> <u>silence</u> permeated as if gravity lost its balance. It was <u>deep</u>, <u>cold silence</u> like 50,000-year old stones that had been locked in a glacier. The 15 bell tones completely changed the quality of the air around me."
(*Nejimakidori to Kayōbi-no Onnatachi* by Haruki Murakami; https://hyogen.info/scate/290192)

The adjective *koi* "thick, dense" in (72a) seems to me to belong to the touch domain, serving as a synesthetic modification for *seijaku* "silence": *koi seijaku* "dense silence" evokes an image that the silence is not easily breakable or escapable. The term *chinmoku* "(verbal) silence" in (72b) is itself a metaphor (personification) for *yami* "darkness," but the collocation of the coldness of the sea, the darkness (of the night), and the personified silence of the darkness creates an intense silence of the atmosphere. The darkness of the night (vision) and silence (hearing) present in parallel two kinds of void in two sense modalities. Although the silence described in this example is of the verbal nature, the darkness of the night is staged in total ambient silence. Based on the storyline of this novel, the stubborn silence of the darkness is understood that God does not respond to the priest's prayer. In addition, the chilling scene with a rich religious connotation is further explicated by the coldness of the sea, compounding the urgency of the situation. Descriptors appealing to vision (darkness of the night) and touch (coldness of the sea) as well as the personification metaphor of the darkness being silent (hearing) jointly heighten the urgency of the situation and desperation. In (72c) the versatile synesthetic metaphor *hukai* "deep" (sight: dimension) appears twice to detail the intensity of the silence. Its second occurrence is juxtaposed with another adjective *tsumetai* "cold," which belongs to the touch domain. The phrase *hukaku tsumetai chinmoku* "deep, cold silence" is indeed preceded by a simile that likens the degree of coldness to the surroundings created by a glacier. It is natural to infer that the silence in this scene is far from a pleasant or comforting one.

synesthetic expressions involving smell

(73)   Wakimichi-ni soreru-to totanni hitoke-ga nakunarimasu. Nodoka-na den'en-hūkei. Yuhudake-no yūshi. Haru-no kaori-ga suru shizukesa.

脇道にそれると途端に人気がなくなります。のどかな田園風景。由布岳の勇姿。春の香りがする静けさ。

"As soon as turning to a side road, there is no sign of life. A calm rural landscape. A majestic figure of Mt. Yuhu. A tranquility with the spring fragrance."
(Takemashuran, n.d.)

synesthetic expressions involving taste

(74)   a. Yoru-no kehai-ga oto-mo naku otozureru yūguredoki-no sabishisa-ni-mo nita amai shizukesa-ni tsutsum-areru shādē-no akōsutikku-bosa-kavā

夜の気配が音もなく訪れる夕暮れどきの寂しさにも似た甘い静けさに包まれるシャーデーのアコースティック・ボサ・カヴァー

"Sade's acoustic Bossa cover,[30] enveloped by a sweet calm like the loneliness around the sunset when a sign of evening appears without a sound"
(Après-midi Seleção, n.d.)

b. Makuwauri-no usu-amai shizukesa-wa, yoru-ni yoku kikoe-sō-da-kara reizōko-kara dashite-oita-noni.

まくわうりのうす甘い静けさは、夜によくきこえそうだから冷蔵庫から出して置いたのに。

"(although) I took out the melon from the refrigerator because I thought its slightly sweet silence seems to be heard more in the evening."
(Hibi-no Sara 2019)

Specification and intensification of silence by descriptors in the smell and taste domains are not all that common but still can be sporadically found, as those in (73–74) illustrate. The spring fragrance mentioned in (73) for modifying tranquility in a rural landscape is not a concretely identifiable smell as such. Nevertheless, the olfactory reference adds a detailed description of the scene that is free of sounds—at least of a disturbing kind—and people. The other mentions of the rural landscape and Mt. Yufu additionally enrich the nature-oriented, comforting milieu that is expressed in the silence characterized in association with the olfactory reaction. The examples in (74) both employ the adjective *amai* "sweet" to detail silence. Of the two examples, the nuance in (74a) is perhaps more straightforwardly ascertained since there are parallel expressions like *amai neiro* "sweet tune," *amai koe* "sweet voice," and *amai sasayaki* "sweet whisper" where the same taste adjective synesthetically modifies sounds. When it qualifies terms for silence as in (74a), the silence is felt—or heard in this case of a music piece—with a pleasant and delightful experience just as a sweet taste in the mouth is dear to average folks (i.e., not to those who shy away from sweets and sweet-tasting food and drinks). In contrast, interpreting (74b) seems to require quite a bit of imagination especially since the "sweet" silence is depicted to belong to a (yellow-colored) melon. Whatever relation a melon may be assessed to have with silence in this example, there are two points of relevance: the silence portrayed in (74b) is said to be "heard" in the text, and related to this, the silence, as a tangible target, has a sweetness in it, just like music tunes and human voices.

Linguistic expressions across multiple modalities help the characterization of silence and in many cases bring it a great level of depth. It is worth noting that unlike the positive connotations that nature sounds bring about in evoking ambient silence, many of the collocated linguistic words and phrases discussed above demonstrate an opposite effect and evoke negative images that silence could lead to. Typical references are darkness and coldness, and with them, silence is virtually always viewed to signal something unpleasant, unwelcomed, or feared. In addition to darkness and coldness, silence can also be closely associated with death, and thus we see silence is linguistically collocated with words that denote death or pertain to it, as is illustrated by the examples in (75).

(75) a. <u>Yoru</u>-no <u>seijaku</u>-to-wa kasuka-na mono'oto-mo tatanu-to iu koto-de-wa nakatta. <u>Yami</u>-ga kodachi-o kasumeru kaze-no-yō-ni, <u>shi-no osoroshisa</u>-o totsuzen, shisai-no kokoro-ni hakonde-kita.

<u>夜の静寂</u>とはかすかな物音もたたぬということではなかった。<u>闇</u>が<u>木立</u>をかすめる風のように、<u>死の怖ろしさ</u>を突然、司祭の心に運んできた。

"It was not that the <u>stillness</u> of <u>the night</u> was completely without sound. Just as the <u>darkness</u> floats over the trees, <u>the awfulness of death</u> suddenly descended upon him, filling him with <u>terror</u>."

(*Chinmoku* by Shusaku Endo, 253; translation by William Johnston, 257)

b. <u>Yoru</u>-ga <u>shinin</u>-no yō-ni <u>shizumari-kaeru</u>
夜が死人のように静まりかえる
"<u>The night</u> falls <u>silent</u> like <u>the dead</u>."

(*Kamisori* by Naoya Shiga;
https://hyogen.info/content/353394667)

Both examples in (75) place silence, the darkness of the night, and death in the same plane. In (75a) the meaning of the silence at night is far beyond the absence of noticeable sounds, extending to the fear of death. Similarly, in (75b), the density of silence is likened to the total absence of any sign of life.

NOTES

1. The source is https://unitedpeople.jp/silence/.
2. Sato's commentary on the tea ceremony appeared at http://www.ucon.co.jp/cha/cha1-1.html.
3. The blog appeared at http://www.rhythmtherapy.jp/blog/2007/06/post_24.html.
4. The blog appeared at http://blog.livedoor.jp/rh1-manyo/archives/46608617.html.
5. Basho's haiku poems with the imaginary insects' sounds are: 蜘何と音をなにと鳴く秋の風; and 蓑虫の音を聞きに来よ草の庵. Horikiri comments on the former poem that Basho is asking a spider to sing in the lonesome atmosphere that the autumn wind creates. As for the latter, Horikiri's interpretation is "come to my hut and let's enjoy the autumn elegance while listening to the sounds of bagworms" (Horikiri 1998, 301; my translation, NT).
6. The Japanese word *omomuki* (趣), which appears in many of the definitions of *wabi*, *wabiru*, *sabi*, and *sabiru* in (41–44), is somewhat difficult to translate uniformly. The word has been translated into "(cultivated) taste, elegance, (refined) sensibility, atmosphere, charm, beauty, flavor" in *Shin Waei Daijiten*. Although my exact choice of wording for the translation of the term varies, it should be understood to refer to the same basic notion.
7. The definition of wabi in *Kojien* is virtually identical with that in *Nihon Kokugo Daijiten*.
8. These four English adjectives are not to be understood to form an exhaustive list, as there are also additional adjectives such as *serene* and others with similar nuances that can be included. Needless to say, listing translation equivalents is not quite sufficient to elucidate the fundamental nature of what "silence" means in the Japanese context.
9. However, Suzuki and Iwai's (2006) study extensively discusses the (fuzzy) origin of the words and concepts of *wabi* and *sabi* vis-à-vis *chanoyu* "tea ceremony."
10. The same line of an aesthetic view has been taken by some Western scholars and professionals who essentialize differences in aesthetic values between the East and the West (e.g., Keene 1969; Ernst 1969; Koren 1994).

11. Kawabata's speech is indicative of this implication, as is suggested by a line to that effect in his speech, 論理よりも直観 "intuition and immediate feeling over reason and argument."

12. A "recycled" notion of aesthetics I discuss here may be thought of in terms of "re-invented tradition" based on Hobsbawm's (1983) term "inventing tradition." Hobsbawm (1983) explains the phrase to mean "essentially a process of formalization and ritualization, characterized by reference to the past, if only by imposing repetition" (p. 4).

13. A parallel interpretation has been made of Basho's poem in (18). For instance, Sano (1991, 91) characterizes the nuance underlying the poem as "silence/stillness in the middle of motion (sounds)."

14. Parallel to Kawabata's aesthetic view mentioned earlier, Koren (1994) also takes a similar approach by trying to reduce wabi-sabi to an essence which includes "intuitive worldview."

15. I would like to thank Ms. Juri Furukawa for her permission to reproduce her paintings here.

16. The paintings can be viewed at https://emuseum.nich.go.jp/detail?content_base_id=100151&content_part_id=001&content_pict_id=003&langId=ja&webView=.

17. Nakagawa (2015) explains that Tohaku considered his ideal work to be "quiet painting," and that Shōrinzu was painted around the time that Tohaku attempted to produce such "quiet paintings."

18. I take their "global metaphor" to be equivalent to Lakoff and Johnson's (1980) conceptual metaphor.

19. I should point out that the sound in (53) is not the frog's natural voice, but instead, it was produced when it jumped into a pond; and the action of jumping into a pond does not typify frogs' inherent behavior or sound quality. That is, the sound that Basho mentions in the poem does not represent an intrinsic characteristic of frogs in any unique way, unlike the cicada's sound in (52).

20. This interpretation of their analysis is confirmed by a more straightforward statement in Hiraga's (2005) earlier work. Specifically, for the cicada poem in (52), she sets up two conceptual (her "global") metaphors, VOICE IS LIQUID and SILENCE IS ROCK, and explains: ". . . the rocks appear to absorb these voices and so to recapture the silence. Indeed, *the two natural entities of the poem, rocks and the cicada, are metaphors for silence and sound*" (Hiraga 2005, 147; emphasis added, NT).

21. For example, Toyama (1997) discusses a vigorous exchange between the poet Mokichi Saito and the literary critic Toyotaka Komiya in the 1920s.

22. This poem was reprinted with permission: Poem by Chang Jian: 題破山寺後禪院 "Inscribed on the Meditation Hall Behind Poshan Monastry" (translated by Ivo Smits) in Ivo Smits, *The Pursuit of Loneliness: Chinese and Japanese Nature Poetry in Medieval Japan, ca. 1050–1150*, Münchener Ostasiatische Studien Band 73, Franz Steiner Verlag, Stuttgart (Germany), 1995, p. 95. I thank the publisher and Dr. Ivo Smits for their permission.

23. I am grateful to Tie Xiao for pointing out to me the significance of Wang Ji's and Chang Jian's poems and directing me to the relevant literature.

24. My sincere thanks go to Dr. Janis Cole for sharing her thoughts with me, and also to Dr. Brenda Nicodemus for her ASL interpretation.

25. I thank Donna Jo Napoli for calling my attention to this film. The source of the film is https://www.youtube.com/watch?v=zXNrqKPsac0.

26. I am fully aware that most deaf people are not completely unable to hear. Here, by a silent world, I mean a situation with a limited auditory sense.

27. I would like to thank Dr. Daniel Roush for pointing this out to me. Below I consulted the websites https://www.handspeak.com/word/search/index.php?id=1967 and https://www.handspeak.com/word/search/index.php?id=301 regarding the signs for "silent" and "calmness," respectively.

28. One clear difference is that crickets are not present or actually heard at the scenes described in the English examples.

29. The use of polar oppositions will be illustrated again with mimetics for silence in chapter 3.

30. The loanword term *kavā* (more likely to be pronounced as *kabā*) カヴァー, corresponding to the English word "cover," is a technical term used in popular music to mean an arrangement of an original song/music to a different style. The type of music mentioned in (74a) is arranged to the bossa nova style. I thank Kazuto Tsujimura for the information about the music terminology.

Chapter Three

Mimetics and Silence

The mimetic vocabulary in Japanese is extensively attested, and by appealing to our five senses—sound, vision, taste, smell, and touch—and emotions, it facilitates vivid depictions of a wide range of manner and states. The pervasiveness and rhetorical magnetism that mimetic words display cannot be underestimated as they play an indispensable role in any medium of Japanese communication on a daily basis. Their communicative power is enriched by a single word that encapsulates sensual and emotional appeals. To illustrate, the catch phrase in (1), which appeared in a commercial poster, speaks to the commanding feature of mimetics.[1] The notation "Q" stands for a geminate consonant, homorganic to a consonant that follows it.[2] Additionally, throughout the chapter, long vowels in mimetic words will be represented by a sequence of two identical letters, rather than using a macron over the vowel letter, to reflect the phonetic realization of vowel length.

(1) **JuuQ**-to   ki-tara,   **guiQ**-to   iki-tai-ne.
    mimetic-quotative   when came   *mimetic*-quotative   go-want-particle

ジューッときたら、グイッと行きたいね

"When it goes 'juuQ,' I want to go 'guiQ.'"

It goes without saying that what is said in (1), when interpreted word-by-word, may not seem to make much sense, because it is vastly abbreviated and does not provide any context that might make the message immediately transparent. However, as Otsubo (1989, 496) elaborates on it, the phrase is construed on par with ジューッと肉が焼けて来たら、グイッと飲みたい, which says "When the meat is getting cooked, 'juuQ,' I want to drink (beer), 'guiQ.'" The two mimetics respectively refer to the sound of the meat being cooked, an equivalent of sizzling, and the sound of gulping liquid. I have presented the phrase in (1) to four native speakers of Japanese, two residing in Japan and two in the US, without any contextual background or visual cues for the phrase, and asked them what they associate the two mimetics with. Not surprisingly, all of them uniformly interpreted the phrase as Otsubo describes. Furthermore, in their reactions and explanations, they commonly used the terms *meat*, *grill*, *griddle*, and *sizzle* for *juuQ*, and *beer* and *gulp* for *guiQ*. One speaker additionally made clear that *guiQ* corresponds to "gulp" rather than "sip." Underlying these native speakers' responses is a strong association that *juuQ* and *guiQ* have with human senses as well as circumstances to which they are pertinent. For instance, the sound *juuQ* relates to a specific food item—meat rather than fish or vegetables; and the food is being cooked by a specific cooking method, i.e., grilling, during which the fat and juice of the meat drips over the coals or its equivalent, raising a strong flame. This image forms the foundation for the speakers' terms "meat," "grill," "griddle," and "sizzle." The word *guiQ* refers to a sound mimicking liquid consumption, but the manner of the ingesting activity is presumed to be done in a rigorous fashion rather than in a reserved and elegant style. This is why one of the speakers specified "gulp" instead of "sip." And, putting all these circumstances together, beer is the beverage that is thought of as (at least one of) the most common type with meat-grilling and meat-eating activities. At the same time, gulping, as opposed to sipping little by little, characterizes beer-drinking. So, the two mimetic expressions bring about sensual reactions that involve sound and vision (e.g., flame) at the very minimum—perhaps as well as the smell of grilled meat—and supplementary situational images based on personal and cultural experiences.

The consistent reaction to (1), despite its rather meager verbal context, is a brief validation of the communicative power that the mimetic vocabulary can exert, and serves as a prelude to an important role that this vocabulary class plays in verbal expressions of silence in broader contexts. All this, however, should not be taken to mean that verbal descriptions by the non-mimetic vocabulary cannot achieve the kind of vivified images that the mimetics do in (1). Literature on narrative descriptions (e.g., Lodge 1990; Clark and van der Wege 2001) testifies that discourse constructed in narratives consists of a variety of ways through which the audience is able to participate in sharing experiences, and a number of such experiences are sensual (including cross-modally) and emotional. This is true of Japanese and presumably many other languages. Nevertheless, as researchers of mimetics in Japanese and their equivalent words in the world's languages have repeatedly explained, the ability to induce imagery and affective reactions is a fundamental word-level attribute of the mimetic word class, and it is this asset that alleviates the need for an elaborate context in leading the audience to sensual and emotional experiences.

The primary goal of this chapter is to demonstrate that mimetics add another means to the catalog of linguistic and rhetorical resources in Japanese that richly express and depict ambient silence. It will be shown that mimetics of silence and mimetics for silence are linguistic means that are suitable for portraying silence. Their exceptional aptitude for depicting ambient silence is due to their sensual and affective characteristics, which sharply distinguish them from prosaic (non-mimetic) words. I believe it is such a lexical trait that makes the use of the mimetic word class coherently in line with the concept of silence constructed in the Japanese cultural context. First, though, we must consider the linguistic characteristics and conceptual basis of the mimetic vocabulary.

1. CONCEPTUAL BASIS OF THE MIMETIC VOCABULARY

1.1 General Introduction to Japanese Mimetics

The mimetic vocabulary in Japanese is extremely pervasive across genres and styles of communication. Scholarly importance and general interest by language users are evidenced not merely by the extensive literature in Japanese linguistics that exclusively deals with this word class (e.g., Hamano 1986, 1998; Kakehi and Tamori 1993; Kita 1997; Tamori and Schourup 1999; Nasu 2002; Akita 2009) and in literary discussions regarding its rhetorical (i.e., literary) effects but also by the number of dictionaries that solely compile mimetic entries culled from broad sources. Mimetic words belong to one of the four major vocabulary strata in Japanese, the other three being native, Sino-Japanese (long-standing loanwords from Chinese), and foreign (loanwords other than those originated from Chinese). Although they show some overlapping properties, these four classes have been established based on linguistic characteristics that distinguish each one from the others. (Martin 1952; McCawley 1968; Ito and Mester 2003; Kageyama and Saito 2016) McCawley (1968, 64) provides a general description of the mimetic vocabulary class while suggesting deeper functions to be spelled out: they "function syntactically as manner adverbs and may refer to just any aspect (visual, emotion, etc.) of the activity involved, rather than just its sound." Japanese is by no means an isolated language that has this word class. Basque, Chichewa, Finnish, Korean, Pacho, Quechua, Tamil, and Turkish are some of the languages in the world that are reported to have similar classes of vocabulary, and relevant discussions are found under the terms like onomatopoeia, ideophones, expressives, and sound-symbolic words.[3] For terminology, I make a distinction between mimetics and non-mimetic words by referring to the latter as "prosaic" following Diffloth (1979) and Newman (2001).

It is commonly acknowledged that Japanese mimetics is wide-ranging in terms of meaning and function, as McCawley's quotation above implies. In much of the Japanese literature on the topic, mimetics are divided into semantic-based categories under the Japanese terms of *giseigo* (擬声語)/ *giongo* (擬音語), *gitaigo* (擬態語), and *gijōgo* (擬情語). *Giseigo* and *giongo* mimic voices (for the former) and sounds (for the latter), corresponding to what onomatopoeic words generally describe. *Gitaigo*, which constitutes the largest membership of the Japanese mimetic vocabulary, is said to depict general manner and conditions of entities. *Gijōgo* refers to psychological states and physical feeling. These three sub-classes are labeled respectively as phonomimes, phenomimes, and psychomimes (Akita 2009), but most discussions, particularly those written in Japanese, use the two-way distinction of *giongo* (for *giseigo* and *giongo*) and *gitaigo* (for *gitaigo* and *gijōgo*).[4] Selective examples of phonomimes, phenomimes, and psychomimes are given in (2), taken from Akita (2009, 12–13), although the transcriptions and some of the English translations have been modified from the original.[5] Following the transcription pattern of Japanese linguistics, I use "N" for moraic nasal (or coda nasal, syllable-final nasal) and "Q" to represent a geminate consonant.[6] As noted before, "Q" should be interpreted as being identical with the consonant that follows it. However, the word-ending "Q," which assumes the suffixation of the quotative particle *-to*, does not normally appear at the end of a word, except for emphatic and/or casual speech. The meanings for the examples are kept as they are assigned in the original for the most part, but, as it will be further discussed below, it should be understood that what mimetics "mean" is quite different in nature from denotations of prosaic words and it also varies depending on the context.

(2) a. Phonomimes: bakiQ "crack," buubuu "oink-oink," gorogoro "thunder," kotoN "plonk," kusukusu "chuckle," putsuQ "snap," shuQ "swish," chariN "clink," doshiN "thud"

b. Phenomimes: shiQtori "moist," niyari "grinning," nebaneba "sticky," chokomaka "bustling restlessly," koNgari "toasted lightly brown," koNmori "swelling," pikaQ "shining," poiQ "tossing," subesube "smooth," suQkari "completely," jirori "staring sharply," zuraQ "lined up"

c. Psychomimes: biQkuri "surprised," gaQkari "disappointed," haQ "noticing," kurakura "dizzy," ukiuki "feeling happy and lighthearted," zoQ "fearful," zukiQ "feeling one's head/tooth throb"

The examples in (2) demonstrate the variety of morphological forms in which mimetics appear, but some recurring shapes such as reduplication, geminate ending (indicated by the final Q), and the word-final *-ri* are typical of mimetics. Morphological patterns that are associated with mimetic words are often schematically represented, including more common templates like CVCV-CVCV (e.g., *pakupaku* "the manner of widely opening and closing the mouth repeatedly when eating or speaking"), CVCVQ (e.g., *pakuQ* "the manner of opening the mouth wide, usually to bite or swallow something"), CVCVN (e.g., *pakuN* "the manner of opening the mouth wide, usually to bite or swallow something"), CVCVri (e.g., *pakuri* "the manner of opening the mouth wide and/or biting or snapping at something"), and CVCCVri (e.g., *paQkuri* "the manner of opening the mouth wide and/or biting or snapping at something") (Hamano 1998; Akita 2009).[7,8,9] As shown in these examples, a shared base (e.g., *paku*) serves as the semantic thread of the variant forms. The finite set of these morphological patterns is a helpful indicator in partially identifying members of the mimetic vocabulary.

Morphophonological and morphosemantic aspects of mimetics have widely been studied, and the systematic relationships between a restricted number of templatic representations and their iconic meanings have been noted (e.g., Hamano 1998; Akita 2009). Hamano (1998, 104–107), for one, gives generalizations over the form-meaning relationships underlying the morphological templates expanding from a CVCV-base form, as in (3).

(3) a. CVCVN: involvement of elastic objects or accompaniment of a reverberation

b. CVCVQ: movement in one direction with forcefulness or vigorousness

c. CVCV*ri*: quiet ending of the movement

d. CVCV-CVCV: continuous, stative, distributive, or repetitive movement[10]

To illustrate, *tsuruN*, *tsuruQ*, *tsururi*, and *tsuru-tsuru* are all attested mimetic words that share the CVCV-base of *tsuru*. Kakehi et al. (1996) give them the identical definition of "the state in which the surface of something is smooth and slippery," but the subtle semantic differences among them are attributed to the nuance that is associated with each of the morphological templates. In another set of examples, *pin~piin~pin-pin* (CVN~CVVN~CVN-CVN), where the first is presumed to be the base form in this sequence, "the state in which something is stretched tight" (Kakehi et al. 1996) is the general meaning common across them, but the lengthened vowel [i] in *piin* corresponds to spatial and temporal lengthening or strenuous action, according to Hamano's characterization (p. 72). The morphological templates of the sort shown above are not available to all mimetic words, but nevertheless, at least to the extent that several forms share a base and follow the templatic patterns pertinent to the mimetic stratum, the formal representations serve as one measure for distinguishing between mimetics and prosaics.[11]

1.2 What Do Mimetics Mean and Do?

While linguistic characterizations of Japanese mimetics and their equivalents in other languages have been richly documented and given descriptive and theoretical analysis, defining this vocabulary class has been a contentious issue, especially in the attempt to distinguish it clearly enough from prosaic words. McCawley's characterization for Japanese mimetics given above is indeed vague, allowing much room, in particular, for semantic (and functional) specification. Although the language-internal semantic classification and the terminology given for its categories such as those in (2) are commonly used in the literature, I wish to further discuss the "meaning" aspect of mimetics, as it is decisively germane to the current topic.

The challenge of determining essential characteristics for the mimetic vocabulary is well known among scholars of mimetics and ideophones in the world's languages. To cite in part from Hinton et al. (1994, 10), the semantic scope runs the gamut from "mimicry of environmental and internal sounds," "expression of internal states of being, both physical and emotional," "salient characteristics of objects and activities, such as movement, size, shape, color, and texture," to "expression of the evaluative and affective relationship of the speaker to the subject being discussed."[12] Despite the wide semantic range of mimetics and the difficulty in characterizing it with a coherent and concise set of criteria, there are indeed a few semantic aspects scholars have largely agreed on. Standing out most prominently are their reference to an experienced vividness and the underlying sensual nature that gives rise to the liveliness.[13] Samarin (1970, 157) comments, ". . . take them [=ideophones] out, and the narration becomes as tasteless as oatmeal without salt." Samarin's distinction between the sensual reference of ideophones and the cognitive reference of prosaic words (p. 163) also has a parallel in Diffloth's (1972, 445) "expressive mode of meaning" for ideophones vs. "cognitive mode of meaning" for prosaic words. Building on these observations and consolidating reports cross-linguistically, Voeltz and Kilian-Hatz (2001, 3) summarize that mimetics and ideophones "simulate an event, an emotion, a perception through language," exhibiting "a special dramaturgic function."

Related to these observations and insights, Kita (1997) enunciates the semantic contrast between mimetics/ideophones and prosaic words in his two-dimensional approach. The basic tenet of his proposal is that meanings of words are not represented uniformly but in two distinct dimensions: the affecto-imagistic dimension and the analytical dimension. The former represents the semantics of mimetics (and ideophones) whereas the latter represents the semantics of prosaic words. The two dimensions are defined as in (4).

(4) a. Affecto-imagistic dimension: the level at which language has direct contact with sensory, motor, and affective information (p. 380)
b. Analytical dimension: the level of decompositional and hierarchical representation in terms of decontextualized semantic partials (p. 409)

Kita further explains the affecto-imagistic dimension as follows (p. 387):

In the affecto-imagistic dimension, different facets of an experience are represented. *These include the affective, emotive, and perceptual activation in an experience but do not include the rational construal of it based on such things as agentivity and causality.* Iconicity is an important architectural principle in this dimension, and thus various facets of an experience do not stand in syntagmatic relationships. Rather, they are merely spatiotemporally contiguous. In the affecto-imagistic dimension, various kinds of information from different cognitive modalities remain modality-specific, *creating the subjective effect of evoking an image or "re-experience."* (emphasis added, NT)

The characterization of mimetics in connection with the affecto-imagistic dimension perfectly aligns with the afore-mentioned insights into the semantic properties of ideophones and expressives commented on by Samarin, Diffloth, and Voeltz and Kilian-Hatz, making even sharper the fundamental semantic differences between mimetics and prosaic words. In Kita's two-dimensional approach, it is important to view the semantic nature of mimetics as stemming from the "affective, emotive, and perceptual" realms from which iconic images are evoked, and such images—sometimes multiple images for a single word—are linguistically represented as the "meaning" of a mimetic expression. The iconicity that underlies phenomimes in particular and psychomimes may not be straightforwardly apprehensible since there do not seem to be concrete and direct associations between linguistic form and meaning. However, it is to evoked images based on individual experiences that the "meaning" of a mimetic word corresponds. This is why verbally giving a dictionary-like definition for a mimetic item in prose form is extremely difficult and sometimes misleading. As pointed out by many, instead, the speakers are compelled to rely on gestures and facial expressions to convey exactly what they "mean" by the mimetic (e.g., Diffloth 1972; Kita 1997; Dingemanse and Akita 2016; Akita and Dingemanse 2019).

In the attempt to shed even more light on the essential semantic nature underlying the mimetic vocabulary, some discussions center on its depictive feature, which is considered in comparison with descriptive representation of what is observed and referred to (e.g., Dingemanse and Akita 2016; Akita and Dingemanse 2019). The general semantic characterization as "marked words that depict sensory imagery" by Dingemanse (2012), for instance, is indicative of this perspective. The difference between depiction and description has been examined in linguistics and other disciplines (e.g., philosophy, literature) alike, where depiction is thought to take the form of pictorial representations (e.g., pictures, paintings, sculptures) (Goodman 1976; Walton 1976) and to be interpreted "through direct perceptual experience" (Clark and Gerrig 1990, 767). Clark and Gerrig use the dichotomy of description vs. depiction as a critical criterion in considering quotations to be a type of demonstration, and claim that quotations depict, rather than describe, the referent.[14] Regarding quotations as depiction becomes relevant to analyzing the semantic role of mimetics as depiction. It has been cross-linguistically observed that mimetics, ideophones, and expressives are commonly accompanied or introduced by grammatical marking like quotative particles and complementizers. In Japanese, the quotative particle -*to* is frequently observed following mimetic words, some obligatorily while others optionally.[15] The two mimetic words in (1) provide sufficient examples to show the point: *juuQ-to* and *guiQ-to* are both marked by the quotative particle. Although we do not take up the issue here regarding the optionality of the quotative marker, the generic tendency that points to the juxtaposition of a mimetic word and the quotative particle suggests that what precedes the quotative particle -*to* (i.e., mimetics) in Japanese shares common properties with what is quoted. Analyzed on par with quotations, it follows that mimetics are demonstrations and, as such, they are depictions.

In trying to understand the distinction between depiction and description as they apply to the difference between mimetics and prosaics, I find it beneficial to look at potentially similar instantiations of this dichotomy from slightly different perspectives that are entertained in fields including anthropology, aesthetic studies, and music (e.g., Armstrong 1971, 1975; Goodman 1976; Feld 1988). In my view, these standpoints pertain to the general purview of mimetics, but I shall discuss them particularly with my later discussion of mimetics of silence and mimetics for silence in mind.

In his discussion of "affective things" and "affecting presence," motivated by an examination of Yoruba arts but driven by broader implications to anthropological aesthetics, Armstrong (1971, 1975) makes a distinction between *presentation* and *representation*, which are associated respectively with "immediation" and mediation. He defines immediation as "the self-sufficiency of the agents in the affecting transaction" (Armstrong 1971, 56). Presentation assumes physical similarity or identity without any intervention for perception and interpretation, namely, *im*-mediation. In contrast, representation is *re*-presentation, made possible by mediation of a symbol. To use his example, in uttering "I am feeling sad," the speaker is not presenting her/his feeling but instead is representing how s/he feels through the mediation of words. To apply this distinction to our discussion, both mimetics and prosaics are words and thus linguistic symbols, but what they *do* is different. The mimetic vocabulary presents the sensate and affects, and what is presented is visceral and needs no reification. Prosaic words, on the other hand, are symbols that bear rationalized ideas as their meaning. Put slightly differently, in Feld's (1988) terms, mimetics execute the process of "adaptation" from the sensate and affect to a new context of the linguistic form (i.e., a sound sequence) for direct presentation of sensual and emotional reactions; whereas prosaic expressions re-present those visceral reactions through another linguistic symbol that bears "rationalization" of what is perceived and felt. The former brings forward the feeling in actuality, as if one were in effect living through the very sensual and emotional experience, leading to the "in-it" feeling; and the latter corresponds to ideation of the sensate and affect by which one can speak *of* the experience, generating the "of-it" feeling.[16,17] The dichotomy of presentation-immediation-"in-it" vs. representation-mediation-"of it" as applied, in its core, to the mimetic vs. prosaic vocabulary contrast is analogous to the two dimensions that Kita lays out in (4). It is also parallel to the difference between depiction and description as those terms relate to the literature on mimetics and ideophones. But additionally, it offers a different angle from which we can understand the unique path that each of the two sets of vocabulary takes in contributing to linguistic expressions of our experiences.[18]

In light of our observations and interpretations of the essential differences between the two vocabulary types, mimetics are regarded to show stronger and more direct appeal to human senses than what their prosaic counterparts could generally achieve, at least in a word-level comparison. The degree to which mimetic modifiers and their prosaic counterparts demonstrate vividness in various communication acts has been illustrated by Tamori (2002, 2–3) in the contrastive examples in (5–6) below, where the mimetics in (5) and their corresponding prosaic expressions in (6) are supposed to have the same function as adverbial modifications.[19] The definition of each mimetic in (5) has been added, based on Kakehi et al. (1996); I have also added English translations to Tamori's Japanese examples, where the abbreviation "Acc" indicates the accusative case.

(5) a. kao   zentai-o **suppori** ōtte,   hiyake-o   husegu
       face   all-Acc   *mimetic* cover   sunburn-Acc   prevent

       san baiza   [ad for sun visor]
       sun visor

   "a sun visor that prevents you from getting a sunburn by **completely** covering the entire face"

   suppori: The manner of covering something or sinking into something completely.

   b. kahanshin-o   yurayura-sasete,   **kyuQ-to**
      lower body-Acc   *mimetic*-do   *mimetic*

      hikishime!   [ad for beauty appliance]
      tighten

   "get **tightened** by swaying the lower body"

   kyuQ: The manner of tightening, grasping or pressing something firmly; or the state of being tight, narrow, etc.

   c. tsume-o   yasashiku   **sakuQ-to**   kiru   [ad for nail clipper]
      nail-Acc   gently   *mimetic*   cut

   "cut the nail **crisply**"

   sakuQ: A single crisp crunching sound produced when cutting or biting something.

(6) a. kao   zentai-o   **kanzen-ni** ōtte,   hiyake-o   husegu
       face   all-Acc   completely cover   sunburn-Acc   prevent

       san baiza
       sun visor

   "a sun visor that prevents you from getting a sunburn by **completely** covering the entire face"

   b. kahanshin-o   yurayura-sasete,   **kitsuku**   hikishime!
      lower body-Acc   *mimetic*-do   firmly   tighten

   "get **tightened** by swaying the lower body"

   c. tsume-o yasashiku   **keikai-ni**   kiru
      nail-Acc gently   smoothly/lightly   cut

   "cut the nail **smoothly/lightly**"

Tamori explains that while the mimetics in (5) give "concrete and vivid descriptions" (p. 4), the prosaic adverbs in (6) that are supposed to have parallel meanings end up "blurring the images that are evoked" by the mimetics.

Tamori's point speaks directly to the contrast between the "in-it" feeling of mimetics and the "of-it" feeling of prosaic words. The contrast demonstrated in (5–6) further highlights the commercial motivation behind the use of mimetics in the advertisement catch-phrase in (1). Simply saying the Japanese equivalent of "upon hearing the sound of meat being cooked, I want to drink beer" all in prosaic expressions without a single mimetic word would not draw an ideal level of consumers' attention. Instead, the driving force for widespread use and success of the mimetic vocabulary in marketing can be attributed straightforwardly to the multisensory experience and emotional involvement made accessible by mimetic words. The sense of vividness that mimetic expressions exude is a direct and natural consequence of the presentation and immediation aspects of their vocabulary class. The examples in (5) and the advertisement phrase in (1) are convincing testaments to these assets that are characteristic of mimetic expressions.

Returning once again to the characterization of the two dimensions in (4), the "modality-specific" nature of the information accessed in the affecto-imagistic dimension—as opposed to the "amodal" system of the analytical dimension—that gives rise to subjective images has significant implications. Peek (1994) points out that our experiences are multisensory, and recognizes that "we must also anticipate differing cultural foci for the senses" (p. 476). It follows from the multisensory nature of experience that a mimetic word can highlight several individual modal aspects, creating polysemous situations. Furthermore, these sensual reactions that the mimetic presents may not always have clear-cut connections among each other, comparable to, for example, the kind of metaphorical extensions that account for the several meanings of a prosaic word. Some of the entries that are listed in mimetic (and general) dictionaries are more conventionalized than others, and seem to have a finite number of common so-called definitions just like prosaic words. Even then, the perceptual bases are independently recognized without having to share common ground to trace their underlying semantic relations. To illustrate, the mimetic words in (7–10), taken from Kakehi et al.'s (1996) mimetic dictionary, list multiple definitions in the prose style. "S" and "M" stand respectively for sound-based and manner-based definitions. These selective examples are Kakehi et al.'s own but I have added minor modifications in transcription.

(7) goroQ (p. 432)

    a. S: A short rumbling sound.

        Kaminari-ga **goroQ**-to natta-node, akachan-ga naki-dashita.

        "Thunder **rumbled** and made the baby cry."

b. M: The manner of rolling briefly; [of persons or animals] the manner of flopping down or the state of lying somewhere.

Terebi-o miyō-to omotte **goroQ**-to yoko-ni natta-ga, sonomama nete-shimatta.

"I **flopped down** to watch television, but fell asleep instead."

(8) gosoQ (p. 438)

a. S: A short, loud rustling sound.

Kuroi kage-ga **gosoQ**-to ugoku-no-ga mieta-ka-to omou-to, yami-no naka-ni kieta.

"Just when I heard **a rustle** and saw a shadowy figure move, whatever it was disappeared into the darkness."

b. M: The manner of taking or receiving something in one large amount.

... kōkana hōseki-ga **gosoQ**-to nusum-areta.

"... **much** valuable jewelry ... was stolen."

(9) korokoro (pp. 595–99)

a. S: The chirping sound of a cricket; the merry laughter of a child or young girl.

Tonari-no ie-kara musume-san-ga **korokoro**(-to) waratte-iru koe-ga hotondo mainichi-no-yō-ni kikoete-kuru-ga, ...

"The sound of the neighbor's daughter's **gay laughter** can be heard coming from the house next door almost every day, ..."

b. M: The manner of a round or cylindrical object rolling.

... Saikoro-wa **korokoro** korogari, tomarimashita.

"... The dice **rolled** across the floor, and came to a stop."

c. M: The manner of occurring easily and successively.

... Kayo-no, tanin-ni taisuru hyōka-wa, **korokoro** kawaru-to iu tokuchō-ga aru.

"... Kayo's opinions of people had a way of changing **at the drop of a hat**."

(10) shiQtori (pp. 1109–11)

a. M: The state of being agreeably moist or damp.

Sono hi, machi-ni-wa **shiQtori**-to haru-no ame-ga hutte-ita.

"On that day, **light** spring rain was falling in the town."

b. M: The state of being gentle, tranquil or refined.

Yamada-san-no okusan-wa ocha-o oshiete-iru-dake atte, **shiQtori**(-to) ochitsuite, nakanaka jōhin-na hujin-da.

"Yamada's wife is a **calm, composed** and self-possessed woman, as befitting someone who teaches the tea ceremony."

The sound-based meanings under "S" find their sources in the auditory sense, but the meanings that have to do with various types of manner, i.e., phenomimes and under "M," are sometimes particularly difficult to compartmentalize. For instance, *goroQ* in (7b) primarily evokes vision but it is not totally straightforward to recognize *goroQ* as a sound that accompanies the motion. Furthermore, the connection between the sound-based (noted by "S") and manner-based (noted by "M") interpretations in (7–9), as well as between the manner-based meanings in each of (9–10), does not seem to be readily made by analogical mechanisms. With *korokoro* in (9), for instance, it seems clear that the sound of crickets and the sound of girls' laughter do not resemble each other; nor is either type of sound perceived analogously to the manner in which something rolls or to the state in which someone lies down. The situations under which the mimetic word is multiply listed for its semantic properties are independent of each other, and the domains to which different perceptive reactions and evaluations belong do not have to find a unique thread for a commonality. The sensual images and affective reactions that mimetics present are subjectively constructed based on the individual language user's experiences. As such, the images and the "definitions" labeling them may vary according to the specific context in which they occur and the specific language user's individual experiences.

The fluidity or variability with which a given mimetic word is interpreted under situation-specific, individual-specific, or culture-specific contexts, as exemplified in (7–10) and widely observed in larger samples, is in part reminiscent of Clark and Clark's (1979) discussion of innovative denominal verbs in English like those in (11).

(11) a. He **wristed** the ball over the net.
 b. Will you **cigarette** me?
 c. We all **Wayned and Cagneyed**.
 d. She would not try to **stiff-upper-lip** it through.
 e. They **timbered** off the hills in the 1880s.

(Clark and Clark 1979, 767–68)

Clark and Clark explain that innovative denominal verbs such as *wrist, cigarette, Wayne and Cagney, stiff-upper-lip,* and *timber* in (11) have "a shifting sense and denotation," which they characterize as "one that depends on the time, place, and circumstances of their use" (p. 768). They further claim that these words, which they label "contextuals," are distinguished from indexical and denotational expressions in that they satisfy the three criteria in (12).

(12) a. Contextuals should possess not a small finite number of potential senses, but an indefinitely large number of senses.
b. The interpretation of contextuals depends on the context.
c. The interpretation of contextuals requires cooperation between the speaker and the listener.

To demonstrate the difference between contextuals on the one hand and indexical and denotational expressions on the other, they give examples like (13–14).

(13) a. My sister **Houdini**'d her way out of the locked closet. ("escape by trickery")
b. Joe got **Houdini**'d in the stomach yesterday. ("hit hard without warning")
c. I would love to **Houdini** those ESP experiments. ("expose as fraudulent by careful analysis'") (Clark and Clark 1979, 784)

(14) a. bottle the beer, bottle the wine
b. We were stoned and **bottled** by the spectators as we marched down the street.
c. ... battered wives may be stabbed or **bottled** as well as punched.
(Ibid., 785)

The proper noun *Houdini* does not have a sense, but each of its denominalized verb uses in (13) receives a specific sense under its particular contexts. Clark and Clark argue that the three senses of the denominal verb *Houdini* in (13) must rely on the speaker and the listener's knowledge about Houdini, that is, his being an escape artist, his manner of death, and his investigations of fake mediums. The denominal verb *bottle* presents another example of contextuals. While *bottle* is typically used as a location verb as in (14a), it is clear that the particular context that illustrates a political demonstration or a violent act, for example, makes it possible for the same verb to receive a sense as an instrument verb in (14b) and (14c), which is very different from the sense of *bottle* as a location verb as in (14a). In this regard, both *Houdini* and *bottle* have shifting senses and denotations, and are considered contextuals. Clark and Clark conclude that "what they mean depends on the time, place, and circumstances in which they are uttered" (p. 809). Interpreting innovative denominal verbs relies heavily on a specific context under which they are used, and in many cases (particularly examples like those with *Houdini*), cultural information critically participates in figuring out what the most appropriate interpretation might be. On the one hand, innovative denominal verbs that Clark and Clark consider to be part of contextuals are indeed prosaic words that belong to the analytical dimension within Kita's two dimensional approach to lexical classifications. Furthermore, the subjective image-forming that can give rise to individual variation in meaning assignments for Japanese mimetics also separates contextuals from them. That is, the criterion stated in (12c) does not enter into a uniquely crucial requirement for mimetics beyond general conventional principles like Grice's cooperative principle, for instance. On the other hand, the degree of elasticity in meaning possibilities as well as the situational and cultural contribution to narrowing down the word's sense to a unique interpretation shares the basic insight into the semantic characterizations while at the same time separating mimetics from prosaic words within Japanese.

In light of the subjectivity of our experiences and the "in-it" feeling presented by mimetic words, it follows that there is room for nonconventional interpretations of conventionalized mimetics and for innovative mimetic expressions, both of which are broadly attested in human communication. There are copious samples of both these types of divergence that are documented and analyzed in the linguistics literature (e.g., Tamori 2002; Tsujimura 2016, 2017). The first type will be discussed later, but here I touch briefly on the second type by giving one example of a newly created mimetic that, to my knowledge, is absent from both mimetic dictionaries and common use. In the following paragraph, the word *zaun(-to)* is such a mimetic innovation.

(15) Hudan, amari hi-ga haitte-konai hiraya-no wagaya-na-noda keredo, haru-kara natsu-ni kaketa asa-no ichijikan-dake, asahi-ga shinshitsu-no mado-o tataite yatte-kuru. Hantōmei-no madogoshi-ni awaku kakusan-sareta hikari-wa sono kehai-o heyajū-ni akaruku mitasu. Boku-wa machiwabita raikyaku-o mukaeru-yō-ni mado-o akeru. **Zaun**-to kūki-ga ire-kawaru. Nigiyaka-ni raihō-suru hikari-wa, huton zentai-ni huri-kakaru.

普段、あまり日が入ってこない平家の我が家なのだけれど、春から夏にかけた朝の一時間だけ、朝日が寝室の窓を叩いてやってくる。半透明の窓ごしに淡く拡散された光は、その気配を部屋中に明るく満たす。ぼくは待ちわびた来客を迎えるように窓を開ける。**ざうん**と空気が入れ替わる。にぎやかに来訪する光は、布団ぜんたいに降りかかる。

"Ours is a one-story house into which not much sun usually shines, but the morning sun knocks on the bedroom window only for one hour between spring and summer. A sign of the ray that faintly spreads through the translucent window fills the entire room bright. I open the window as if welcoming a guest that I have long been waiting for. The air is exchanged with a **zaun**. The ray that pays us this lively visit pours all over the futon mat."

(Saito 2019, 66)

The novel mimetic, *zaun*, in this context is intended to refer to the manner in which the fresh outside air forces its way to the bedroom, replacing perhaps the morning stuffiness of the room. Although *zaun* is not listed in any dictionary and I at least have never heard of it before, the instant entry of fresh air that is depicted in this passage is readily imagined. The evoked image around *zaun* seems to me to be constructed by drawing multisensory reactions. I would even imagine the scene with some tactile feeling of the warmth of the sunshine and the breeze in the air and, added to that, a fresh scent as an olfactory impression. That the author, Harumichi Saito, is a photographer and essayist who is hearing impaired only makes the coinage of this mimetic more captivating. So, Saito's coinage is likely based not on his auditory experience alone, if any, but on other sensory domain(s) from which the particular image emerges as presentation of what he perceives the sudden flow of fresh air to be like. The mimetic word *zaun* is a linguistic symbol consisting of the phonetic sequence of consonants and vowels available in the language, but the phonetic sequence does not serve as a mediating agent that simply describes the image. Rather, it directly presents the image that Saito intends to project. It is this direct arrival at a perceived image that *zaun* affords, and this is why it is effective in adding vividness and the "in-it" feeling to the context in which incoming refreshing air is presented.

The number of mimetics that are highly recognized and regularly used is large, and these mimetics are mainly conventionalized with a finite number of fixed denotations, as is demonstrated by mimetic dictionaries. As such, conventionalized mimetics have the guise of prosaic vocabulary. However, the nature of the meaning of mimetics is fundamentally different from that of prosaic words for the variety of reasons that have been discussed in this section. Sensually and affectively grounded, mimetics directly appeal to our senses and emotions, evoking vivid images according to individual language users' specific perceptions and experiences. The subjective nature of the images that mimetic words call up can yield non-uniform reactions among speakers, depending on the context in which the words appear and individuals' own memories. As a consequence, we may encounter different interpretations of a given mimetic word depending on individuals and situations. The semantic profile that mimetics display in contrast with prosaic words is an important background for our discussion of mimetics of silence and mimetics for silence. Below, I will occasionally use the term "meaning" or "definition" for ease of exposition, especially when I refer to interpretations listed in dictionaries, simply as a way to speak of the images evoked by mimetics.

Throughout the discussion, however, I maintain that the semantic nature is fundamentally different between mimetic and prosaic expressions for the reasons explained above.

2. MIMETICS OF SILENCE

In chapter 1, I briefly introduced mimetics as a linguistic means deployed in portraying ambient silence. The question to be asked is the following: Given the miming nature of the mimetic vocabulary, what is it that a mimetic word of silence mimics when there is no or little sound? Critical to answering this question is an understanding of the fundamental nature of the mimetic vocabulary in comparison with prosaic vocabulary, as was detailed above. With a single word of the mimetic class, a silent scene is simulated as an image by calling up sensual (not limited to hearing) and affective reactions in the language user's mind. The direct connection between mimetics and evoked images with associated senses and feelings is immediate and intuitive, not through rationalization. Moreover, since our sensual and emotional reactions are personal, based on subjective views and experiences, a mimetic word and the expressions around it can run a gamut of interpretations depending on the individual language user. These are the important characteristics of the mimetic vocabulary that distinguishes it from the prosaic class of words; and, it is just such spontaneity and subjectivity that give mimetics their remarkable linguistic potential for, and an advantage in, depicting ambient silence.

In what follows below, I will survey mimetic words used for depictions of ambient silence and its intensity. It should be kept in mind that mimetics are of the affecto-imagistic dimension, in which "sound" in the form of a phonetic sequence (i.e., the phonetic representation of a mimetic word) directly connects to—namely, presents—sensual and affective experiences. As central ingredients of the affecto-imagistic dimension, evoked images cannot be decomposed into analyzable semantic components; nor can they be generalized into a cookie-cutter semantic norm. Instead, in a single word, mimetics of and for silence present a panoramic view that would correspond to the prosaically represented silent scenes. As such, mimetics are a narrative authority in depictions of ambient silence.

2.1 Mimetics of Silence in Japanese

Central to our discussion are mimetics *hiso*, *shin*, and forms that are derivationally related to them, as listed in (16).[20] The mimetic words in (16) are largely conventionalized in Modern Japanese and widely considered to be descriptors of silence, as is verified by their listing in Japanese language dictionaries, mimetic or otherwise. Their typical definitions found in mimetic dictionaries that are relevant to ambient silence and representative examples are given in (17–24).[21]

(16) a. hiso, hisohiso,[22] hisori, hissori, hissorikan
b. shin, shiin [しいん; しーん; シーン], shinshin

(17) hiso: The state of being quiet and lonesome. The state of fallen silent.

Kono suirikuji-wa hito hanarete aru hodo-ni, **hiso**-to-shite yoizo.

此の水陸時は人離れてある程に、**ひそ**としてよいぞ。

"This Suirikuji here is nice and **quiet**, without a soul."
(M. Ono 2007, 362)

(18) hisohiso: The state of being quiet without a sound.

Taiboku-ga taoreta ato-no sabishii-yō-na, **hisohiso**-shita shōgatu-ga kita.

大木が倒れた跡の淋しいやうな、**ひそひそ**した正月が来た。

"A **quiet** New Year's Day came, like being saddened after a large tree has fallen." (Ibid.)

(19) hisori: The state of being quiet and solitary without any sound. The state of being lonesome with few people.

Huyugomori-to mieru ie-ga noki-o narabete **hisori**-to shizumatte-iru bakari-de aru.

冬籠りと見える家が軒を並べて**ひそり**と静まっている許りである。

"It is **silent and solitary** with only a row of houses that appear to be winter quarters." (Ibid.)

(20) hissori: The state of being quiet and still.

Sakuya natsumatsuri-de anna-ni nigiyaka datta mura-mo, ichiya akeru-to **hissori**(-to) shizumari-kaette-shimatta.

昨夜夏祭であんなに賑やかだった村も、一夜明けると**ひっそり**（と）静まり返ってしまった。

"The village which was so lively last night with the summer festival had become **still and quiet** by this morning." (Kakehi et al. 1996, 530)

(21) hissorikan: [emphatic form of hissori] The state of being quiet and still.

Ichinichi **hissorikan**-to shite-ita hama-mo, kono shibaraku-no aida-dake-wa, sasuga-ni nigiyaka-na kibun-ni naru.

一日**ひっそりかん**としていた浜も、この暫くの間だけは、さすがに賑やかな気分になる。

"The shore, which is **deserted** most of the day, certainly becomes lively during this short period." (Ibid., 531)

(22) shin: The state of perfectly still and quiet.

Jogingu-wa, nan-to itte-mo, sōchō **shin**-to shizumari-kaetta mada usugurai michi-o hashiru-no-ga ichiban-da.

ジョギングは、何といっても、早朝**しん**と静まり返ったまだ薄暗い道を走るのが一番だ。

"As far as jogging goes, there's nothing nicer than running along a still dark, **perfectly quiet** street early in the morning." (Ibid., 1102)

(23) shiin: [emphatic form of shin] The state of being perfectly still and quiet.

Shiin-to shizumari-kaette-iru-ga, betsudan ie-no naibu-ni kawatta koto-ga okotte-iru hū-ni-mo miuke-rare-nakatta.

しいんと静まり返っているが、別段家の内部に変わったことが起こっている風にも見受けられなかった。

"Although the house was **silence itself**, there did not appear to be anything unusual going on inside." (Ibid., 1095)

(24) shinshin [深深、沈沈、森森]: The state being profoundly silent, deeply tranquil. A state of having fallen completely silent.

Atari-wa **shinshin**-to shite inakamichi-no koto-tote hitogoe-mo nanimo kikoezu.

四方は**沈々**として田舎道の事とて人声も何も聞こえず。

"It is **completely silent**; even at a country road no human voice is heard."

Neshizumatta kanji-de atari-wa **shinshin**-to shite-ita.

寝静まった感じで四辺は**森々**としていた。

"Everything seems to have fallen asleep and there was **stone silence**."
(M. Ono 2007, 524–25)

In both of (16a) and (16b), we can recognize the mimetic forms in templatic patterns characteristic of mimetics that we discussed earlier: building on *hiso* (CVCV) and *shin* (CVN), reduplication is observed with both—*hiso-hiso* (CVCV-CVCV) and *shinshin* (CVN-CVN); -ri suffixation shows up on *hisori* (CVCV-ri) and *hissori* (CVCCV-ri); and, *hissori* (CVCCV-ri) and *shiin* (CVVN) exhibit an additional consonant and vowel, respectively, for lengthening the segment. Only *hissorikan* shows a pattern that is somewhat outside the typical templates of mimetics. Not only are the variants in each example set in typical molds of the lexicon's mimetic stratum, but the fact that they appear in a series of related morphological templates, rather than occurring only in a single pattern, confirms their membership status as mimetics. Importantly, it follows that the words in (16), solidly identified as mimetic words, construct their meanings grounded in a variety of images that are evoked through subjective, sensual, and affective experiences.

Some of the mimetic words in (16) are more prevalently used than others, and *hissori, hissorikan, shin(-to)*, and *shiin(-to)*, for instance, are listed in general dictionaries as well.[23] As conventionalized mimetics, the words in (16) commonly share the meanings provided by the mimetic and general dictionaries. As demonstrated above, these mimetics uniformly refer to lack of sounds, stillness, and tranquility; and in the case of the variants of *hiso* in (16a), solitary, lonesome sentiments are added to the silent state. (16a) and (16b) are thus very similar in referring to quiet scenes. However, drawing from a number of literary examples over a span of some 500 years to date, Nakazato's (2005) analysis concludes that *hissori* (and presumably its variants) describes the silence resulting from no sign of people and as such further adds a nuance of lonesomeness. In contrast, she characterizes *shin(-to)* as no sound being made or as the quiet state leading to it.

The stratum of mimetics has existed in the Japanese lexicon since the earliest texts. Just like the members of the native stratum, some mimetic words have been added relatively recently, while others have continued to be in use although in some cases the exact range of what they refer to (i.e., received interpretations) may have changed over time.[24] Tracing back the historical origins of mimetics is not always straightforward, but Nakazato (2005, 354) relates *hissori* to the old prosaic word, *hisoka-ni* "secretly, without being noticed by others." On the other hand, scholars (e.g., Kadooka 1993, 2001; Nakazato 2005, 2017; M. Ono 2007) seem to agree that *shin* and related forms in (16a) originate from Chinese. I will come back to detailed discussion of the origin and derivation of *shin* and its variants later.

While mimetics in general are ubiquitous in a variety of communication media, the mimetics in (16) tend to appear more prevalently in—although not limited to—literary works. The extent to which the mimetic vocabulary is used varies depending on authors, but there is no denying that writers make great use of the vividness afforded by the vocabulary class. Nakazato (2009) examines the array of mimetics by the writer Shusei Tokuda (1872–1943), who is known to use mimetics extensively in his novels. Based on several of Tokuda's literary pieces, she observes that *hissori* and *shin(-to)* are noticeable in the number of occurrences as well as the degree of their efficacy. For example, in the story *Ashiato, hissori* appears nine times and *shin-to* four times;

and in the work *Kabi*, Tokuda uses *hissori* three times and *shin-to* four times. Nakazato notes that these mimetics in Tokuda's novels acutely depict "dark silence and solitude in contrast with lively brightness" that fills a deserted house and the atmosphere surrounding it (p. 137). Fujita (2009) surveyed 304 haiku pieces written by the poet Santoka Taneda (1882–1940). She reports that out of 304 haiku poems she surveyed, *hissori* (25 times), *hissorikan* (1), *shinshin* (11), and *shin* (1) are detected, and furthermore, *hissori* counts as the third most frequently used mimetic word in her sample of Taneda's haiku pieces. As we will discuss more later, the Japanese poetry forms of tanka and haiku are written within the limited numbers of syllables, and it is imperative to devise efficient and effective ways in which poems appeal to the poet and the reader maximally within the boundary of the length requirements. For writers and poets who opt for verbal expressions with a rich image impact, mimetics offer an excellent tool to that end. Interestingly, Nakazato and Fujita discern that Tokuda and Taneda each are notable not only in their common use of mimetic expressions but also in the frequent innovation of new mimetic forms.

The following are additional examples of variants of *hiso* in (16a), most of which are taken from literary sources in the modern era.

(25) Marude daichi-no naka-ni merikonda yō-ni, atari-wa **hissori**-to shizumari-kaette-iru.

まるで大地の中にめりこんだように、あたりは**ひっそり**と静まりかえっている。

"It has fallen completely silent [=in **hissori** manner], as if it has sunk under the ground."   (*Yama-no Kanata-ni* by Yojiro Ishizaka; https://hyogen.info/content/674800004)

(26) **Hissori**-to shite, shinkū-no yō-ni shizuka

ひっそりとして、真空のように閑（しず）か

"It is very quiet [=in the state of **hissori**], silent like a vacuum"
(*Tairiku-no Hosomichi* by Shohei Kiyama; https://hyogen.info/content/810982927)

(27) Husuma-o akete rōka-ni deta. Marude yume-no naka-de miru nihonkaoku-no yō-ni **hissori**-shite-iru.

ふすまを開けて廊下に出た。まるで夢の中で見る日本家屋のように**ひっそり**している。

"I opened the sliding door and got out to the corridor. It is silent [=in the state of **hissori**], as if it were a Japanese house that appears in a dream."
(*Kanashii Yokan* by Banana Yoshimoto; https://hyogen.info/content/680076691)

(28) Dono heya-no mado-no kāten-mo mina orite **hissorikan**-to shite-iru.

どの部屋の窓のカーテンも皆下りて**ひっそり閑**としている。

"It is utterly quiet [=in the state of **hissorikan**], with the curtains of every room being closed." (*Maru-no Uchi* by Kyoshi Takahama; https://www.aozora.gr.jp/cards/001310/files/47742_37751.html)

(29) Mon-kara, genkan-atari-mo **hissorikan**-to shite-iru.

門から、玄関あたりも**ひっそりかん**としている。

"It is totally quiet [=in the state of **hissorikan**] from the gate to the entrance area." (Kiyama 2015)

In isolation, mimetic words are generally unspecified for grammatical category (i.e., parts of speech categories), but categorial identification can be made based on the morphological and syntactic environments in which they occur. In (25) *hissori* is followed by the quotative -*to*, and *hissori-to* then serves as an adverbial that modifies the main predicate, *shizumari-kaette-iru* "is fallen completely silent." The light verb *suru* "do" appears directly after *hissori* in (27) while after *hissori-to* in (26). In both of these examples, the verbal complex of *hissori-(to)-suru* depicts the silent state of the scene. The morphological make-up around *hissorikan* in (28–29) is similar to that in (26–27) in that the mimetic word is in the sequence of –*(to) suru*: -*(to) shite-iru* [=the gerund form of *suru*, *shite*, followed by the verb *iru* "be"] adds the aspectual nuance that the quiet state of the scene is unchanged and sustained for an observed period of time.[25]

Many mimetics appear with prosaic predicates, as in (25), and play the adverbial role of further elaborating on what is described by the predicates.

(25) Marude daichi-no naka-ni merikonda yō-ni, atari-wa **hissori**-to shizumari-kaette-iru.

まるで大地の中にめりこんだように、あたりは**ひっそり**と静まりかえっている。

"It has fallen completely silent [=in **hissori** manner], as if it has sunk under the ground." (*Yama-no Kanata-ni* by Yojiro Ishizaka; https://hyogen.info/content/674800004)

The quiet scene in (25) can easily be portrayed without *hissori-to*, while maintaining what is linguistically denoted, but *hissori-to* additionally evokes related images that vividly intensify the depth of silence prevailing in the scene. That is, the prosaic expression, *shizumari-kaette-iru* "has fallen completely silent," makes an analytical contribution while the mimetic word, *hissori-to*, makes an affecto-imagistic contribution. Together, their contributions are not only to the conceptual description of ambient silence but to the sensual impact that accompanies it.

In (26) the mimetic word in the phrase of *hissori-to shite* has the status of an independent predicate, but it cooccurs with another predicate formed by a prosaic adjectival noun *shizuka* "quiet."

(26) **Hissori**-to shite, shinkū-no yō-ni shizuka

ひっそりとして、真空のように閑（しず）か

"It is very quiet [=in the state of **hissori**], silent like a vacuum"
(*Tairiku-no Hosomichi* by Shohei Kiyama;
https://hyogen.info/content/810982927)

Hissori-to shite, the gerundive form of *hissori-to suru*, is used as a verbal form connecting onto what follows it. Just as in (25), the delineation of the sheer silent scene by collocating the prosaic expression and the mimetic predicate not only informs us objectively of the fact that no other sounds are heard but provides leeway for constructing subjective images that are associated with the silent scene. In this particular case, the additional simile, *shinkū-no yō-ni* "as in a vacuum," rids all possible external stimuli in the scene described. These three ways of detailing silence together make the rhetorical force for the depiction comprehensive and maximally experiential. Contrastively, in (27–29), it is exclusively the mimetic expressions that directly present silent scenes since there is no prosaic word that refers to or suggests lack of sound in each of the sentences.

(27) Husuma-o akete rōka-ni deta. Marude yume-no naka-de miru nihonkaoku-no yō-ni **hissori**-shite-iru.

ふすまを開けて廊下に出た。まるで夢の中で見る日本家屋のようにひっそりしている。

"I opened the sliding door and got out to the corridor. It is silent [=in the state of **hissori**], as if it were a Japanese house that appears in a dream."
(*Kanashii Yokan* by Banana Yoshimoto;
https://hyogen.info/content/680076691)

(28) Dono heya-no mado-no kāten-mo mina orite **hissorikan**-to shite-iru.

どの部屋の窓のカーテンも皆下りてひっそり閑としている。

"It is utterly quiet [=in the state of **hissorikan**], with the curtains of every room being closed." (*Maru-no Uchi* by Kyoshi Takahama; https://www.aozora.gr.jp/cards/001310/files/47742_37751.html)

(29) Mon-kara, genkan-atari-mo **hissorikan**-to shite-iru.

門から、玄関あたりも**ひっそりかん**としている。

"It is totally quiet [=in the state of **hissorikan**] from the gate to the entrance area." (Kiyama 2015)

In these examples, the mimetics, *hissori* and *hissorikan*, serve as the exclusive sources that explicate the presence of silence as well as its quality and extent. These mimetics take center stage in depicting residential scenes around which no human activities are detected. The mimetics, thus, are no less important than prosaic expressions, proving their invaluable function and remarkable value as rhetorical and aesthetic means.

In all of these examples, prosaic expressions like *shizuka* "quiet," *muon* "no sound," and *shizumari-kaetta* "fallen silent" would be sufficient if the intended message is simply to make a statement that a soundless or quiet state is observed and described. The presence of the mimetics, either by themselves or with prosaic expressions, conveys the same base-line message, but at the same time opens up to a vivid panoramic experience that can be relived or imagined, though not just by visual images but potentially accompanying reactions to other senses evoked by the mimetic words. For instance, it seems to me that the slight darkness of the dusk, crisp air, or even some mustiness can be sensed from the mimetics in a few of these examples, although these reactions are presumably closely tied to the absence of human presence or activities that Nakazato (2005) pinpoints as the underlying nuance of *hissori*. These multi-layered and multi-modal semantic shades contributing to the details of silent settings as well as the inclusion of "lonesome" and "solitary" in the conventionalized definitions of *hissori* and *hissorikan* are indeed attributed to the affecto-imagistic dimension to which mimetics belong.

We now turn to variants of *shin* listed in (16b): *shin*, *shiin*, and *shinshin*. Earlier in (22–24), we have given examples from mimetic dictionaries. Additional samples presented in (30–41) below have been found in various types of descriptions of silent environments, ranging from literary works to social media sites. Some of the examples here are shown in longer discourse contexts to furnish the clearer background in which mimetics are used.

(30) Jimen-no soko-ni shizunde-iku yō-ni **shin**-to shizuka-ni naru.

地面の底に沈んでいくように**しん**と静かになる。

"It falls silent [=into the state of **shin**] as if going down to the bottom of the ground."

(*Oka-wa Hanazakari* by Yojiro Ishizaka; https://hyogen.info/content/423612025)

(31) Nezumi-ga damaru-to atari-wa **shin**-to shite, tokei-no oto-dake-ga kikoeta. Yuki-ga sore igai-no subete-no oto-o suikonde-ita. Marude uchū-no naka-ni wareware hutari-dake-ga torinokos-areta yō-na kibun-datta.

鼠が黙るとあたりはしんとして、時計の音だけが聞こえた。雪がそれ以外の全ての音を吸いこんでいた。まるで宇宙の中に我々二人だけがとり残されたような気分だった。

"Once the mouse became quiet, it fell **silent** all around, and only the sound of the clock was heard. Snow swallowed all other sounds. I felt as if only the two of us were left behind in the universe."

(*Hitsuji-o Meguru Bōken* by Haruki Murakami; https://hyogen.info/content/710909185)

(32) Wareware-wa hidoku **shin**-to shita matsubayashi-no naka-o aruite-ita. Michi-no ue-ni-wa natsu-no owari-ni shinda semi-no shigai-ga karakara-ni kawaite chirabatte-ite, sore-ga kutsu-no shita-de paripari-to iu oto-o tateta.

我々はひどくしんとした松林の中を歩いていた。道の上には夏の終わりに死んだ蝉の死骸がからからに乾いてちらばっていて、それが靴の下でぱりぱりという音を立てた。

"Now we were walking through the **frightful silence** of a pine wood. The desiccated corpses of cicadas that had died at the end of the summer littered the surface of the path, crunching beneath our shoes."

(*Noruwē-no Mori* by Haruki Murakami, 19; translation by Jay Rubin, 8)

(33) Boku-wa **shin**-to shizumari-kaetta heya-no naka-ni ita. Seikaku-ni iu-to, tsumetai hurōringu-no yuka-ni suwari-konde-ita. Soko-ni aru-no-wa minareta keshiki. Terebi-to shiroi sofa-to shiroi tēburu-to, tatta sore-dake-no sabishii ribingu. Sukoshi mae-made kabe-ni-wa tokei-ga kakatte-ita-ga, ima-wa mō nai.

Seijaku-ni tsutsum-areta kono heya-o, boku-wa kekkō ki-ni itte-ita. Iki-o hisomeru-dake-de dokomademo shizuka-ni natte-kureru. Sono tsumetaku-mo odayaka-na kūkan-ga yui'itsu anshin dekiru ibasho.

僕はしんと静まり返った部屋の中にいた。正確に言うと、冷たいフローリングの床に座り込んでいた。そこにあるのは見なれた景色。テレビと白いソファと白いテーブルと、たったそれだけの寂しいリビング。少し前まで壁には時計がかかっていたが、今はもうない。

静寂に包まれたこの部屋を、僕は結構気に入っていた。息を潜めるだけでどこまでも静かになってくれる。その冷たくも穏やかな空間が、唯一安心できる居場所。

"I was in the room that had fallen silent [=in the state of **shin**]. More accurately, I was sitting on the cold flooring. It is a familiar scene. A lonely living room only with a TV, a white sofa, and a white table. The clock that hung on the wall until a while ago is gone now.

I was quite fond of this room, which was covered with silence. It falls forever silent by holding my breath. The cold yet tranquil space offered me a sole place for peace of mind." (Kiyu, n.d.)

(34) 2013-nen-ni USEN-ga okonatta chōsa-ni yoru-to, ofisu-de hataraku bijinesuman 400-mei-no uchi 68.8%-ga shizuka-na kankyō-de shigoto-o shite-ori, shizuka-sugiru (**shiin**-to shita) shokuba-ni kan-shite, hansū-ijō-no 53.0%-ga "igokochi-ga warui"-to kanjite-imashita.

2013年にUSENが行った調査によると、オフィスで働くビジネスマン400名のうち68.8%が静かな環境で仕事をしており、静か過ぎる(**シーン**とした)職場に関して、半数以上の53.0%が『居心地が悪い』と感じていました。

"According to the study conducted by the USEN, 68.8% of the 400 office employees did their work in quiet environments, but more than half, 53%, thought that work places that are too quiet [=in the state of **shiin**] are uncomfortable." (Kosumosu Moa, n.d.)

(35) Kenketsusha-no naka-wa kurakute, **shiin**-to shizuka-da, to omotte-imasen-ka.

献血車の中は暗くて、**シーン**と静かだ、と思っていませんか。

"Aren't you thinking that it is dark and silent [=in the state of **shiin**] in the bloodmobile?" (Suzakashi Shakaihukushi Kyogikai 2018)

(36) **Shiin**-to shite-iru ninensei-no kyōshitsu. Minna shinchō-ni shinchō-ni kattānaihu-no tsukai-kata-o renshūchū-desu.

しーんとしている2年生の教室。みんな慎重に慎重にカッターナイフの使い方を練習中です。

"A second-year classroom that has fallen silent [=in the state of **shiin**]. The students are all practicing how to use box cutters extremely carefully." (Kawasakishiritsu Nishimiyuki Shogakko 2021)

(37) Kaze-ga nai-node mori-no naka-wa **shiin**-to shite-ite totemo shizuka-desu. Tokiori [tori-]tachi-no nakigoe-ya ki-o tsutsuku oto-ga kikoeru koto-mo arimasita.

風がないので森の中は**シーン**としていてとても静かです。時折[鳥]達の鳴き声や木をつつく音が聞こえることもありました。

"With no wind, it is silent [=in the state of **shiin**] and very tranquil in the woods. Occasionally we heard the sounds of birds' singing and pecking trees." (Nopporo Shinrin Koen 2019)

(38) Neshizumatta kanji-de atari-wa **shinshin**-to shite-ita.

寝静まった感じであたりは**しんしん**としていた。

"Everybody seems to have fallen asleep, and it was dead quiet all around [=in the state of **shinshin**]." (*An'ya Kōro* by Naoya Shiga; https://dictionary.goo.ne.jp/word/森森/)

(39) Hoshi-akari-no moto-ni, **shinshin**-to shite mono-oto hitotsu shinai.

星明りの下に、**しんしん**として物音一つしない。

"Under the starlight, not a sound is heard [=in the state of **shinshin**]." (Wakayamaken Kikakubu Kikakuseisakukyoku Bunkagakujutsuka, n.d.)

(40) Samusa-ga hukamari-yuku naka, **shinshin**-to shizuka-na jikan-no naka-de homura-ga shinkan-ni yotte taki-ager-areru.

寒さが深まりゆくなか、**しんしん**と静かな時間の中でほむら（炎）が神官によって焚き上げられる。

"As the cold deepens, a Shinto priest makes a fire in the quiet [=in the state of **shinshin**], serene time." (Seimei Jinja, n.d.)

(41) Hayashi-no naka-wa **shinshin**-to shite tori-no koe-nado, hoohoo-te kikoeru-dakede hanayome mitsukannen-da-do.

林の中は**しんしん**として鳥の声など、ホーホーて聞えるだけで花嫁見つかんねんだど。

"It was totally quiet [=in the state of **shinshin**] in the woods; only birds' 'hoohoo' sounds were heard. We could not find the bride." (Tohoku Bunkyo Daigaku Tanki Daigaku Minwa Kenkyu Senta 2006)

All of the examples show that *shin*, *shiin*, and *shinshin* are immediately followed by the quotative -*to*, and either serve as adverbials—as in (30), (33), (35), and (40)—or appear in the verbal complex of *shin/shiin/shinshin-to suru*—as in (31), (32), (34), (36), (37), (38), (39), and (41). Many of them cooccur with prosaic words that denote silence, such as *shizuka* "silent, quiet" (30, 35, 37, 40), *shizumarikaeru* "fall silent" (33), *shizuka-sugiru* "too quiet" (34), *neshizumaru* "fall asleep (and quiet as a result)" (38), and *mono-oto hitotsu shinai* "not a sound is heard" (39), contributing to the depictions of the quiet scenes. In contrast, the mimetics are the only words in (31), (32), (36), and (41) that directly portray silent environments.

These mimetics evoke, at the very least, a base-line image of profoundly silent and still scenes, but that image exudes a feel of reliving the experience of being there, thereby simulating the "in-it" feeling. The affecto-imagistic effect of the mimetics is often supplemented by cooccurring expressions (either mimetic or prosaic) and specific nuances that arise from the overall context, so that the content of the presented image can be further narrowed down and particularized. In (30) some surreal sensation stemming from the total silence could be felt due to the accompanying metaphorical/simile phrase, *jimen-no soko-ni shizunde-iku yō-ni* "as if going down to the bottom of the ground."

(30) Jimen-no soko-ni shizunde-iku yō-ni **shin**-to shizuka-ni naru.

地面の底に沈んでいくように**しん**と静かになる。

"It falls silent [=into the state of **shin**] as if going down to the bottom of the ground." (*Oka-wa Hanazakari* by Yojiro Ishizaka; https://hyogen.info/content/423612025)

The examples in (31) and (32) are taken from two novels by Haruki Murakami, who makes frequent and effective use of mimetic expressions in his literary works.

(31) Nezumi-ga damaru-to atari-wa **shin**-to shite, tokei-no oto-dake-ga kikoeta. Yuki-ga sore igai-no subete-no oto-o suikonde-ita. Marude uchū-no naka-ni wareware hutari-dake-ga torinokos-areta yō-na kibun-datta.

鼠が黙るとあたりは**しん**として、時計の音だけが聞こえた。雪がそれ以外の全ての音を吸いこんでいた。まるで宇宙の中に我々二人だけがとり残されたような気分だった。

"Once the mouse became quiet, it fell **silent** all around, and only the sound of the clock was heard. Snow swallowed all other sounds. I felt as if only the two of us were left behind in the universe." (*Hitsuji-o Meguru Bōken* by Haruki Murakami; https://hyogen.info/content/710909185)

The ticking of the clock as the sole audible sound in (31) is reminiscent of the role that secondary sounds play as discussed in chapter 2: the perceptible degree of the ticking sound suggests the intensity of the pervading silence in the scene. At the same time, the metaphor of snow swallowing other sounds and the reference to the unique human existence in the universe serve as an agent that mysteriously thickens the silence surrounding the two individuals portrayed. The passage in (32) contains three mimetic expressions including *shin*; the other two are *karakara* for complete dryness and *paripari* for crisp texture.

(32) Wareware-wa hidoku **shin**-to shita matsubayashi-no naka-o aruite-ita. Michi-no ue-ni-wa natsu-no owari-ni shinda semi-no shigai-ga karakara-ni kawaite chirabatte-ite, sore-ga kutsu-no shita-de paripari-to iu oto-o tateta.

我々はひどく**しん**とした松林の中を歩いていた。道の上には夏の終わりに死んだ蝉の死骸がからからに乾いてちらばっていて、それが靴の下でぱりぱりという音を立てた。

"Now we were walking through the **frightful silence** of a pine wood. The desiccated corpses of cicadas that had died at the end of the summer littered the surface of the path, crunching beneath our shoes."

(*Noruwē-no Mori* by Haruki Murakami, 19; translation by Jay Rubin, 8)

The mimetic *paripari*, a tangible sound made upon stepping on desiccated leaves, cooccurs with *shin*, a mimetic of silence, and serves to highlight the intensity of silence that fills the woods. I have added the translation by Jay Rubin, who is one of the main professional translators of Murakami's literary works. Rubin's translation of *shin* as "frightful silence" reflects the emotive aspect pertinent to the affecto-imagistic dimension that is part of the image evoked by the mimetic in this context.

(33) shows an interesting combination of factors that contribute to elucidating the type of silence in the room.

(33) Boku-wa **shin**-to shizumari-kaetta heya-no naka-ni ita. Seikaku-ni iu-to, tsumetai hurōringu-no yuka-ni suwari-konde-ita. Soko-ni aru-no-wa minareta keshiki. Terebi-to shiroi sofa-to shiroi tēburu-to, tatta sore-dake-no sabishii ribingu. Sukoshi mae-made kabe-ni-wa tokei-ga kakatte-ita-ga, ima-wa mō nai.

Seijaku-ni tsutsum-areta kono heya-o, boku-wa kekkō ki-ni itte-ita. Iki-o hisomeru-dake-de dokomademo shizuka-ni natte-kureru. Sono tsumetaku-mo odayaka-na kūkan-ga yui'itsu anshin dekiru ibasho.

僕は**しん**と静まり返った部屋の中にいた。正確に言うと、冷たいフローリングの床に座り込んでいた。そこにあるのは見なれた景色。テレビと白いソファと白いテーブルと、たったそれだけの寂しいリビング。少し前まで壁には時計がかかっていたが、今はもうない。

静寂に包まれたこの部屋を、僕は結構気に入っていた。息を潜めるだけでどこまでも静かになってくれる。その冷たくも穏やかな空間が、唯一安心できる居場所。

"I was in the room that had fallen silent [=in the state of **shin**]. More accurately, I was sitting on the cold flooring. It is a familiar scene. A lonely living room only with a TV, a white sofa, and a white table. The clock that hung on the wall until a while ago is gone now.

I was quite fond of this room, which was covered with silence. It falls forever silent by holding my breath. The cold yet tranquil space offered me a sole place for peace of mind." (Kiyu, n.d.)

The image of total silence is set out by the single mimetic word *shin*, but it is further elaborated on not only by the synesthetic reference to the coldness of the floor but also by the lonesome space that very little furniture creates. These prosaic descriptions in the narrative generate vivid imagery on par with the single mimetic word *shin*. The text informs us that the silence characterized by the tactile sensation and the emotional impact of the space creates a precious serene place in which one can be at peace. In this context, the silence in the room presented by the mimetic and complemented by the solitary and comforting atmosphere that permeates the room through the prosaic descriptions is explicated as a spiritual antidote. It does not seem to be an accident that the manner in which the silence in the room is perceived, evaluated, and appreciated through the deployment of multiple senses and their affective consequences is consistent with the concept of silence in the Japanese cultural context and its aesthetic grounding.

(34) is contrastive with the soothing and comforting silence portrayed in (33).

(34) 2013-nen-ni USEN-ga okonatta chōsa-ni yoru-to, ofisu-de hataraku bijine-suman 400-mei-no uchi 68.8%-ga shizuka-na kankyō-de shigoto-o shite-ori, shizuka-sugiru (**shiin**-to shita) shokuba-ni kan-shite, hansū-ijō-no 53.0%-ga "igokochi-ga warui"-to kanjite-imashita.

2013年にUSENが行った調査によると、オフィスで働くビジネスマン400名のうち68.8%が静かな環境で仕事をしており、静か過ぎる(**シーン**とした)職場に関して、半数以上の53.0%が『居心地が悪い』と感じていました。

"According to the study conducted by the USEN, 68.8% of the 400 office employees did their work in quiet environments, but more than half, 53%, thought that work places that are too quiet (in the state of **shiin**) are uncomfortable."
(Kosumosu Moa, n.d.)

The prosaic *shizuka-sugiru* "too quiet" tints a silent ambience presented by the single mimetic word of *shiin* with a negative nuance. In this example, the basic mimetic word *shin* is emphasized by the lengthened vowel, *shiin*, projecting a deepened degree of silence. This emphatic form perfectly aligns with the prosaic compound expression for an excessive degree of silence, *shizuka-sugiru* [lit: quiet-exceed] "too quiet." The prosaic description of a very quiet work place and the immediately following parenthetical depiction of silent ambience by the intensified mimetic form *shiin* together give the greatest level of quietness. Unlike (33), however, the juxtaposition of *shizuka-sugiru* and *shiin* in (34) illustrates an atmosphere that is ill at ease for a majority of employees as a work environment. Notwithstanding the contrast in the overall emotional reactions to these two instances of ambient silence, i.e., solitary but soothing in (33) vs. uneasy in (34), a vivid image of an environment that is filled with barely a minimal level of sound or noise is evoked by *shin* and *shiin* as a sensory and affective experience. In these two cases, moreover, it is the prose narrative that further details the "in-it" experience of silence presented by the mimetics. Coming from distinct sources, depiction and description of silence coalesce into a concerted rhetorical effectiveness.

The mimetic *shiin* in (35–36) evokes somewhat serious environments.

(35) Kenketsusha-no naka-wa kurakute, **shiin**-to shizuka-da, to omotte-imasen-ka.

献血車の中は暗くて、シーンと静かだ、と思っていませんか。

"Aren't you thinking that it is dark and dead silent [=in the state of **shiin**] inside the bloodmobile?" (Suzakashi Shakaihukushi Kyogikai 2018)

(36) **Shiin**-to shite-iru ninensei-no kyōshitsu. Minna shinchō-ni shinchō-ni kattānaihu-no tsukai-kata-o renshūchū-desu.

しーんとしている2年生の教室。みんな慎重に慎重にカッターナイフの使い方を練習中です。

"A second-year classroom that has fallen silent [=in the state of **shiin**]. The students are all practicing how to use box cutters extremely carefully." (Kawasakishiritsu Nishimiyuki Shogakko 2021)

Appearing in a community newsletter, the line in (35) is intended to encourage blood donations. The depiction of a bloodmobile being very quiet inside reflects the solemn image that we have of helping others who need intense medical care. The collocation of the silence, darkness, and also blood may even call to mind some somber situations that we would rather avoid. The message that follows in the public announcement, however, assures that the uncomfortable impression of (35) is just a false belief and that the donation site, instead, is surrounded by smiling staff and pleasant music. (36), too, presents a very quiet place—a classroom in an elementary school. It would be surprising to see a classroom full of active pre-teen pupils being very quiet. Yet, the second sentence, especially with repeated *shinchō-ni* "carefully," emphasizes the depth of concentration that they display as they practice handling sharp tools. Upon realizing *shiin* results from the students' engrossed activities, the absence of standard classroom noise is to such an extent that we could hear their breathing.

The passage in (37) exhibits an interesting interaction of the role of nature sounds examined in chapter 2 and the mimetic word *shiin*.

(37) Kaze-ga nai-node mori-no naka-wa **shiin**-to shite-ite totemo shizuka-desu. Tokiori [tori-]tachi-no nakigoe-ya ki-o tsutsuku oto-ga kikoeru koto-mo arimasita.

風がないので森の中は**シーン**としていてとても静かです。時折[鳥]達の鳴き声や 木をつつく音が聞こえることもありました。

"With no wind, it is silent [=in the state of **shiin**] and very tranquil in the woods. Occasionally we heard the sounds of birds' singing and pecking trees."
(Nopporo Shinrin Koen 2019)

It should be remembered that the sounds like those made by birds embody silent and peaceful surroundings. The mimetic *shiin*—an emphatic form—is not just congruent with the silent scene represented by those nature sounds but also with the prosaic word *shizuka*. Additionally, the mimetic immediately links up to an image of a subjective experience in which tranquility and peace of mind are felt as a reality. The mimetics' "immediate" (i.e., direct evocation without mediation) connection guarantees silence as a sensate experience. All in all, the three types of expressions, i.e., the mimetic *shiin*, the prosaic word *shizuka* "silent," and the references to the sounds that birds make, afford a maximally effective presentation of a silent, tranquil scene in (37).

The mimetic complex in (38–39), *shinshin-to shite*, sets an utterly silent sight staged at night.

(38) Neshizumatta kanji-de atari-wa **shinshin**-to shite-ita.

寝静まった感じであたりは**しんしん**としていた。

"Everybody seems to have fallen asleep, and it was dead quiet all around [=in the state of **shinshin**]." (*An'ya Kōro* by Naoya Shiga; https://dictionary.goo.ne.jp/word/森森/)

(39) Hoshi-akari-no moto-ni, **shinshin**-to shite mono-oto hitotsu shinai.

星明りの下に、**しんしん**として物音一つしない。

"Under the starlight, not a sound is heard [=in the state of **shinshin**]."
(Wakayamaken Kikakubu Kikakuseisakukyoku Bunkagakujutsuka, n.d.)

While *shinshin* in these examples does not suggest a specific nuance, whether positive or negative, this mimetic word commonly connects to a night scene as it is illustrated here: everybody has fallen asleep in (38); and the background contains only the starlight in (39). They jointly create an image of tranquil air in the atmosphere. The juxtaposition of the darkness of the night and *shinshin* is indeed a recurring setting for many poems including Mokichi Saito's and Akiko Baba's tanka pieces, as we will examine closely later.[26]

(40) appears in a website of a Shinto shrine, reporting a November event of a religious ritual.

> (40) Samusa-ga hukamari-yuku naka, **shinshin**-to shizuka-na jikan-no naka-de homura-ga shinkan-ni yotte taki-ager-areru.
> 寒さが深まりゆくなか、しんしんと静かな時間の中でほむら（炎）が神官によって焚き上げられる。
> "As the cold deepens, a Shinto priest makes a fire in the quiet [=in the state of **shinshin**], serene time." (Seimei Jinja, n.d.)

The fire-burning ritual by a Shinto priest at the end of the fall season signifies revival of the impoverished soil that has resulted from harvests earlier in the year. The combination of *shinshin* and *shizuka* "silent" bring forth the image of a sacred and serene atmosphere in this religious setting. The chilly November air in the outdoor scene further has the cross-modal effect of highlighting the holiness of the silence. The description of the event on the website adds that visitors experience *shizuka-na kandō*, a quiet kind of inspiration, through the ritual process. That is, the calmness transcends the space and time and reaches one's soul. Note that the state of stillness in (40) could be expressed with *shizuka* "quiet" alone without the mimetic *shinshin*; conversely, it could also be stated with the mimetic alone (e.g., *shinshin-to shita*) without the prosaic word. They are factually parallel; yet, an underlying distinction resides in the nature of nuanced appeals or imprints that each of these words rhetorically puts forward. As we have repeatedly illustrated, mimetics enable us to deploy our senses and emotions in recognizing and observing that which prosaic words analyze into target concepts and objects. Standing as an individual word, the prosaic word *shizuka* describes the scene through a rationalized concept; whereas the mimetic *shinshin* evokes a certain image that arises in an individual person's mind as "quiet" atmosphere. Consequently, immediacy to an actual scene is more direct and visceral with mimetics. Emerging from the mimetic word (*shinshin*), juxtaposed with the prosaic word (*shizuka*), is sacred calmness that is displayed for aesthetic and spiritual experiences that would match *shizuka-na kandō* "calm inspiration" mentioned above.

Finally, we see in (41) no prosaic expressions that straightforwardly denote a soundless atmosphere, but the mimetic *shinshin* and a reference to the sounds that birds make are fully successful in staging a silent environment in the woods.

(41) Hayashi-no naka-wa **shinshin**-to shite tori-no koe-nado, hoohoo-te kikoeru-dakede hanayome mitsukannen-da-do.

林の中は**しんしん**として鳥の声など、ホーホーて聞えるだけで花嫁見つかんねんだど。

"It was totally quiet [=in the state of **shinshin**] in the woods; only birds' 'hoohoo' sounds were heard. We could not find the bride."

(Tohoku Bunkyo Daigaku Tanki Daigaku Minwa Kenkyu Senta 2006)

The mimetic word, through its immediation function, presents us with a silent image to which we respond with our senses and affects. And, the reference to the bird sounds is reminiscent of the nature sounds expressed in (37): the sounds that the birds make in the woods symbolize, rather than contradict, hushed tranquility as part of the concept of silence. Similar to the previous example, a single appearance of the mimetic or the birds' sounds (i.e., not necessarily both) would perfectly be a sufficient linguistic tool to depict the quiet state of the woods, but the dual use of the two linguistic means enhances and intensifies the presence of deep silence in the atmosphere, yielding a static scene deprived of living souls in sight.

It should be underscored that in all the samples with mimetics of silence commented on thus far in (30–41) and in many more like them that are ubiquitous across genres of communication, the role that the mimetics of silence play can be likened to a visual and overall sensual aid that presents language users with panoramic views of silent scenes and virtual experiences of being at those scenes. In the examples that contain both mimetics and prosaic descriptions, silent scenes are described and the intended messages are conveyed successfully. I should hasten to add that I do not mean to discount the ability of verbal narratives with prosaic expressions to achieve descriptive and depictive effectiveness. Skillful narrative discourse and metaphors, for instance, indeed evoke the vibrant imagination in us enough to elicit subjective reactions of the type that mimetics are claimed to bring about (Lodge 1990; Clark and van der Wege 2001). The tremendous advantage of mimetics that I want to stress is that they offer word-level resources that shorten the path to "the sense of reality" and "the reality of personal experience," using Lodge's terms, so that its rhetorical impact is immediate. A single mimetic word enables such a real "in-it" sense to be provoked in the minds of language users. I view this side of their functionality as a sharp contrast with the linguistic role of the prosaic vocabulary.

2.2 The Synchronic and Diachronic Status of *shin~shiin~shinshin*

The ultimate semantic distinctions between the mimetic and prosaic vocabularies of Japanese have already been extensively elaborated on, but in a way at a more fundamental level, it is vital that a word be recognized as mimetic in its core. This is indeed a relevant point to consider because prosaic words can be recognized as mimetic, as I have briefly noted in note 11. Many prosaic words, in fact, have come to be viewed as mimetics over time. I previously referred to the analysis by scholars like Kadooka (1993, 2001), Nakazato (2005), and M. Ono (2007) that *shin*, *shiin*, and *shinshin* are of Chinese origin. Recall that these three mimetics of silence all conform to the morphological hallmarks of mimetic templates: *shiin* is an emphatic form of *shin* by lengthening the vowel; and reduplication in *shinshin* is the most frequent templatic pattern of the mimetic vocabulary. So, based on their morphological structure, they are readily recognized as mimetics. Interestingly, while *shin* and *shiin* are fully conventionalized as their entries in mimetic dictionaries attest to, *shinshin* is actually not placed as a mimetic of silence in any of the mimetic dictionaries that I have consulted. Although we have been assuming that *shinshin* is the reduplicated form of the base *shin*, it has been claimed that *shinshin*, independent of *shin*, is diachronically traced back to Chinese with a very close semantic definition of describing silent situations. In fact, *shinshin*, written with the Chinese characters of 深深 or 沈沈, appears as a prosaic word in standard Japanese dictionaries with the definition of silence and quietness.[27] Nakazato (2005) and M. Ono (2007) independently claim that *shinshin* in Chinese is not a mimetic expression, but since reduplication is a very common morphological shape that is suggestive of the Japanese mimetic vocabulary, they conclude that it is reasonable to think *shinshin* has come to be regarded as a member of the mimetic stratum. There are several other words of a similar type that have been perceived as mimetics despite their prosaic origin in Chinese, and they are sometimes termed as *kango-onomatope* (漢語オノマトペ) "onomatopoeia of the (prosaic) Chinese origin" (Nakzato 2005; M. Ono 2007) or *giji-onomatope* (擬似オノマトペ) "pseudo onomatopoeia" (Kadooka 1993, 2001).[28] M. Ono (2007), for example, lists *shinshin* separately from "full-fledged" mimetics in his mimetic dictionary, and treats it under the independent rubric of *kango-onomatope*.

Although *shinshin* is generally not listed in contemporary Japanese mimetic dictionaries presumably because of its more technical status as *kango-onomatope* or *giji-onomatope*, its morphological relation to *shin* and *shiin* can be readily established when we consider the morphological structure pertinent to the mimetic stratum, as we have already touched on. A number of Japanese mimetic lexemes of the reduplicated CVN-CVN form (with a coda nasal) such as *panpan*, *dondon*, and *gungun* have variants consisting of the respective monosyllabic form, *pan*, *don*, and *gun*, as well as the form with the lengthened vowel, *paan*, *doon*, and *guun*, for its emphatic counterpart. (Akita 2009) Thus, *shin* (CVN), *shiin* (CVVN), and *shinshin* (CVN-CVN) should be viewed as forming a morphological paradigm parallel to *pan~paan~panpan* and *don~doon~dondon*. That is, notwithstanding the diachronic origin of *shinshin*, the lexical entries of *shin~shiin~shinshin* are synchronically better accounted for as constituting a morphologically related family rather than giving them individual treatment, since the morphological patterns of these three words follow the general characteristics of the mimetic stratum.

The synchronic status of *shinshin* as mimetic, or more relevant to our purpose, native speakers' perception of the word as mimetic, is further solidified by the fact that it is written in the hiragana syllabary (しんしん) rather than in the Chinese characters (深深 or 沈沈). Observing that mimetics are overwhelmingly, if not exclusively, written in the *kana* (i.e., hiragana or katakana) syllabary, M. Ono (2007) (also Kadooka 1993 for the role that the orthography plays) explains that writing *kango-onomatope* "onomatopoeia of the (prosaic) Chinese origin" in hiragana and katakana masks its Chinese origin, thereby giving the language users the impression, or leading them to the perception, that they are full-fledged mimetic expressions. Orthographical representations of the Japanese vocabulary, thus, greatly contribute to distinguishing among the lexical strata. Furthermore, drawing on the critical difference between Chinese characters as ideograms and Japanese kana as phonograms, Kadooka (1993) emphasizes that Japanese mimetics (i.e., mimetics of Japanese origin) "do not base their meanings on orthographical symbols unlike Chinese counterparts" (p. 213; my translation, NT). This remark by Kadooka aptly explains the synchronic recognition or perception of *shinshin* as a full-fledged Japanese mimetic word by contemporary language users. It is of further interest that Nakazato (2005) displays a set of data from early twentieth-century literature where the mimetics of silence we have been discussing were once written in Chinese characters but are accompanied by *hurigana* or *rubi*, which indicates their Japanese pronunciations scripted by hiragana. *Rubi* can be added to relatively complicated Chinese characters to aid in reading, but it is also utilized to impose on Chinese characters specific readings that are different from their standard readings. To illustrate, the words written in Chinese characters, 「理由」、「半分」、and 「料理人」, are read with *riyū* "reason," *hanbun* "half", and *ryōrinin* "cook, chef" as their standard readings. However, when particular contexts or purposes such as advertisements and some particularly intended connotations are deemed suitable or convenient, other Japanese words or loanwords with the same meanings are imposed as their newly assigned (often temporary) readings. In each of the examples above, the native Japanese word *wake* "reason" (written in hiragana) and English and French loanwords, *hāhu* "half" and *shehu* "chef" (written in katakana), are respectively added on top of the Chinese characters. The examples in (42) are those that Nakazato found of the words written in Chinese characters with mimetics of silence as their imposed readings. They all describe silence. For each word, I indicate in Romanization the standard reading of the Chinese character(s) followed by a mimetic reading written in hiragana (i.e., as *rubi*). The mimetics imposed on the Chinese words are *shin* or *shiin* in (a), and *hissori* in (b).

(42) a. 寂然 jakunen—shin, 寂 jaku—shin, 沈々 shinshin—shiin
 b. 静寂 seijaku—hissori, 沈静 chinsei—hissori, 森閑 shinkan—hissori

Nakazato does not provide information as to how long and how extensive this orthographical practice was adopted, but in light of the remarks by Kadooka regarding the contrast between ideograms and phonograms, the prosaic words and their imposed mimetic readings are totally amalgamated into a concept compounded with an affective and sensual impact.

Returning to our focus on *shinshin* again, written in the kana syllabary and regarded as belonging to the mimetic vocabulary, it also distinguishes itself from reduplicated native (prosaic) words. It has been observed that the sequential voicing phenomenon, Rendaku, applies to the native vocabulary but not to mimetics, as the contrast in (43) demonstrates. Although all of the examples in (43) take the reduplicated morphological form, those in (43a) are prosaic words whereas those in (43b) are mimetics. (The "*" indicates an ungrammatical pronunciation.)

(43) a. hito-bito "people" (*hito-hito)
 toki-doki "sometimes" (*toki-toki)
 saki-zaki "the distant future" (*saki-saki)
 kuni-guni "countries" (*kuni-kuni)

 b. pata-pata "pattering" (*pata-bata)
 toko-toko "jog-trot" (*toko-doko)
 saku-saku "crunchy" (*saku-zaku)
 kata-kata "clattering" (*kata-gata)

(Nasu 2015, 261–62; minor modifications added)

The initial voiceless consonants in the repeated bases of native words in (43a)—phonetically represented as [ç, t, s, k]—undergo Rendaku, and failure to do so would derive ungrammatical forms. In contrast, the reduplicated mimetics in (43b) do not undergo voicing; and this is the pattern *shin-shin* follows (*shin-jin*). It is true that Rendaku serves as a diagnostic test that isolates native words from the other three lexical strata (Sino-Japanese, loanword, and mimetic), and it alone does not separate mimetics from Sino-Japanese words. Nevertheless, it shows that *shinshin* displays the phonological behavior that is at least consistent with the mimetic stratum but not with the native word class.[29]

2.3 Mimetics of Silence in Japanese Poetry

The availability of the mimetic vocabulary as an expressive verbal tool for portraying silence indeed comes as no surprise in connection with the basic insight of Japanese aesthetic appreciation through sensual and emotional experiences. The connection in its most pronounced form is often attested in Japanese poetry, such as in tanka and haiku, where its common pervasiveness is broadly sampled below. The aesthetic aspect in other languages of the world that employ the equivalent word class has actually been recognized and discussed regarding the role that these words play in the verbal arts, especially in poetry and as part of ritualistic events in specific cultures (Noss 1989; Nuckolls 1996; Dingemanse 2011, 2012, 2014).

Whether or not *shinshin* originally belonged to the vocabulary category of mimetics in the Chinese source language, the synchronic status of *shinshin* and its variants as part of the mimetic stratum in contemporary Japanese is recognized by the language users who may not know its linguistic history. It is worth underscoring that *shinshin*, once acknowledged as a mimetic word (contrastive with a prosaic word), enters into the affecto-imagistic dimension, rather than the analytical dimension. As a semantic consequence, *shinshin* as well as *shin* and *shiin* all appeal to our affects and senses in their presentation of direct images associated with silent scenes according to our individual experiences and subjective reactions. They simulate silence by evoking images that emerge from our affective and sensual experiences—the property that is shared by other mimetics of silence that we have been discussing. The impression and perception regarding the mimetic status of *shinshin* that is motivated by the orthographical representation is unequivocally observed among poets and commentators of haiku and tanka, and is very likely shared by Japanese literary and general audiences as well.

Especially in the poetic world of tanka and haiku, *shinshin* is regarded as a mimetic expression which some poets favor in order to effectively express silence or the depth of silence in their poems. Yukitsuna Sasaki, who is a contemporary tanka poet, critic, and judge in various tanka contests, commented on two important tenets in writing tanka poems on an educational TV program on tanka, "NHK [=Nippon Hōsō Kyōkai] Tanka," which aired in February, 2016: (i) sound and rhythmic effects that words and combinations of words make, and (ii) not expressing everything in a poem, leaving some room for the reader's imagination and interpretation. A similar view is echoed by Fujishima (2007), also a renowned award-winning tanka poet. Acknowledging the widespread use of mimetics in tanka poetry, Fujishima particularly recognizes that the two main functions of the vocabulary class are memory search and imagination arousal. For instance, the former reminds one of a sound that s/he remembers to have heard before, and the latter leads one to imagine the tactile sensation of wringing clothes even if s/he has never wrung clothes before (p. 55). So, the significant role that mimetics play in the poetry form of tanka and haiku and the reasons for it are firmly acknowledged and widely agreed on.

Mimetics are ideal in fulfilling the need for concise verbal expressions to be delivered most vibrantly. What appeals to poets' thoughts and emotions must be intoned within a limited number of syllables[30] (5-7-5 for haiku and 5-7-5-7-7 for tanka), and single-word expressions by mimetics that are packed with direct "in-it" effects serve its purpose most economically. Sasaki himself is one of several tanka poets who are known to be frequent users of mimetic expressions (e.g., others include Akiko Baba, Yuko Kawano, Mokichi Saito, Machi Tawara). Of these notable tanka poets, Mokichi Saito and Akiko Baba, in particular, have been commented on for using *shinshin* often in their poems. Professional commentaries on haiku and tanka pieces by Saito, Baba, and others indeed recognize *shinshin* as a mimetic word and discuss its interpretations and rhetorical effects. For example, two critics (Itsumi 2009; Moriyama 2009) appraise the poetic value that the mimetic *shinshin* brings out in Mokichi Saito's poems in (44–45).

(44) Shi-ni chikaki / haha-ni soine-no / **shinshin**-to / tōda-no kawazu / ten-ni kikoyuru

死に近き母に添寝のしんしんと遠田のかはづ天に聞こゆる

"dying mother on my side / frogs' croaking in rice paddies far away / echoes to the heaven / through tranquility"[31]   (*Shakkō* by Mokichi Saito)

(45) Hita-hashiru / waga michi kurashi / **shinshin**-to / koraekanetaru / waga mich kurashi

ひた走るわが道暗ししんしんと怺えかねたるわが道くらし

"running in earnest / on my dark path / unbearable in stillness / on my dark path"   (Ibid.)

In the celebrated tanka in (44), the poet Saito uses *shinshin* to evoke pure and solemn tranquility penetrating the atmosphere in his and the reader's minds. The calmness and serenity exuding from the image presented by *shinshin* tactfully sets the stage for, and connects to, his mother's approaching departure. (45) is written when Saito was on his way to his friend's house to share the sad news about his teacher's passing. In both there is no word but *shinshin* to refer to a silent ambience; and critics' commentaries on them base their own interpretations of silence focusing on the word *shinshin*. Undoubtedly identifying *shinshin* as a mimetic expression, Moriyama (2009) generalizes various occurrences of *shinshin* in Saito's poems that the mimetic commonly evokes "serene silence of nature as a background holding up the magnitude of the author's strong emotions. In other words, the author's personal emotions organically blend together with the universe that is described as '*shinshin*,' so that they become enlarged and generalized. The reader savors all that" (p. 59; my translation, NT). In another commentary of the tanka in (44), Yoshikazu Shinada interprets *shinshin* to describe Saito's severe emotional pain upon attending his mother's deathbed (https://tankanokoto.com/2018/03/sinitikaki.html). According to M. Ono's (2007) mimetic dictionary, *shinshin* as a mimetic to refer to strong pain is written in different Chinese characters, 岑岑. However, written in hiragana, *shinshin* creates an ambiguity in its interpretation between the two homophonous mimetics. Whether Saito himself intended the double meaning based on the homophones, *shinshin* certainly benefits from its sound and rhythmic representation, illustrating Sasaki's first point mentioned above. Shinada's interpretation of *shinshin* as referring to an emotional pain in fact may well be applied to (45) as well. The possible dual interpretations of *shinshin* as they are demonstrated in (44–45) further confirm that mimetics in tanka prove to be an excellent tool as a verbal shortcut to affective and sensual images and reactions.

Akiko Baba is another tanka poet who is a frequent user of *shinshin* in her poems such as in (46).

(46) Gassan-no / humoto **shinshin** / shimoyo-nite / ugokanu yami-o / mura-to yobu nari

月山のふもとしんしん霜夜にて動かぬ闇を村とよぶなり

"At the foot of Mt. Gassan / immovable darkness in a frosty night / we call it a village"　　　　　　　　　　(*Budō Karakusa* by Akiko Baba)

Poet and critic, Satoshi Ichihara comments on Baba's tanka piece in (46): "Akiko Baba likes to use the phenomime '*shinshin*.' It is also a phonomime that is silent with a sense of urgency" (2009, 66; my translation, NT). While *shinshin* is recognized as part of the mimetic vocabulary, it is intriguing to see in addition that he views *shinshin* as mimesis of sound as well as mimesis of manner and state. Not too distant in essence from Yoshitsuna Sasaki's view of relevant factors for poetic expressions, Ichihara singles out musicality, imagination, and linguistic creation. Of the three, moreover, he even considers linguistic creation to be the heart of poetic activities which amount to "the presentation of new thought, knowledge, and feelings that transcends common linguistic norms," asserting that mimetics "can give rise to highly symbolic poetry" (pp. 66–67; my translation, NT). Not only is Ichihara's acknowledgement of *shinshin* as mimetic apparently oblivious of its Chinese origin, but his conception of the role of mimetics in general in Japanese poetry confirms the affecto-imagistic nature of this vocabulary class. Particularly telling is his recognition of mimetics as means for "highly symbolic" literary artifacts. It seems reasonable to understand that his reference to "common linguistic norms" is to prosaic expressions. (46) is his choice of a tanka by Akiko Baba to illustrate *shinshin*'s contribution to linguistic creativity. The remark that Baba herself made on the very tanka piece in (46) is helpful in appreciating the role of *shinshin* in the tanka and also in Ichihara's commentary. Baba explains that the poem was written when she visited Mt. Gassan. During the day, the mountain top was shrouded in silence, and later in the afternoon, a quiet and deeply cold air surrounded the area. And, once the sun set, the village was in total darkness. She then describes the cold nightfall as in (47).

(47) じっと耳を傾けると霜の降る音が聞こえるような夜がある。しんしん、しんしん、という音ともない音の中に、静かに、重く、動かぬ闇が広がっている。それが村そのものなのだ。

"There is a night through which I feel as if I could hear the sound of frost falling when I pay close attention. In the sound '**shinshin, shinshin**'— although I cannot be sure if it is a sound—quietly and heavily extends unmovable darkness. That is the village itself." (Baba 2016)

In this passage, Baba describes *shinshin* as something like a sound whose exact nature she cannot ascertain. She perceives a sound-like sensation, *shinshin*, in a frosty scene, but it is not necessarily the sound itself but an image of total silence encapsulated in the darkness of the frosty night that she pictures with *shinshin*. This appears to be virtually a contradictory statement but nevertheless it may be precisely what Ichihara calls linguistic creativity and a presentation of Baba's perceptions and emotions that "transcends common linguistic norms."

Note that the silent or tranquil scenes or the backgrounds that are evoked by the mimetic *shinshin* in at least one of Saito's and Baba's tanka are also placed in the darkness of the night. The juxtaposition of silence and darkness is commonly used not just in literary works, as we have observed in our earlier examples above. Silence and darkness are arguably parallel phenomena, as auditory and visual voids, respectively, and the union of the two seems to mutually deepen the two types of voids and to enrich the evoked images even further. These three tanka poems and their commentaries (both by critics and by the poets themselves) suffice to confirm that *shinshin* is without doubt regarded as mimetic. They further suggest that if *shinshin* were to be taken as a prosaic word, it would not bring about the wide and subjective range of affective and sensual reactions that it does. It is highly unlikely that prosaic expressions are capable of exhibiting such a high level of expressive power while at the same time achieving the set of literary goals in only the 31 syllables that comprise tanka.

3. MIMETICS FOR SILENCE

The role that mimetics play in depicting silent scenes is further recognized when they are used to measure the intensity of silence or to characterize its nature. There are basically two ways of modifying silence by mimetics. One is by using mimetics of sound. The other is by way of mimetics that belong to modality categories other than the auditory sense, thereby achieving synesthetic effects. The Japanese expressions equivalent to "cold silence" and "stinging sensation of silence" serve as examples to illustrate the second type, where the attribute and depth of silence is synesthetically detailed by mimetics. In this fashion, the mimetic vocabulary can serve as an efficacious metaphorical tool in minutely characterizing and measuring the auditory void by bridging one sensual domain to another.

In what follows below I will discuss the two ways in which mimetic modifiers contribute to a portrayal of ambient silence particularly by providing a means for detailing its degree and extent. Just as with mimetics of silence, mimetics for silence make their affecto-imagistic contribution to enriching the overall verbal expression of silence. And, ultimately, the juxtaposition of a prosaic word (or expressions of similar functions) that represents a rationalized idea of silence on the one hand and a mimetic word that presents an enacted sensation of silence on the other, coalesces into a refined discourse that accentuates the visceral experience of silent scenes.

3.1 Mimetics of Sounds

Mimetics of sounds, phonomimes or onomatopoeic words, are numerous in Japanese, and many are considered iconic with arguably more concrete auditory images. There are at least two ways in which mimetics of sounds can qualify ambient silence. The first way, or pattern, is similar to the role that is played by the ticking sound of a clock and the sound of dripping water in the description of deep silence discussed in chapter 2. This is the type that is accounted for in figure-ground terms. It can be achieved either with or without verbal characterizations of silent scenes, whether they be by prosaic or mimetic expressions. The two passages below from Haruki Murakami's novel,

Noruwē-no Mori, set up silent views in the woods by stating as such in the prose form in (48) and by using a mimetic of silence *shin* in (49), while phonomimes, *sarasara* in (48) and *paripari* in (49), help explain the kind or depth of the silence. The mimetics *sarasara* and *paripari* as phonomimes are given the following meanings in Kakehi et al.'s mimetic dictionary (1996): "[t]he soft, murmuring sound of gently flowing water; the rustling sound made by leaves, cloth, etc., brushing against something; the sound made when rhythmically eating *o-chazuke* [rice with hot green tea poured over it]" (p. 1073); and "a repeated cracking or splitting sound made when crunching something crisp in the mouth, or tearing a stiff, thin material, such as cellophane or ice" (p. 885). In the examples below, mimetics of sounds are in bold-face, and clear assertions of silence are underlined. The passages have been professionally translated by Jay Rubin, who frequently translates Murakami's novels.

(48) Kaze-wa sōgen-o watari, kanojo-no kami-o kasuka-ni yur-asete zōkibayashi-ni nukete itta. Kozue-ni ha-ga **sarasara**-to oto-o tate, tōku-no hō-de inu-no naku koe-ga kikoeta. Marude betsu-no sekai-no iriguchi-kara kikoete-kuru-yō-na chīsaku kasunda nakigoe-datta. <u>Sono hoka-ni-wa donna mono'oto-mo nakatta. Donna mono'oto-mo wareware-no mimi-ni-wa todokanakatta.</u>

風は草原をわたり、彼女の髪をかすかに揺らせて雑木林に抜けていった。梢に葉が**さらさら**と音を立て、遠くの方で犬の鳴く声が聞こえた。まるで別の世界の入り口から聞こえてくるような小さくかすんだ泣き声だった。<u>その他にはどんな物音もなかった。どんな物音も我々の耳には届かなかった。</u>

"A puff of wind swept across the meadow and through her hair before it slipped into the woods to **rustle** branches and send back snatches of distant barking—a hazy sound that seemed to reach us from the door-way to another world. <u>We heard no other sounds.</u>"

(*Noruwē-no Mori* by Haruki Murakami, 9; translated by Jay Rubin, 4)

(49) Wareware-wa hidoku <u>shin</u>-to shita matsubayashi-no naka-o aruite-ita. Michi-no ue-ni-wa natsu-no owari-ni shinda semi-no shigai-ga karakara-ni kawaite chirabette-ite, sore-ga kutsu-no shita-de **paripari**-to iu oto-o tateta.

我々はひどく<u>しん</u>とした松林の中を歩いていた。道の上には夏の終わりに死んだ蝉の死骸がからからに乾いてちらばっていて、それが靴の下で**ぱりぱり**という音を立てた。

"Now we were walking through the <u>frightful silence</u> of a pine wood. The desiccated corpses of cicadas that had died at the end of the summer littered the surface of the path, **crunching** beneath our shoes."

(*Noruwē-no Mori* by Haruki Murakami, 19; translated by Jay Rubin, 8)

There seem to be two ways of construing (48) regarding the silence in the woods portrayed in this context although they are not exclusive of each other. The last two original Japanese sentences in (48) literally mean: "[t]here were no other sounds. No other sounds reached us (=our ears)," which leaves the *sarasara* sound of rustling branches and a barking of a dog from a distance the only tangible sounds in the setting. These two perceptible sounds in nature, then, can be interpreted to be a direct embodiment of silence as it is conceptualized in the cultural context. Under that interpretation, the underlined prosaic sentences complement the mimetic and prosaic references to the nature sounds, and together express deep hushed tranquility in the woods. The other interpretation, however, may perhaps better illustrate the role of the mimetic of sound, *sarasara*, as a modifier for silence. The tangible sounds in (48)—rustling branches and distant barking—are normally in the background and would not be easily noticed. In particular, the mimetic *sarasara*, conventionally and in this example as well, stands for a very gentle sound of grass and leaves. In the analytical terms of figure and ground, the sounds from branches and a dog are figure and the silence spread throughout the woods is ground. By virtue of the fact that such otherwise inaudible or unnoticeable sounds are indeed heard, the passage conveys an intense silence in the woods. That is, the audible sounds are foregrounded in the background of intense silence. The soundscape image in (49) is similar to that in (48). In (49), though, instead of directly announcing in prosaic words, phrases, and sentences that there is no audible sound of significance, the mimetic word *shin*, modified by the prosaic intensifier *hidoku* "very," presents an extremely silent setting, as it is reflected by the professional translation, "the frightful silence of a pine wood." As mentioned above, the mimetic *paripari* corresponds to the sound made when cracking or crunching something dry and crisp like rice crackers, and is fitting for the sound of stepping on dead cicadas whose corpses have been dried up. Just like (48), the sound of desiccated cicadas being stepped on is foregrounded and highlighted because of the intense silence filled in the woods. While these mimetics of sounds in (48–49) refer to very soft, subtle sounds in natural environments, foregrounding them in the soundscape has the effect of magnifying the penetrating degree of depicted silence.

The haiku poem by Sojin Harutachi in (50) pictures a virtually soundless world in nature.

(50)   Tonbō-no / ato **sarasara**-to / kusa-no oto

   蜻蛉のあとさらさらと草の音

   "A dragonfly flutters away, leaving behind **the rustling sound** of the grass"
   ("Haikurei," n.d.)

Unlike (48–49) there is no verbal assertion of silence in this setting. Yet, the prosaic phrase, *kusa-no oto* "the sound of the grass" informs us that there is indeed a very subtle sound in nature that is heard. The mimetic of sound, *sarasara*, further projects an auditory image of the unobtrusive and gentle nature sound as well as other sensate reactions including the tactile one from the breeze, for instance. They jointly confirm the profound quietness imbued in the air that a dragonfly leaves behind. Although the aesthetic nuance that one receives from this haiku (as with others in general) is subject to non-uniform ways in which individuals interpret and appreciate poetry, Miyao Sakamoto's (2014) remark on the haiku in (50) is indicative of the same line of literary appreciation. Sakamoto, a poet herself, comments that writing on the tender sound of the grass in (50) makes stillness stand prominent and the world depicted in the poem puts one in the space of silence. The sole sound, conveyed by the prosaic *kusa-no oto* "the sound of the grass" and its modifying mimetic *sarasara*, generates a symbiotic relation between sound and silence. At the same time, we can construe that the soft sound of the grass that *sarasara* presents prominently takes the center stage, reflecting a pronounced depth of silence.

The second pattern of mimetics of sounds qualifying the intensity of silence is by way of a metaphorical use of polar opposition between total lack of sound and the presence of loud penetrating sound. It parallels English expressions like *deafening silence*. The haiku by Kakio Tomizawa in (51) illustrates that the presence, rather than the absence, of a loud sound by way of the mimetic *wanwan* alludes to intense silence.[32]

(51) zeppeki-no / **wanwan**-to naru / toki hekiraku

絶壁のわんわんと鳴るとき碧落

"A cliff stands / **crying out** / under the blue sky"[33]

("Tomizawa Kakio," n.d.)

First, Kakehi et al. (1996) gives the definition of *wanwan* as "a loud echoing sound" (p. 1256). An example of the typical use under this meaning is taken from Kakehi et al.'s mimetic dictionary, given in (52).

(52) Tonneru-no naka-de ōgoe-o dasu-to **wanwan**(-to) hibiite omoshiroi node, gakkō-e iku kodomo-tachi-wa ōgoe-o dashi-nagara tonneru-o tōtte iku.

トンネルの中で大声を出すとわんわん（と）響いて面白いので、学校へ行く子供達は、大声を出しながらトンネルを通って行く。

"If you yell loudly in the tunnel, it **echoes**, which is enjoyable to listen to, so the children on their way to school walk along yelling loudly."

(Kakehi et al. 1996, 1256)

The loudness of *wanwan* is indisputable, and particularly the echoing aspect of the sound is clearly reflected both in (52), in a tunnel, and in (51), at a cliff. In (51), the loud sound of *wanwan*, of course, does not actually exist in the scene, but the degree of the virtual sound is metaphorically equated to the intensity of the silence that is being portrayed in the poem. The scene is reminiscent of an experience that haiku poet, Ms. Fumiko Sakai (personal communication, 2015) had of the breathtaking view of Yosemite. Interpreting the haiku to be about silence, she visualizes standing at a cliff, overpowered, facing an ever-expanding blue sky. Even though in reality absolute silence dominates at the cliff, she feels as if she could hear the silence in the guise of a penetrating sound emerging from the magnificent view that echoes through the surroundings up to the sky. The sound, although virtual, is simulated by the mimetic *wanwan*, whose intensity is superimposed on the silence persisting throughout the scene. A similar sensation is spoken of in a haiku appreciation commentary by Takano (2014). Connecting the mimetic *wanwan* directly to silence, Takano goes on to say, "the author's ears have sensitively perceived the roaring sound hidden in silence" (p. 36; my translation, NT).

Another example of marking intense silence by a mimetic of forceful sounds is found in novels, as illustrated in (53), in which attention should be paid to the cooccurrence of the mimetic *jiin* and the prosaic word *seijaku* "silence."

(53) kūki-no oto-ga **jiin**-to jimushi-no yō-ni kikoeru <u>seijaku</u>

空気の音が**ジーン**と地虫のように聞こえる<u>静寂</u>

"<u>silence</u> in which the air makes **the ringing sound** of a grub"

(*Yasagure Keiji* by Giichi Fujimoto;
https://hyogen.info/content/962871154)

In this phrase the presence of silence is prosaically asserted by *seijaku* while the remainder adds a qualification to further characterize the kind of the silence. According to mimetic dictionaries, *jiin* as a phonomime is described as "a ringing sound in the ears" (Kakehi et al. 1996) or "a continuously, quickly, and strongly reverberating low-pitch sound" (M. Ono 2007). On the one hand, *jiin* in (53) is likened to the sound of a grub, and may not strike one as presenting an overwhelmingly forceful sound that can be considered the polar opposite of silence. On the other hand, *jiin* often collocates with the ringing in the ear. Coupled with the meanings listed in the mimetic dictionaries cited above, then, the degree of the sound that *jiin* refers to falls within the realm of intense sounds, if the sound intensity is measured by the degree of unpleasant reactions (presumably synesthetically in this case). This in fact parallels one of the examples of synesthetic metaphors discussed in chapter 2. I repeat the relevant example below as (54).

(54) Komaku-ga hen-ni naru yō-na <u>shizukesa</u>

鼓膜が変になるような<u>静けさ</u>

"deafening <u>silence</u>" (lit: silence that would make the ear-drum lose control)
(*Shukkotōki* by Toshio Shimao;
https://hyogen.info/content/451535202)

Loss of control in the ear drum in (54) due to the depth of the silence is an instance of cross-modal transfer between touch and hearing. Turning to (53), there is literally no such thing as the perceptible level of the sound of air (at least in a non-technical sense), but the mimetic *jiin* disguises it while its uncomfortably resonating degree in turn speaks to an overwhelming silence. Once again, a maximum level of amplitude is equally applied to sound and silence, where the former is presented by mimetics. The degree of the virtual—and hence inaudible—sound resonates to the audience with extreme intensity.

A variant of *jiin*, the reduplicated mimetic *jiinjiin* in (55) demonstrates the variability in interpretation arising from the subjectively formed perspectives of individual experiences.

(55) Hana moteru / natsugi-no ue-o / ā "toki"-ga / **jiinjiin**-to / sugite-yuku-nari.

花もてる夏樹の上をああ「時」が**じいんじいん**と過ぎてゆくなり

"Above blossoming summer trees, 'time' seems to be passing with **a ringing sound**." (*Hyōgen* by Susumu Kagawa;
http://sakuramitih31.livedoor.blog/archives/17926085.html)

In addition to the entry as phenomime, the mimetic base *jiin* has another conventionalized use as a phenomime that describes "the manner in which one's senses are strongly stimulated or one's emotions are deeply aroused" (Kakehi et al. 1996). Commentaries of the tanka in (55) uniformly report that the poet Kagawa despairingly wrote this poem when he heard the news that Japan lost the Pacific War.[34] An opinion shared by one reader treats *jiinjlin* as a means to express the grief Kagawa felt toward the loss in the war, consistent with the conventional meaning listed in the mimetic dictionary cited above.[35] Another commentary, however, reports the explanation that Kagawa himself gave about the mimetic: *jiinjiin* refers to the manner in which "the time that [it seems to him] had been halted in silence [due to the war] suddenly started to flow rapidly."[36] The poet's intended use of *jiinjiin*, thus, refers to the contrastive fast speed of time going by after the war. In addition, Dr. Kozue Uzawa, a tanka poet herself, shared yet another interpretation with me (personal communication, 2013). In her appreciation of this poem, she envisions a very quiet summer day—quiet to the extent that she could hear the sound of time;

jiinjiin, although reflecting a sound, expresses surrounding silence. It is not clear whether she is familiar with the historical background of this poem and Kagawa's mindset in relation to it, but she evidently connects *jiinjiin* with ambient silence in the image evoked in her mind upon reading the poem. Setting aside the importance of the diverse interpretations that the haiku in (55) generates of the poem as a whole, as well as of the mimetic, for our present purposes, the last view voiced by Dr. Uzawa is particularly suggestive that mimetics of tangible sounds are prevalently and effectively employed to add a heightened degree to an embodiment of silence.

Finally, the use of the mimetic in (56) presents an intriguing example in which a mimetic of silence, *shinshin*, is treated as if it carried a sound content by mimicking it, and yet the apparent contradiction targets an intense level of absolute silence.

(56) Anmari <u>shizuka</u>-na-node, mimi-no naka-ga **shinshin**-to naru.

あんまり<u>静か</u>なので、耳の中がしんしんと鳴る。

"It's so <u>quiet</u> that my ears ring '**shinshin**.'"
(*Hōrōki* by Humiko Hayashi; https://aozora .hyogen.info/detail.html?url=915550278)

As we have previously discussed, *shinshin* is a mimetic of silence, specifically falling under the type of phenomime, but since *shinshin* is juxtaposed with the verb *naru* "ring," the mimetic is best understood to be a phonomime that metaphorically maximizes the magnitude of the silence in the depicted space. The first part of the sentence in (56) announces tremendous quietness by way of the prosaic adjective *shizuka* "quiet," which then serves as a pretext for the metaphorical sonic effects on the ears. That is, put side by side, the annulled presence of sound by *shizuka* and the (imaginative) pronouncement of sound by *shinshin* do not negate or contradict each other, but instead their attributes are merged into one by equating their intensity level. What is particularly ingenious about this example is the use of a mimetic of silence rather than a mimetic of sound like the examples we have discussed above. The metaphorical tool that involves polar oppositions in the auditory domain has been doubly applied in ultimately leading to intensification of silence: first for linking the phenomime *shinshin* of silence with the phonomime *shinshin* of sound, and again for linking ambient silence with the phonomime *shinshin*. In each application, the distance between the presence and absence of sound is kept in opposition, and it is why the intensification mode adopted in (56) is remarkably creative and effectual at the same time.

3.2 Synesthetic Mimetics

We have discussed synesthetic metaphors and similes in section 3.2 of chapter 2, in which prosaic expressions that belong to the sense domains pertinent to smell, vision, and touch play an important role in intensifying the degree of silence. To that end, mimetics can achieve the same level of rhetorical success, helping us relive silent environments by evoking additional images arising from a modal domain other than the auditory sense. Since many instances of sensual appeals are cross-modal or multi-modal, the targeted silence is more richly presented by cross-modal mimetics with extraordinary vividness.

In general terms, there have been studies that demonstrate Japanese native speakers' relative partiality to mimetics over prosaic equivalents for synesthetic metaphors. For instance, Ono et al. (2011) find that synesthetic metaphors expressed by mimetics are easier to understand than those by prosaic adjectives. Takada (2008) also observes the prevalent use of mimetics in Japanese in contrast with standard "descriptive expressions" in English.[37] Furthermore, Ohno (2009) reviews linguistic patterns of innovative mimetics in contemporary haiku and tanka poetry that are derived from existing vocabulary, both mimetic and prosaic. In this survey, she reports that one of the recurrent patterns is to use mimetics cross-modally. Examples include: *hirihiri*, which is a conventional reference to pain resulting from a burn, for instance, but is instead used for smell [touch → smell]; *tokutoku*, which generally corresponds to the sound of liquid flowing but innovatively used for the smell (of soy sauce) [sound → smell]; and *pirapira*, which is a mimetic for some thin object fluttering, but stands for the sound that a skylark makes [touch/vision → sound]. Though in varying degrees, all these examples are somewhat stretched from their standard use that is more familiar to language users. However, Ohno suspects that they may be considered to replace prosaic expressions (perhaps for the purpose of reducing the number of syllables as required by the poetry format). More importantly, she comments that the novel use of synesthetic mimetics is transparent enough to the reader for appreciating the poet's intention.

In chapter 2 we discussed an example of (verbal) silence metaphorically qualified by a prosaic adjective describing cold temperature. The same type of modification is carried out by the mimetic vocabulary as well. The word *hiyari* in (57) and its morphological variant, *hin'yari* in (58–59), both directly appeal to a tactile reaction to a cold temperature. According to Kakehi et al. (1996), *hiyari* is referred to as "[t]he state in which something is felt to be cool or cold" (p. 536). Regarding *hin'yari*, the dictionary gives the following: "[t]he state of being cool [usually connotes a pleasant feeling]" (p. 521).

(57) Ame-ga huru sukoshi mae-ni kūki-ga **hiyari**-to suru-yō-na, sonna <u>shi-zukesa</u>-ga kanjir-are-masu.

雨が降る少し前に空気が**ひやり**とするような、そんな<u>静けさ</u>が感じられます。

"**Cool** air little before it starts to rain—that sort of <u>silence</u> is felt."

(fujiokashinya 2019)

(58) <u>Shiin</u>-to shita <u>seijaku</u>-de **hin'yari**-to shita kūki

<u>シーン</u>とした<u>静寂</u>で**ひんやり**とした空気

"the air that is <u>silent</u> and **cool**" (Tanaka 2021)

(59) Kyōto-no otera-no naka-no **hin'yari** shita <u>shizukesa</u>-to-mo, oranda-no yoru-no haritsumeta <u>shizukesa</u>-to-mo mata chigau.

京都のお寺のなかの**ひんやり**した<u>静けさ</u>とも、オランダの夜のはりつめた<u>静けさ</u>ともまた違う。

"It is neither like the **cool** <u>silence</u> in a temple of Kyoto, nor like the tense silence at night in the Netherlands." (Tanno 2010)

In all of the three examples, the mimetics, *hiyari* and *hin'yari*, modify and specify the prosaic word denoting silence, *shizukesa* in (57) and (59), and *seijaku* in (58). Furthermore, in (58), the cooccurrence of the prosaic *seijaku* and the mimetic of silence, *shiin*, evokes an even sharper image of a silent scene, without being redundant. Concrete physical sensation upon touching something cold or being exposed to the chilly air is aroused by the mimetics of tactile sensation (i.e., *hiyari* and *hin'yari*), adding further explications of the silent scenes through cross-modal sensations. The common nature of silence expressed via *hiyari~hin'yari* in (57–58) is simultaneously of a refreshing and yet solemn feel. Likewise in (59), *hin'yari* simulates the coolness imbued and perceived in the quiet and ceremonial ambience typical at temples in Kyoto. The depiction is suitably linked to the calming level of silence characteristic of a temple setting.

There are mimetic words that correspond to perhaps a stronger tactile sensation in order to detail the nature of silence or to intensify its degree. I discuss *jin* for illustration. Consider (60), where the mimetic *jin* is used as a synesthetic metaphor for silence.

(60) Mimi-no oku-ga **jin**-to hurueru mitai-ni <u>shizuka</u>

耳の奥が**じん**と震えるみたいに<u>静か</u>

"<u>silent</u>, as if the inner ear would **quiver**"

(*Ninshin Karendā* by Yoko Ogawa, 25)

Jin (or its intensified variant *jiin*) is more commonly used in conveying a strong emotional surge that accompanies a stinging sensation in the nose or the chest. Mimetic dictionaries differ in their explanations, but M. Ono (2007) and H. Ono (1984) additionally include heavy numbness resulting from an exposure to severe coldness and electricity. Referring to a sensation in the ear, the mimetic *jin* in (60) is similar to *tsuun*, but it is perhaps with a higher intensity and more closely aligns with the numbing sensation described in the two aforementioned mimetic dictionaries. Just as all the examples we have reviewed thus far, silence, confirmed by the prosaic word *shizuka* in (60), unquestionably gives little or no room for tangible sounds in the setting. The absence of verbal means that literally describes the depth of silence is made up for by the simile phrase with the mimetic *jin*, i.e., that there is a quiver or numbness in the manner or state of *jin* that is felt deep inside the ears. The severity with which no sound stimulus of any sort can be found is conveyed parallel to the concrete physical sensation that is experienced with the tiniest quiver or numbing feeling. In particular, since the sensation of *jin* is said to occur in small and narrow cavities of the body, the corporeal impact is felt even more amplified and reverberated. This analogy holding between silence and the tactile image evoked by *jin* serves the purpose of furthering the silent ambience.

4. IDEOPHONES OF SILENCE IN CROSS-LINGUISTIC PERSPECTIVE

As stated in the introduction of this chapter, languages with a rich inventory of mimetic vocabulary (or under its equivalent labels like ideophones and expressives) are widely distributed in the languages of the world. Primarily due to the Euro-centric focus on scholarly issues, the word class has long been sidelined as a peripheral matter in linguistic examinations and analyses. Especially ideophones that are attested in many African languages have been dealt with in disciplines like anthropology and folklore since ideophones play important rhetorical and sonic roles in oral traditions, performing arts, and some ritualistic events. It is not surprising that a substantial level of aesthetic values is inherent to the vocabulary class of ideophones and thus there is a logical motivation for their extensive use as a verbal means for communicating in those cultural activities.

Ideophones in these languages, like Japanese mimetics, extend far beyond so-called onomatopoeia (or phonomimes) that mimic audible sounds, and include types of words that correspond to phenomimes and psychomimes. For instance, Childs (1994, 189) gives the following list of sense-based ideophones in Kisi (Niger-Congo), spoken in West Africa.

(61) a. Hearing   bakala-bakala   "sound of rain falling in single droplets"
      b. Sight   hiaŋ-hiaŋ   "loose-jointed, floppy"
      c. Touch   cam-cam   "lukewarm"
      d. Taste   paŋ   "tasteless, insipid, unpalatable"
      e. Smell   kpiini-kpiini   "offensive smelling"

Within the sonic realm, furthermore, Japanese is not an isolated language that has mimetics of silence, as ideophones that are said to depict silence have been documented in many of the African languages as well as in other languages families spoken outside the African continent. Many of the sources I have consulted give examples only at the word level without detailed explanations on the exact kind of silence, so some instances may refer to ambient silence as well as verbal silence. To the extent that I was able to gather relevant information and based on the glosses provided, however, the samples in (62) seem to be close to the Japanese mimetics of silence discussed in this chapter regarding what these ideophones refer to. (63) and (64) provide additional examples of expressions of silence within a context.

(62) Gbaya (Niger-Congo): séléle "absolute silence"   (Noss 2001)
      Siwu (Niger-Congo): kananana "quietness, lacking noise or sound," kpoo
          "stillness, nocturnal silence"   (Dingemanse 2011)
      Emai (Niger-Congo): híí "silence"   (Egbokhare 2001)
      Wolof (Niger-Congo): miig "extreme silence"   (Baglini 2018)
      Llogoori (Bantu—Niger-Congo): zi "cold, still, quiet"
                                                  (Bowler and Gluckman 2018)
      Zulu (Bantu—Niger-Congo): tu "silent"   (Voeltz and Kilian-Hatz 2001)
      Hausa (Chadic): tsít "in complete silence, hush"   (Newman 2001)
      Katuena (Cariban): ti "silent"   (Smoll 2014)
      Pastaz Quichua (Quechuan): chun "sound of silence"   (Hatton 2016)
      Kamberra (Austronesian): pàdi "quiet, silent" (without sound)
                                                            (Klamer 1999)

(63) Gbaya
      Ŋgalaŋ   a leap
      Pingoŋ   whoosh
      Séléle   silence
      Dawa iɲa só te   how the monkey knows trees   (Noss 1989, 33)

(64) Katuena
      Ti::::.   Tu:na   ti   nititbamu.
      IDEO(silent)   water   REP   3s-IDEO(silent)-INCH

      "There was silence. The rain was stopping."   (Smoll 2014, 45)

A few comments are added to elaborate on further details about some of these ideophones. Drawing from a poem on a Gbaya community gathering, Noss (2001) explains that the ideophone *sélélé* in (62) describes silence that signals the community members' agreement on a decision they have reached after some discussion. While this use of *sélélé* represents more of a verbal silence, an internet source on Gbaya ideophones notes that *sélélé* is a word for "silence of a peaceful night," suggesting that it can describe silence of the surroundings.[38] The ideophone poem in (63) by the Cameroonian performing artist, Dogobadomo Béloko, consists of four lines all together, with each of the first three presenting an image expressed by an ideophone. Noss (1989) explains that the first ideophone in this poem evokes an image of an animal (monkey) leaping from the ground to a tree; the second presents an image that a leafy branch swings and dips downward with the rustling sound of the leaves as the monkey moves. Noss further states that the movement of the branches and the sounds from the leaves are foregrounded in these images, while the monkey is not, because it is "hidden by the foliage" (p. 33). With the third ideophone *sélélé* a sudden silence emerges: "[t]hen there is nothing but silence *sélélé*. No more is the movement of the monkey to be seen, no more are there swaying branches to betray its presence. There is only the silence of the empty forest. The monkey is gone or so well hidden that all that can be felt is silence" (p. 34). The first and second ideophones put primary foci on appeal to vision and hearing senses, respectively, while *sélélé* relates to the image that "describes the setting, affirming the presence of absolute quiet, or the total absence of sound and movement" (p. 34). In Siwu, as seen in (62), there are several ideophones of silence, both of verbal and ambient types, but *kananaa* and *kpoo* seem to be appropriate for referring to silence and stillness in the surroundings (Dingemanse 2011). Bowler and Gluckman (2018) identify *zi* as an ideophone in Llogoori that serves as a degree intensifier. Noting that "*zi* combines with lexical items describing stillness or coldness" (p. 34), they provide examples like *zi-zilu* "cold, still" and *zi-chinganu* "quiet," where *-zilu* (adjective) and *-chinganu* (adjective) are both lexical items. The semantic class that subsumes stillness and coldness under the same rubric for the ideophone *zi* is reminiscent of the darkness of the night (and falling snow, as noted in note 26) juxtaposed with the Japanese mimetic of silence, *shinshin*. A synesthetic undertone is suggestive for the range of images evoked by these expressive vocabulary items. Finally, for *chun* in Pastaz Quichua, while considering the ideophone to depict the sound of silence, Hatton (2016) comments, "instead of depicting sound, it depicts the path of silence falling" (p. 107). I take it to be a more dynamic conceptualization of silence, as opposed to capturing silence as a static state of silence.

Japanese is one among a mosaic of languages that have rich inventories of ideophones and their equivalent lexical class. It is indisputable that in these languages, an auditory void finds words to express it by way of the vocabulary type that centralizes sensory experiences as its core. Since those experiences are multi-sensory, the apparent absence of perceptible stimuli is articulated and conveyed by such vocabulary items with clarity and vividness as productively as their presence. Notwithstanding minute differences in precise references and various nuances underlying them, it is noteworthy that languages with extensive ideophones and mimetics are able to add expressive and rhetorical richness to the prosaic vocabulary. Ideophones and mimetics belong to the affecto-imagistic dimension, and silence is portrayed by taking a path different from prosaic words through multisensory and affective appeals. The richness that the expressive vocabulary provides does not end up with a semantic overlap or redundancy with what prosaic vocabulary denotes; instead, it expands the range of linguistic and rhetorical conduits for communicative expressiveness.

NOTES

1. According to Otsubo (1989), the source of the phrase in (1) is Osaka Kintetsu Railway. It is not clear to me how its message is related to the company business, as further contextual information including visual props is not available to me.

2. This means that *juuQ-to* and *guiQ-to* in (1) are equivalents of *juut-to* and *guit-to* in their Romanized transliterations. In the Hiragana and Katakana syllabary, "Q" corresponds to the small characters 「っ」 and 「ッ」 (促音).

3. Onomatopoeic words like *bow-wow, buzz, bang, pitter-patter, click-clack,* and *helter-skelter,* are English examples of the vocabulary class corresponding to mimetics in Japanese. English exhibits a far smaller number of words that belong to this class.

4. Generally in Japan, *giongo* and *gitaigo* are subsumed under the loanword term *onomatope* "onomatopoeia." Although onomatopoeia in the source language of English means sound-imitating words, *onomatope* as an English loanword used in Japan includes both phonomimes and phenomimes.

5. Although maintaining the three-way division of phonomimes, phenomimes, and psychomimes, McVeigh (1996) labels phonomimes (based on sounds) and phenomimes (including other senses, sight, touch, taste, and smell) under "sensate" while psychomimes (subsuming emotions, cognition, attitude, and personal characteristics) under "nonsensate." I will come back to the term "sensate" later when discussing differences between mimetic and prosaic words.

6. The linguistic notation of "N" corresponds to 「ん」 (撥音) in the Japanese Hiragana syllabary.

7. Morphological templates are schematized by using the abbreviations "C" for consonants and "V" for vowels.

8. The meaning definitions of the five examples including the base *paku* are taken from Kakehi et al. (1996).

9. I refrain from including the accentual properties pertinent to the mimetic templates. See Hamano (1998) and Akita (2009) on the topic and discussions relevant to it.

10. Hamano (1998) gives this characterization in contrast with a single CVCV sequence, whose semantic content is explained as "momentary or single movement" (p. 105).

11. The common templatic representations as in (3) and their alternants with epenthetic elements like a lengthened vowel and a geminate consonant for emphasis indeed play an important role as a morphological frame for newly coined mimetics, however short-lived they may be, as is discussed, for example, in Tsujimura (2016). It is important to note, furthermore, that such innovative words that are molded in common morphological shapes are recognized by the language user as mimetics, even though the original word from which the innovative mimetic is derived may be prosaic. A crucial implication is that once identified as mimetic, the language user considers its semantic property on par with that of mimetics rather than of prosaic words. As I detail in section 1.2 of this chapter, the distinction in the semantic nature between mimetics and prosaics is of great significance to our examination of mimetics of silence.

12. Hinton et al. (1994) include some pragmatic and social functions that ideophones and mimetic words in some languages have been reported to show. Such areas are described as: "expressions of social relationships (as in diminutive forms and vocatives and imperatives); also the expression of opprobrium and stigma"; and "grammatical and discourse indicators, such as intonational markers of discourse and sentence structure, and distinctions between parts of speech" (p. 10). It seems to me that these two areas are not instantiated by the Japanese mimetic system.

13. There have been investigations, such as Osaka (1990) and Dingemanse and Majid (2012), that use experimental methods to demonstrate the status of mimetics as "sensory vocabulary."

14. In their discussion of quotations, Clark and Gerrig (1990) qualify that their use of the term "demonstration" corresponds to the sense of "illustrate by exemplification" rather than the meaning "point to" and "indicate" (p. 764).

15. The obligatory vs. optional status of the quotative particle *-to* for mimetics raises an interesting topic of linguistic analysis, and various related issues have been discussed from different linguistic perspectives. See Tamori (1980), Tamori and Schourup (1999), Nasu (2002), Asano (2003), Toratani (2006, 2017), Kageyama (2007), and Akita and Usuki (2016), for discussion.

16. Lodge (1990) discusses the role of mimesis (as opposed to diegesis), which is parallel to the "in-it" feeling that we are referring to here in characterizing the function of mimetic words: "[r]oughly speaking mimesis gives us the sense of reality in fiction, the illusion of access to the reality of personal experience" (p. 144). As Lodge discusses in detail, verbal narratives are fully capable of achieving vividness in descriptions. I am in complete agreement with Lodge and others on this point. My emphasis in the current work is on the word-level depictive capacity that mimetics inherently demonstrate.

17. The basic idea regarding the "in-it" feeling is echoed by Noss (1989), who comments on ideophones in Gbaya as follows: "[t]hrough the ideophone and his [=the poet, Dogobadomo] own experience, the listener participates directly in the event being recounted" (p. 34).

18. McVeigh (1996) considers phonomimes and phenomimes to be sensate but psychomimes to be based on the first two. He claims that through the objective phase and then the subjective phase, phonomimes and phenomimes are "psychologized" to receive the non-sensate meaning. Many mimetics are polysemous, and in some cases metaphorial extensions can be argued for. In this book, however, I regard the mimetic vocabulary in itself as presenting sensual and affective experiences without any derivational relations.

19. See also Tsujimura (2016) where I discuss the difference in nuance and degree of vividness that mimetics and their prosaic equivalents contrastively exhibit.

20. In addition to the mimetic words in (16), *shittori* can be recognized as describing ambient silence although it is more customarily used to depict the state of being lightly wet, as is demonstrated in (10). A few mimetic dictionaries include *shittori* as a mimetic of silence with the following definitions: "the state of being quiet and calm; the state of having fallen deeply silent" (M. Ono 2007, 168) (my translation, NT); "to be calm and tasteful, giving a pleasant feeling of tranquility" (H. Ono 1984, 143); and "to be calm and delicate (said of an atmosphere which gives a pleasant feeling of tranquility and good taste)" (Chang 1990, 375). The examples under these definitions indeed depict silent, quiet, calm, or tranquil scenes in an atmosphere. Despite the attested availability, its contemporary use seems to center primarily on the "light wetness" sense; and, for this reason, I will not include *shittori* in the list of mimetics of silence to be discussed.

21. Translations of the definitions and examples in (17), (18), (19), and (24), originally given in Japanese, are mine.

22. The mimetic *hisohiso* usually describes the whispering manner of speaking so that confidentiality is kept, rather than referring to ambient silence. Of all the dictionaries I have consulted, only M. Ono's (2007) mimetic dictionary has an entry of *hisohiso* with the definition corresponding to ambient silence. I have included (18) for the expository purpose of its morphological form but will not discuss *hisohiso* as part of the mimetic vocabulary depicting silence.

23. *Kōjien* explains that *hissorikan* is derived by suffixing the Chinese character 閑 [kan], which has a synonymous meaning to *hissori*, suggesting that a prosaic element has been contributing to the formation of the word. On the other hand, *hissorikan* is listed as an independent entry in Kakehi et al.'s (1996) mimetic dictionary. I adopt Kakehi et al.'s listing and will continue to treat *hissorikan* as an expression that is at least conventionally perceived as part of the mimetic vocabulary in Japanese. As I will discuss in connection with *shinshin* below, the question as to which type of vocabulary Japanese speakers consider a given word to belong to (i.e., whether mimetic or prosaic) is a criterion that is relevant to our discussion of how to express silence in Japanese.

24. For instance, *wanwan* is commonly understood to refer to dogs' barking in contemporary Japanese, while *byoobyoo* was in use at least in the seventeenth cen-

tury, judging from a recorded example in a dictionary. The latter, however, is no longer used in contemporary Japanese. Another mimetic *iraira* depicts the irritated state of a person in Modern Japanese, but it had been used to describe a type of prickling pain caused by thorns and the like. The latter interpretation is no longer available.

25. The construction that comprises the gerundive form of a verb, V(erb)-*te/de*, followed by the stative verb *iru* "be" has been extensively explored in the literature on Japanese linguistics. It gives rise to either the progressive or resultative meaning depending on the semantic nature of the base verb, and a number of analyses have been proposed for these two interpretations and additional semantic characteristics that the construction exhibits. In the present discussion, I adopt Jacobsen's (1992) semantic analysis that unifies the progressive and resultative meaning as referring to "a state of affairs as existing in a homogeneous, unchanging fashion over a given interval of time" (p. 200).

26. Another collocation frequently occurring with *shinshin* relates to snow-falling scenes. Given that a number of passages and discourses that use *shinshin* as a descriptor of silent surroundings refer to falling snow or snowy sights, one may wonder if *shinshin* is a mimetic that relates to snow-falling rather than to a quiet atmosphere. In fact, one mimetic dictionary (Chang 1990, 369) gives the sole meaning of *shinshin* as "continuously; thick and fast (describing a scene in which snow is falling steadily on a quiet winter night)." However, other dictionaries, either of mimetics or otherwise, do not include relations to snow or falling snow for *shinshin* if they carry its entry at all. It seems reasonable and appropriate, then, to understand that the image that *shinshin* evokes is often typically captured in people's mind as snowfall that accompanies a tranquil scenery. The whole scene is viewed as being picturesque, where snow-falling and silence are interdependent and totally congruous.

27. It is not clear when the borrowing from Chinese took place, but one of the largest Japanese language dictionaries (*Nihon Kokugo Daijiten*, 2006) gives an example that dates back prior to the thirteenth century.

28. Kadooka (1993) characterizes pseudo onomatopoeia as "Chinese phenomimes that have been borrowed into Japanese" (p. 145; my translation, NT). This view, however, is not shared with Nakazato and M. Ono.

29. Kimi Akita has pointed out to me that the accentuation pattern of *shinshin(-to)* does not follow that of the regular adverbial mimetic: although the accent on reduplicated mimetics of the CVN-CVN pattern, when they appear with the quotative particle *-to*, falls on the first vowel, *shinshin-to* is unaccented. A quick perusal of the entries under *kango-onomatope* (漢語オノマトペ) "onomatopoeia of the (prosaic) Chinese origin" in M. Ono (2007) shows that the majority, if not all, of mimetics under this class that take the CVN-CVN form keep the same unaccented pattern. *Shinshin* and other *kango-onomatope* thus exhibit hybrid linguistic features reflecting the historical paths that they have taken.

30. More technically, the length of haiku and tanka is measured in Japanese by mora, rather than syllable, reflecting the phonological unit of the language. Mora, in brief, corresponds to a single character of kana (i.e., hiragana and katakana).

31. I thank Yasuko Watt for working on the translation of this tanka with me.

32. As indicated by the comments that the poet Yukitsuna Sasaki makes (see section 2.3 of this chapter), Japanese haiku and tanka poems have the propensity to be interpreted subjectively and hence differently by various readers, so that the way in which they are understood and appreciated is left to the audience. To keep neutrality, I generally rely on haiku specialists' interpretations of the haiku and tanka pieces that I discuss in this chapter.

33. I am indebted to Yasuko Watt for discussing this haiku with me and providing me with the translation.

34. The sources of this background information are http://shiika.sakura.ne.jp/daily_poem/2012-07-06-9594.html and http://sakuramitih31.livedoor.blog/archives/2012-06.html?p=3.

35. The commentary appeared in https://detail.chiebukuro.yahoo.co.jp/qa/question_detail/q1150159271.

36. The commentary appeared in http://sakuramitih31.livedoor.blog/archives/2012-06.html?p=3.

37. I interpret his "descriptive expressions" to mean prosaic expressions.

38. The information is taken from http://www.encyclopedias.biz/encyclopedia-of-african-folklore/50884-ideophone.html.

Chapter Four

Epilogue

The small seed of my domestic conversation about something as ostensibly trivial as birds chirping has led me to wonder how many ways there are to describe ambient silence through language. I have subsequently asked other related questions like: Beyond single individual Japanese words like *muon*, *seijaku*, and *shizuka*, how effectively does the language express the absence of tangible sensations like silence? The thinking process has revealed that verbal expressions of ambient silence touch on a number of issues that transcend far more than just linguistic matters. Chief among them, as others have noted, is that the concept of silence is not necessarily structured solely based on the absence or suppression of sound. In order to understand how silence is conceptualized, we need to grasp what silence means to the language user. To that end, it is equally imperative to ascertain what sound means to the language user, and ultimately to elucidate what the relationship between silence and sound means to the members of a linguistic community. Guided by these conceptual premises, I have examined the way to perceive, interpret, and express silence in words, the way to perceive, interpret, and express sound in words, and the way that the two interact. In the Japanese context, suppression of sound and hushed tranquility make major contributions to constructing the concept of silence, and I have shown that hushed tranquility in particular exhibits an intriguing range of linguistic representations in Japanese. Importantly, however, these varied concepts of silence are not strictly compartmentalized, nor do they contradict each other. Instead, they complement one another and should be gauge on a continuum.

In this book I have singled out two types of linguistic mechanisms which Japanese language users make common—and arguably preferred—use of in verbal portrayals of ambient silence. One has to do with references to a cluster of sounds in nature, such as birdsongs, rustling of leaves, and sounds from brooks and the breeze. The other is the mimetic vocabulary, extensively employed in all channels of Japanese-language communication. These two linguistic means may strike one as paradoxical on the surface, given that ambient silence is portrayed by verbal tools that involve some level of sound orientation. A battery of questions has been raised in relation to them that include: What are the fundamental characteristics of nature sounds that capture the essence of silence without nullifying it; and in light of the miming trait of the mimetic vocabulary, what is it that a mimetic word of silence mimics when there is little or no sound to imitate? The role of nature sounds is explained by invoking a culturally contextualized concept of silence, which may be attributed to the *wabi-sabi* principle in relation to an aesthetic perspective. The spiritual connotations and allusions that nature sounds possess constitute a critical part of the connection to which nature sounds contribute in constructing the concept of silence. And, it has been surmised that this connection, which forms a pattern with broader instantiations, can be situated more fittingly in a culturally fostered way of observing what is around us. As for the mimetic vocabulary, despite the apparent "mimicry" aspect of the vocabulary class, mimetics are able to provide a simulation of subjective experiences that the individual language user either relives or imagines. Mimetics are sharply contrastive with prosaic words in that the former is of a sensual and affective orientation whereas the latter is of a cognitive and analytical nature. As such, it is mimetics' immediate (i.e., im-mediated) presentations, as opposed to prosaics' mediated representations, that directly appeal to the language user's senses and emotions. The emphasis on sensual and affective reactions that the mimetic vocabulary intrinsically evokes is indeed in tandem with a cultural stance that values visceral reactions and evaluations. For that reason, mimetics are superbly suitable to depicting silence as an instance of the sensate.

It is common knowledge that multiple linguistic and rhetorical ways to speak about silence are shared by languages in the world, including metaphors, similes, and hypothetical expressions. However, our study points to the availability of linguistic tools that have an advantage over the more commonly adopted ones for reasons of fit to culturally situated practices. That is, our examination has revealed that linguistic mechanisms deployed for verbal portrayals of ambient silence in Japanese follow a recognized pattern of cultural practices and cultural identity that are embedded in the society.

The conceptual thread that puts together the two linguistic means taken up in this book revolves around reliance on immediate, sensate, and affective reactions, which are accordingly of a subjective nature, in our observations and their verbal expressions. Crucially, such a stance is repeated in people's thoughts and across various art forms including poetry (more broadly, literature), music, and painting, as we noted in chapter 2. To give a final illustration, in a recent Linda Hoaglund film that features paintings from the Edo period, *Edo Avant Garde* (2019),[1] Yukio Lippit, an art historian, speaks of an unsigned painting, *Cockscombs* (1600), drawn on a folding screen: "[y]ou would be sitting on the floor on your knees. You weren't looking at the painting. You were surrounded by it. You were in the painting." Another art historian, Noi Sawaragi, also comments on the same painting: "[s]itting on the floor and feeling the breeze, seeing this screen, I feel like I'm a small animal crouched on the ground peering up at the flowers, instead of a human being."[2] These commentaries express instinctive, visceral responses to what the painting presents, creating the "in-it" feeling. A similar stance applies to architecture, sculpture, and food preparation and presentation, and other areas of contemporary culture. These recurring illustrations of the manner in which to observe and assess intuitively by direct experiences certainly form a coherent and cohesive pattern, and comports with Armstrong's (1975, 18) characterization of culture "as a pattern-in-experience." Silence and sound are woven into a fabric of elegant linguistic expression, rather than being rigidly compartmentalized as opposite poles. Through a study of how we describe and depict silence in words, I hope to have demonstrated an interlacing of two essential components that characterize the human experience—language and culture.

NOTES

1. The source is https://www.youtube.com/watch?v=VbiIHSszBlE.

2. Commenting on the Edo paintings highlighted in the same film, Hollis Goodall, curator of Japanese arts at Los Angeles County Museum of Art, compares Japanese and Western paintings. Drawing an example from the painting *Study of Horses* (1490) by Leonardo da Vinci, she explains that Western paintings focus on "very careful depiction of the anatomy, structure of the animal without any emotional content." The contrast she points out seems to infer Japanese paintings' emotional involvement and visceral imaginations that we recurrently see in our discussion of cultural practices.

References

Akita, Kimi. 2009. "A Grammar of Sound-Symbolic Words in Japanese: Theoretical Approaches to Iconic and Lexical Properties of Mimetics." PhD diss., Kobe University.

Akita, Kimi, and Mark Dingemanse. 2019. "Ideophones (Mimetics, Expressives)." In *Oxford Research Encyclopedia of Linguistics*, edited by Mark Aronoff. Oxford: Oxford University Press. DOI:10.1093/acrefore/9780199384655.013.477.

Akita, Kimi, and Takeshi Usuki. 2016. "A Constructional Account of the 'Optional' Quotative Marking on Japanese Mimetics." *Journal of Linguistics* 52 (2): 1–31.

Allende, Isabel. 2017. *In the Midst of Winter*. Translated by Nick Caistor and Amanda Hopkinson. New York: Arita Paperback.

Ando, Makoto. 2010. "Gunjō-no Seijaku" [Ultramarine Silence]. http://hickorywind.jp/blog/2010/09/23/navyblue/.

Après-midi Seleção. n.d. "V.A. 'Ongaku-no Aru Hūkei ~ Haru-kara Natsu-e'" [V.A. "Scenery with Music ~ Spring to Summer]. http://apres-midi.biz/eccube/html/products/detail.php?product_id=22.

Armstrong, Robert Plant. 1971. *The Affecting Presence: An Essay in Humanistic Anthropology*. Urbana: University of Illinois Press.

———. 1975. *Wellspring: On the Myth and Source of Culture*. Berkeley: University of California Press.

Asano, Makiko. 2003. "The Optionality of the Quotative Particle -to in Japanese Mimetics." In *Japanese/Korean Linguistics*, edited by William McClure, 91–102. Stanford, CA: CSLI Publications.

Baba, Akiko.1985. *Budō Karakusa*. Tokyo: Rippu Shobo.

———. 2016. "Gessan-no Humoto Shinshin Shimoyo-nite Ugokanu Yama-o Mura-to Yobu-nari." *Sakuya Kono Hana* [This Flower has Bloomed] 62, February, 2016. http://www.karinnokai.net/sakuyakonohana/sakuyakonohana62.html.

Baglini, Rebekah. 2018. Workshop abstract. International Congress of Linguistics.

Bahan, Benjamin. 2014. "Sense and Culture: Exploring Sensory Orientations." In *Deaf Gain: Raising the Stakes for Human Diversity*, edited by H-Dirksen L. Bauman, and Joseph J. Murray, 233–54. Minneapolis: University of Minnesota Press.

Beauchamp, Glenn. 2017. "I Applied for a Job, Now There's Crickets (Silence). . ." Published December 13, 2017. https://www.linkedin.com/pulse/i-applied-job-now-theres-crickets-silence-glenn-beauchamp.

Bowler, Margit, and John Gluckman. 2018. "Intensifying Ideophones in Three Luhya Languages." In *Proceedings of TripleA* 4, edited by Elizabeth Bogal-Allbritten, and Elizabeth Coppock, 31–47. Tübingen: Universität Tübingen.

Cao, Yuan Chun. 2001. "Oto, Koe-ni-yoru Seijaku Hūkei-no Hyōgen" [Expressions of Silent Scenery by Way of Sounds and Voices]. *Annual Bulletin of General Cultural Studies–Kyoritsu Women's College* 7: 167–87.

Chang, Andrew C. 1990. *A Thesaurus of Japanese Mimesis and Onomatopoeia: Usage by Categories*. Tokyo: Taishukan Shoten.

Childs, G. Tucker. 1994. "African Ideophones." In *Sound Symbolism*, edited by Leanne Hinton, Joanna Nichols, and John J. Ohala, 178–204. Cambridge: Cambridge University Press.

Childs, Margaret H. 1999. "The Value of Vulnerability: Sexual Coercion and the Nature of Love in Japanese Court Literature." *The Journal of Asian Studies* 58 (4): 1059–79.

Clark, Eve V., and Herbert H. Clark. 1979. "When Nouns Surface as Verbs." *Language* 55: 767–811.

Clark, Herbert H., and Richard J. Gerrig. 1990. "Quotations as Demonstrations." *Language* 66: 764–805.

Clark, Herbert H., and Mija M. van der Wege. 2001. "Imagination in Discourse." In *The Handbook of Discourse Analysis*, edited by Deborah Schiffrin, Deborah Tannen, and Heidi E. Hamilton, 772–86. Malden, MA: Blackwell Publishers.

Diffloth, Gérard. 1972. "Notes on Expressive Meaning." *Chicago Linguistic Society* 8: 440–47.

———. 1979. "Expressive Phonology and Prosaic Phonology in Mon-Khmer." In *Studies in Tai and Mon-Khmer Phonetics and Phonology in Honor of Eugénia J. A. Henderson*, edited by Theraphan L. Thongkum, Vichin Panupong, Pranee Kullavanijava, and M. R. Kalaya Tingsabadh, 49–59. Bangkok: Chulalongkorn University Press.

Dingemanse, Mark. 2011. "Ezra Pound among the Mawu: Ideophones and Iconicity in Siwu." In *Semblance and Signification*, edited by Pascal Michelucci, Olga Fischer, and Christina Ljungbert, 39–54. Amsterdam: John Benjamins.

———. 2012. "Advances in the Cross-Linguistic Study of Ideophones." *Language and Linguistics Compass* 6/10: 654–72.

———. 2014. "Making New Ideophones in Siwu: Creating Depiction in Conversation." *Pragmatics and Society* 5 (3): 384–405.

Dingemanse, Mark, and Kimi Akita. 2016. "An Inverse Relation between Expressiveness and Grammatical Integration: On the Morphosyntactic Typology of Ideophones, with Special Reference to Japanese." *Journal of Linguistics* 53 (3): 1–32. DOI:10.1017/S002222671600030X.

Dingemanse, Mark, and Asifa Majid. 2012. "The Semantic Structure of Sensory Vocabulary in an African Language." In *Proceedings of the 34th Annual Meeting of the Cognitive Science Society*, edited by Naomi Miyake, David Peebles, and Richard P. Cooper, 300–305. Austin, TX: Cognitive Science Society.

Editorial Department. 2008. "Furukawa Juri 'Sei'-to 'Dō'-ga Orinasu Seijaku-no Kūkan" [Furukawa Juri, a Silent Space Woven by 'Stillness' and 'Motion']. *Gekkan Bijutsu* 34 (11): 183–86.

Egbokhare, Francis O. 2001. "Phonosemantic Correspondences in Emai Attributive Ideophones." In *Ideophones*, edited by F.K. Erhard Voelts, and Christa Kilian-Hatz, 87–96. Amsterdam: John Benjamins.

Ehon-no Mori. 2017. "'Yoru-no Oto'—Yoru-no Shizukesa-o Kankakuteki-ni Egaita Ehon" ["Sounds at Night"—Picture Book that Sensually Depicted the Silence at Night]. https://iaph-philo.org/2017/12/27/『よるのおと』——夜の静けさを感覚的に描いた/.

Endo, Nachiko. 2013. *Kashū: Seijaku*. Tokyo: Maruzen Shoten Shuppan Service Center.

Endo, Shusaku. 1981. *Chinmoku*. Tokyo: Shinchosha. [*Silence*. 1982. Translated by William Johnson, Tokyo: Kodansha International Ltd.]

Ephratt, Michal. 2011. "Linguistic, Paralinguistic and Extralinguistic Speech and Silence." *Journal of Pragmatics* 43 (9): 2286–307.

Ernst, Earle. 1969. "On Donald Keene's 'Japanese Aesthetics.'" *Philosophy East and West* 19 (3): 307–309.

Feld, Steven. 1988. "Aesthetics as Iconicity of Style, or 'Lift-up-over Sounding': Getting into the Kaluli Groove." *Yearbook for Traditional Music* 20: 74–113.

Fromkin, Victoria, and Robert Rodman. 1993. *An Introduction to Language*. Fifth Edition. Fort Worth, TX: Harcourt Brace Jovanovich College Publishers.

Fujimoto, Giichi. 1981. *Yasagure Keiji*. Tokyo: Shueisha. Quoted from "Nihongo Hyōgen Info" [Information on Japanese Expressions]. n.d. https://hyogen.info/content/962871154.

Fujimura, Makoto. 2016. *Silence and Beauty*. Downers Grove: IVP Books.

fujiokashinya. 2019. "Zedd and Kehlani 'Good Thing': Aishū Tadayou Merodi, Musaishoku-de Egaku Oto-no Rinkaku" [Zedd and Kehlani "Good Thing": Tune Tinted with Sadness, Contour of Sound Drawn in an Achromatic Color], October 8, 2019. https://note.com/iamfjk/n/ne22ac6a64773.

Fujishima, Hidenori. 2007. "Nihongo-no Hen'yō-to Tanka—Onomatope-kara-no Ichi-Kōsatsu" [Transformation of Japanese and Tanka—An Examination from the Perspective of Onomatopoeia]. *Tanka Kenkyu* 10: 54–62.

Fujita, Makiko. 2009. "Onomatopoeia in Haiku by Santōka Taneda." *The Annals of Gifu Shotoku Gakuen University Faculty of Education* 48: 45–65.

Fukuhara, Sachiko. 2002. "Kayō Watashi-no Besuto 3" [My Best 3 Tanka]. http://www.eonet.ne.jp/~rekio/kayouken/backmumber/m-uta052.htm.

Furiya, Linda. 2006. *Bento Box in the Heartland*. Berkeley: Seal Press.

Goodman, Nelson. 1976. *Languages of Art: An Approach to a Theory of Symbols*. Indianapolis: Hackett Publishing Company.

"Haikurei: 201-kume~." n.d. Kigo Tonbo-o Tsukatta Haiku [Haiku with Dragonfly as Season Word]. https://www.haiku-kigo-ichiran.net/tombo/3/.

Hamano, Shoko. 1986. "The Sound-Symbolic System of Japanese." PhD diss., University of Florida.

———. 1998. *The Sound-Symbolic System of Japanese*. Stanford, CA: CSLI Publications.

Haruki. 2007. "Mui-no Kōi-kara-no Oto" [Sound from Inactive Actions]. Essē: Morino Seikatsu [Essay: Life in the Woods]. Institute for Rhythm Therapy. http://www.rhythmtherapy.jp/blog/2007/06/post_24.html.

Hatton, Sarah Ann. 2016. "The Onomatopoeic Ideophone-Gesture Relationship in Pastaza Quichua." PhD diss., Brigham Young University.

Hayashi, Humiko. 1979. *Hōrōki*. Tokyo: Shinchosha. Quoted from "Nihongo Hyōgen Info" [Information on Japanese Expressions]. n.d. https://aozora.hyogen.info/detail.html?url=915550278.

Hibi-no Sara. 2019. "Risshū-no Sora-no Shita" [Under the Sky on the First Day of Autumn]. https://hibinosara.exblog.jp/30440898/.

Hinton, Leanne, Johanna Nichols, and John Ohala. 1994. "Introduction: Sound-Symbolic Processes." In *Sound Symbolism*, edited by Leanne Hinton, Johanna Nichols, and John J. Ohala, 1–12. Cambridge: Cambridge University Press.

Hiraga, Masako K. 1987. "Eternal Stillness: A Linguistic Journey to Bashō's Haiku about the Cicada." *Poetics Today* 8 (1): 5–18.

———. 2005. *Metaphor and Iconicity: A Cognitive Approach to Analysing Texts*. New York: Palgrave Macmillan.

Hiraga, Masako K., and Haj Ross. 2013. "The Bashō Code: Metaphor and Diagram in Two *Haiku* about Silence." In *Iconic Investigations*, edited by Lars Ellestrӧm, Olga Fischer, and Christina Ljungberg, 25–42. Amsterdam: John Benjamins.

Hirai, Takashi. 2019. *Wabi Sabi-no Tetsugaku—Nihonjin-no Tetsugaku-o Motomete* [Wabi-Sabi Philosophy—In Search for the Philosophy of Japanese People]. Tokyo: Kokushokankokai.

Hobsbawm, Eric. 1983. "Introduction: Inventing Traditions." In *The Invention of Tradition*, edited by Eric Hobsbawm and Terence Ranger, 1–14. Cambridge: Cambridge University Press.

Honjo, Mutsuo. 2011. *Ishikarigawa*. Tokyo: Shin-Nihon Shuppansha. Quoted from "Nihongo Hyōgen Info" [Information on Japanese Expressions]. n.d. https://hyogen.info/content/309744552.

Horikiri, Minoru. 1998. *Bashô's Soundscape: Toward the History of Haiku Expression*. Tokyo: Perikansha.

———. 2006. "Exploring Basho's World of Poetic Expression: Soundscape Haiku." Translated by Cheryl Crowley. In *Matsuo Bashô's Poetic Spaces : Exploring Haikai Intersections*, edited by Eleanor Kerkham, 159–71. New York: Palgrave Macmillan.

Hoshigaoka Sanso. n.d. http://hoshigaokasanso.com.

Hosoya, Ryota. 2015. "Honō-no Atatakasa" [The Warmth of A Flame]. *Kurashi-no Techo* 74: 98–99.

Ichihara, Satoshi. 2009. "Onomatope to Shīka." [Onomatopoeia and Poetry] *Tanka Kenkyu* 7: 66–67.

Igarashi, Takahisa. 2006. *Kōshōnin*. Tokyo: Gentosha.
Inagaki, Daishiro. 2017. "150-Nen-Mae-ni Taimu-Surippu? Sunde Ikasu Gasshōzukuri" [Time Slip to 150 Years Ago? Gassho-Style Building Revived by Living (in It)]. Asahi Digital, September 16, 2017. https://digital.asahi.com/articles/ASK8J52GVK8JPTFC00H.html.
Isaka, Kotaro. 2003. *Ōdubon-no Inori*. Tokyo: Shinchosha. Quoted from "Nihongo Hyōgen Info" [Information on Japanese Expressions]. n.d. https://hyogen.info/content/242575515.
Ishizaka, Yojiro. 1954. *Yama-no Kanata-ni*. Tokyo: Shinchosha. Quoted from "Nihongo Hyōgen Info" [Information on Japanese Expressions]. n.d. https://hyogen.info/content/674800004.
———. 1956. *Oka-wa Hanazakari*. Tokyo: Shinchosha. Quoted from "Nihongo Hyōgen Info" [Information on Japanese Expressions]. n.d. https://hyogen.info/content/423612025.
Ito, Junko, and Armin Mester. 2003. *Japanese Morphophonemics: Markedness and Word Structure*. Cambridge, MA: MIT Press.
Itsumi, Kikuo. 2009. "Murinaku Shizenni." [Effortlessly Naturally] *Tanka Kenkyu* 7: 56–57.
Iwai, Shigeki. 2006. "Sadō-no Seishin-to-wa Nani-ka? Cha-to 'Wabi' 'Sabi'-no Kankeishi." [What is the Spirit of Tea Ceremony? A History of the Relation between Wabi and Sabi] In *Wabi Sabi Yūgen—'Nihonteki Naru Mono'e no Dōtei* [Wabi Sabi Yugen–A Journey to 'What is Typical of Japan'], edited by Sadami Suzuki, and Shigeki Iwai, 387–417. Tokyo: Suiseisha.
Jacobsen, Wesley M. 1992. *The Transitive Structure of Events in Japanese*. Tokyo: Kurosio Publishers.
Japan Federation of Landscape Contractors. n.d. "Shishiodoshi-to Suikinkutsu" [Bamboo Fountain and Earthen Jar]. https://jflc.or.jp/index.php?itemid=140&catid=61.
Kadooka, Kenichi. 1993. "Nihongo-no Giji Onomatope—Nihongo-to Chūgokugo-no Setten." [Pseudo Onomatopoeia in Japanese—Intersection of Japanese and Chinese] In *Onomatopia* [Onomatopoeia], edited by Hisao Kakehi, and Ikuhiro Tamori, 145–218. Tokyo: Keiso Shoten.
———. 2001. "Nihongo-ni Okeru 'Kana Giji Onomatope.'" ["Hiragana Pseudo Onomatopoeia" in Japanese]. *Ryukokukiyo* 22: 77–93.
Kaga, Otsuhiko. 1992. *Kaimu*. Tokyo: Shinchosha. Quoted from "Nihongo Hyōgen Info" [Information on Japanese Expressions]. n.d. https://hyogen.info/content/106174224.
Kagawa, Susumu. 1980. *Hyōgen*. Tokyo: Shiki Shuppan. Quoted from "Meika Kanshō" [Tanka Appreciation], June 16, 2012. http://sakuramitih31.livedoor.blog/archives/17926085.html.
Kageyama, Taro. 2007. "Explorations in the Conceptual Semantics of Mimetic Verbs." In *Current Issues in the History and Structure of Japanese*, edited by Bjarke Frellesvig, Masayoshi Shibatani, and John Smith, 27–82. Tokyo: Kurosio Publishers.

Kageyama, Taro, and Michiaki Saito. 2016. "Vocabulary Strata and Word Formation Processes." In *Handbook of Japanese Lexicon and Word Formation*, edited by Taro Kageyama, and Hideki Kishimoto, 11–50. Boston/Berlin: de Gruyter Mouton.

Kaji, Nanaka. 2015. "Seijaku-no Hi-ni, Ji'in-e Sanpai" [Workship at a Shrine on a Silent Day]. Memo Bali Blog, March 21, 2015. https://memobali.blog.fc2.com/blog-entry-59.html.

Kakehi, Hisao, and Ikuhiro Tamori, ed. 1993. *Onomatopia: Gion • Gitaigo-no Rakuen* [Onomatopoeia: Paradise of Phonomimes and Phemomimes]. Tokyo: Keiso Shobo.

———. 1996. *Dictionary of Iconic Expressions in Japanese A–J*. Berlin: Mouton de Gruyter.

Kakehi, Hisao, Ikuhiro Tamori, and Lawrence Schourup. 1996. *Dictionary of Iconic Expressions in Japanese K–Z*. Berlin: Mouton de Gruyter.

Kawabata, Yasunari. 1968. Nobel Lecture. Stockholm, Sweden. https://www.nobelprize.org/prizes/literature/1968/kawabata/25542-yasunari-kawabata-nobel-lecture-1968/.

Kawasakishiritsu Nishimiyuki Shogakko. 2021. "Rokugatsu-no Nishi-Fami Nikki" [June Nishi-Fami Diary], June 30, 2021. https://kawasaki-edu.jp/2/104nisimiyuki/index.cfm/11,1119,15,153,html.

Keene, Donald. 1969. "Japanese Aesthetics." *Philosophy East and West* 19 (3): 293–306.

Kita, Sotaro. 1997. "Two-Dimensional Semantic Analysis of Japanese Mimetics." *Linguistics* 35: 370–415.

Kiyama, Shohei. 2011. *Tairiku-no Hosomichi*. Tokyo: Kodansha. Quoted from "Nihongo Hyōgen Info" [Information on Japanese Expressions]. n.d. https://hyogen.info/content/810982927.

Kiyama, Teruichiro. 2015. "Kingetsu-to Reikō-no Jidai" [Age of Kingetsu and Reiko]. @nifty kokorogu, July 30, 2015. http://rasensuisha.cocolog-nifty.com/kingetsureikou/2015/07/1960-cd99.html.

Kiyu. n.d. "Oto-no Aru Seijaku" [Silence with Sounds]. https://ncode.syosetu.com/n1450bn/1/.

Klamer, Marian. 1999. "Austronesian Expressives and the Lexicon." *Toronto Working Papers in Linguistics* 16 (2): 201–19.

Koike, Mariko. 2002. *Koi*. Tokyo: Shinchosha.

Kojien. Sixth edition. 2008. Tokyo: Iwanami Shoten.

Koren, Leonard. 1994. *Wabi-Sabi for Artists, Designers, Poets & Philosophers*. Point Reyes, CA: Imperfect Publishing.

Kosugi, Riichiro. 2018. "Nōsuwesuto Shizen Tanbō" [Northwest Nature Fieldwork]. Lighthouse. https://www.youmaga.com/odekake/northwest-nature/eco111/.

Kosumosu Moa. n.d. "Anata-no Kaisha-wa Daijōbu? Ofisu-ni Hisomu Sutoresu-no Tane" [Is Your Company OK? Causes of Stress Hidden in Your Office]. https://www.cosmosmore.co.jp/workplace/service/consulting/morenote/column9.

Kurashiki Kokusai Hoteru. n.d. https://www.kurashiki-kokusai-hotel.co.jp/rooms/.

Kuwako, Toshio. 1999. "Yami-to Seijaku-no Hūkei" [Landscape of Darkness and Silence]. *Kokusai Koryu* 21 (2): 54–61.

References

Kuwana City Medical Center. 2017. "11-gatsu Aki-no Nogeshi" [November Common Sow Thistles in Autumn]. Rijichō-no Heya [Managing Director's Room]. https://www.kuwanacmc.or.jp/rijichoblog/6394/.

Lakoff, George, and Mark Johnson. 1980. *Metaphors We Live by*. Chicago: University of Chicago Press.

lisn. 2015. "Sumi-ni Tadayou Ichiru-no Kaori" [A Touch of a Scent in Sumi Ink]. https://www.lisn.co.jp/reading/journey/76/.

Lodge, David. 1990. "Narration with Words." In *Images and Understanding: Thoughts about Images, Ideas about Understanding*, edited by Horace Barlow, Colin Blakemore, and Miranda Weston-Smith, 141–53. Cambridge: Cambridge University Press.

McCawley, James. 1968. *The Phonological Component of a Grammar of Japanese*. The Hague: Mouton.

McVeigh, Brian. 1996. "Standing Stomachs, Clamoring Chests and Cooling Livers: Metaphors in the Psychological Lexicon of Japanese." *Journal of Pragmatics* 26 (1): 25–50.

Marra, Michael. 1999. *Modern Japanese Aesthetics: A Reader*. Honolulu: University of Hawai'i Press.

Martin, Samuel E. 1952. *Morphophonemics of Standard Colloquial Japanese*. Language Dissertation 47. Baltimore, MD: Linguistic Society of America.

Matsuya. 2014. "Seijaku-no Bi" [Beauty of Silence]. https://tochigi-matsuya.jp/blog/332/.

Meikyo Kokugo Jiten. 2008. Tokyo: Taishukan.

Mizuo, Hiroshi. 1971. *Wabi* [Wabi]. Tokyo: Tankosha.

mle*****san. 2010. Yahoo! Chiebukuro [A Fount of Wisdom]. https://detail.chiebukuro.yahoo.co.jp/qa/question_detail/q1341041643.

Moriyama, Harumi. 2009. "Onomatope-wa Kankaku-no Kaihō." [Onomatopoeia as Sensual Release]. *Tanka Kenkyu* 7: 58–59.

Murakami, Haruki. 1982. *Hitsuji-o Meguru Bōken*. Tokyo: Kodansha. Quoted from "Nihongo Hyōgen Info" [Information on Japanese Expressions]. n.d. https://hyogen.info/content/710909185.

———. 2004. *Noruwē-no Mori*. Tokyo: Kodansha. [*Norwegian Wood*. 2000. Translated by Jay Rubin. New York: Vintage International.]

———. 2009. *1Q84*, Book 1. Tokyo: Shinchosha. Quoted from "Nihongo Hyōgen Info" [Information on Japanese Expressions]. n.d. https://hyogen.info/content/185538321.

music.usen.com n.d. "Mushi-no Neiro" [Insects' Tunes]. http://music.usen.com/channel/j52/.

Nakagawa, Shinichi. 2015. "Hasegawa Tōhaku-ni Okeru Yohaku-no Kōsatsu" [Consideration of Open Space in the Pine Trees (Shōrinzu-Byoubu) by Hasegawa Tohaku]. PhD diss., Takarazuka University.

Nakagawa, Yuichi. 1995. "Seijaku-no Bi" [Beauty of Silence]. *Ongaku-no Sekai* 34 (1): 27–29.

Nakane, Ikuko. 2007. *Silence in Intercultural Communication: Perceptions and Performance*. Amsterdam: John Benjamins.

Nakazato, Michiko. 2005. "Seijaku-Chinmoku-o Arawasu Onomatope: Wagokei—Kangokei Onomatope-no Kakawari-kara" [Onomatopoeias of Quietness and of Silence: Relation between Onomatopoeias of Japanese Origin and Those of Chinese Origin]. *Bulletin of Joetsu University of Education* 24: 353–66.

———. 2009. "Tokuda Shūsei Sakuhin-ni Miru Onomatope—'Ashiato,' 'Kabi' o Chūshin-ni" [Onomatopoeia in the Novels of Tokuda Shūsei—in 'Ashiato' and 'Kabi']. *Bulletin of Joetsu University of Education* 28: 131–42.

———. 2017. *Onomatope no Gogi Henka Kenkyū* [Investigation into Semantic Change of Onomatopoeia]. Tokyo: Bensei Shuppan.

Nasu, Akio. 2002. "Nihongo Onomatope-no Gokeisei-to Inritu-Kōzō" [Word Formation and Prosodic Structure of Japanese Onomatopoeia]. PhD diss., Tsukuba University.

———. 2015. "The Phonological Lexicon and Mimetic Phonology." In *Handbook of Japanese Phonetics and Phonology*, edited by Haruo Kubozono, 253–88. Berlin: Walter de Gruyter, Inc.

Newman, Paul. 2001 "Are Ideophones Really as Weird and Extra-Systematic as Linguists Make Them out to Be?" In *Ideophones*, edited by F.K. Erhard Voeltz, and Christa Kilian-Hatz, 251–58. Amsterdam: John Benjamins.

Nihon Kokugo Daijiten. 2006. Tokyo: Shogakukan.

Nikko Kirihurikoogen Kisugedairaenchi. n.d. "Ruribitaki" [Siberian Bluechat]. Nikkō-no Ikimono Nakigoe Kuizu [Living Beings in Nikko—Quizzes on their Sounds]. http://www.kirifuri-kogen.jp/singing/index-seikai.html.

Nopporo Shinrin Koen. 2019. "Kyō-no Masshiro" [Today's Pure White]. Kōryūkan Nikki [Koryukan Diary], January 11, 2019. http://www.kaitaku.or.jp/nfpvc/diary/diary00.htm.

Noss, Philip A. 1989. "The ideophone Poems of Dogobadomo." *Crosscurrent* 2 (3–4): 33–43.

———. 2001. "Ideas, Phones and Gbaya Verbal Art." In *Ideophones*, edited by F.K. Erhard Voeltz, and Christa Kilian-Hatz, 259–70. Amsterdam: John Benjamins.

Nozarashi. n.d. "Dezukurigoya-de" [At a Cottage for Traveling Farmers]. Novel Days. https://novel.daysneo.com/works/episode/6024241b8ff6156cc0e872751d151114.html.

Nuckolls, Janis B. 1996. *Sounds Like Life: Sound-Symbolic Grammar, Performance, and Cognition in Pastaza Quechua*. Oxford: Oxford University Press.

Ogura, Ro. 1977. *Nihon-no Mimi* [Japanese Ears]. Tokyo: Iwanami Shoten.

Ohno, Junko. 2009. "Gendai Tanka/Haiku-ni Miru Shingo Onomatope—Kizon-no Onomatope-kara-no Hasei-o Toriagete" [Newly Coined Onomatopoeia in Modern Tanka and Haiku—On the Derivation from Existing Onomatopoeia]. *Taisho University Research Bulletin* 94: 1–13.

Onda, Riku. 2016. *Mitsubachi-to Enrai*. Tokyo: Gentosha.

Ono, Hideichi. 1984. *A Practical Guide to Japanese-English Onomatopoeia & Mimesis*. Tokyo: Hokuseido Shoten.

Ono, Masahiro, ed. 2007. *Nihongo Onomatope Jiten* [Japanese Onomatopoeia Dictionary]. Tokyo: Shogakukan.

Ono, Masatada, Maki Sakamoto, and Yuichiro Shimizu. 2011. "Onomatope-ni-yoru Kyōkan-Hiyu-ga Rikai Shiyasui-no-wa Naze-ka." [Why are Synesthetic Metaphors by Onomatopoeia Easy to Understand?] *Proceedings of the Tenth Annual Meeting of the Japanese Cognitive Linguistics Association* 11: 170–80.

Osaka, Naoyuki. 1990. "Multidimensional Analysis of Onomatopoeia: A Note to Make Sensory Scale from Words." *Onsei Kagaku Kenkyu* 24: 25–33.

Otsubo, Heiji. 1989. *Giseigo-no Kenkyuu* [Studies of Onomatopoeia]. Tokyo: Meiji Shoten.

Padden, Carol. 1988. *Deaf in America: Voice from a Culture*. Cambridge, MA: Harvard University.

Peek, Philip M. 1994. "The Sounds of Silence: Cross-World Communication and the Auditory Arts in African Societies." *American Ethnologist* 21 (3): 474–94.

Qian, Zhongshu. 2011. *Humans, Beasts, and Ghosts: stories and essays*. Edited with an introduction by Christophor G. Rea with translation by Dennis T. Hu, Nathan K. Mao, Yiran Mao, Christopher G. Rea, and Philip F. Williams. New York: Columbia University Press.

Reservoir. n.d. "Tiefenmesser." https://www.reservoir-watch.com/ja/watch/marine/tiefenmesser/tiefenmesser/.

Saito, Harumichi. 2019. "Yocchi Bocchi—Kazoku Yonin-no Yottsu-no Jinsei: Hoshi-no Jōkei" [Yocchi Bocchi—Four Lives in a Family of Four: A Starry Scenery]. *Kurashi-no Techo* 1: 66–67.

Saito, Mokichi. 1989. *Red Lights: Selected Tanka Sequences from Shakkō by Mokichi Saitō*. Translated by Seishi Shinoda and Sanford Goldstein. West Lafayette, IN: Purdue Research Foundation.

———. 2000. *Shakkō*. Tokyo: Shinchosha.

Sakamoto, Miyao. 2014. [Commentary] *Haiku* 10: 82.

Samarin, William. 1970. "Inventory and Choice in Expressive Language." *Word* 26: 153–67.

Sano, Kiyohiko. 1991. *Oto-no Bunkashi: Tōzai Hikaku Bunkakō* [A Cultural History of Sounds—Cultural Comparison of the East and the West]. Tokyo: Yuzankaku.

Seimei Jinja. n.d. "11-gatsu" [November]. Nenchūgyōji [Annual Events]. https://www.seimeijinja.jp/event/.

Senba, Hisao, Atsushi Ota, Kenji Katakura, and Masaki Takeda. 2015. *Baria Hurī-to Oto* [Barrier Free and Sounds]. Tokyo: Gihodo Shuppan.

Shiga, Naoya. 1989. *Kamisori*. *Shiga Naoya Tanpenshū*. Tokyo: Iwanami Shoten. Quoted from "Nihongo Hyōgen Info" [Information on Japanese Expressions]. n.d. https://hyogen.info/content/353394667.

———. 1990. *An'ya Kōro*. Tokyo: Shinchosha. Quoted from "Shinshin-no Imi" [The Meaning of shinshin]. n.d. https://dictionary.goo.ne.jp/word/森森/.

Shimao, Toshio. 1976. *Shukkotōki*. Tokyo: Shinchosha. Quoted from "Nihongo Hyōgen Info" [Information on Japanese Expressions]. n.d. https://hyogen.info/content/451535202.

"Shinshōhūkei." n.d. ReversoContext. https://context.reverso.net/translation/japanese-english/心象風景.

Shin-Waei Daijiten. Fifth edition. 2008. Tokyo: Kenkyusha.

Sla, MJ. 2014. "IU's Gonzalez Welcomes Renewed Ties with Cuba: 'People Everywhere Want Freedom.'" *The Herald-Times*, December 18, 2014. https://www.heraldtimesonline.com/story/news/local/2014/12/19/ius-gonzalez-welcomes-renewed-ties-with-cuba-people-everywhere-want-freedom/47089015/.

Smits, Ivo. 1995. *The Pursuit of Loneliness: Chinese and Japanese Nature Poetry in Medieval Japan, CA. 1050–1150*. Stuttgart: Franz Steiner Verlag Stuttgart.

Smoll, Laetitia. 2014. "Meːɾuɾu, ɸoku, and t∫itowi: An Analysis of Ideophones in Katuena (Tunayana)." MA thesis, Universiteit Leiden.

Sugawara Jinja. 2019. "Watashitachi-no Shizen—Semi-no Koe" [Our Nature—Cicada Sound]. Mori-no Kotozute [A Message from the Woods], August, 2019. https://www.sugawarajinja.com/message/view/174.

Suzakashi Shakaihukushi Kyogikai. 2018. "Tasukeaiokoshi—Suzaka" [Setup for Help], February 1, 2018. https://www.suzaka-shakyo.jp/pdf/koho/2018_02_no387.pdf.

Suzuki, Sadami, and Shigeki Iwai. 2006. *Wabi Sabi Yūgen—"Nihontekinaru Mono"-e-no Dōtei* [Wabi Sabi Yugen: Journey to "Japanese Things"]. Tokyo: Suiseisha.

Suzumushi-no Sato. n.d. "Itsutsu-no Miryoku" [Five Attractions]. http://suzumushi.jp/suzumushiso/point/.

Takada, Kaoru. 2019. *Akinai Seiden Kin-to Gin* 7. Tokyo: Kadokawaharuki Jimusho.

Takada, Mari. 2008. "Keiyōshi-no Tagisei: Kyōkan-Hiyu-no Imi Nettowāku" [Polysemy of Adjectives: The Semantic Network of Synesthetic Metaphors]. *Proceedings of the Eighth Annual Meeting of the Japanese Cognitive Linguistics Association* 8: 256–62.

Takahama, Kyoshi. 2013. *Maru-no Uchi*. Aozorabunko POD. https://www.aozora.gr.jp/cards/001310/files/47742_37751.html.

Takahashi, Michitsuna. 1994. *Namida*. Tokyo: Kodansha. Quoted from "Nihongo Hyōgen Info" [Information on Japanese Expressions]. n.d. https://hyogen.info/content/950480196.

Takahashi, Yuji. 2004. *Oto-no Seijaku Seijaku-no Oto* [Silence of Sounds, Sounds of Silence]. Tokyo: Heibonsha.

Takano, Kimihiko. 2004. "Onomatope-no Kōyō" [Effects of Onomatopoeia]. *Kadan*: 36–39.

Takayama, Makoto. 2021. "Kokoro Ugoku Toki" [When We Are Moved]. Kyoiku 31, July 2021. https://img-kokugakuin.com/assets/uploads/2021/08/Kyoiku31_low.pdf.

Takemashuran. n.d. "JAL-ga Zen'in-o Shiawase-ni Suru Shikumi-o Kaihatsu" [JAL Has Developed the System That Makes Everybody Happy"]. https://www.takemachelin.com/2017/03/yuhuin.html.

Talmy, Leonard. 1985. "Lexicalization Patterns: Semantic Structure in Lexical Forms." In *Language Typology and Syntactic Description, Vol. III: Grammatical Categories and the Lexicon*, edited by Timothy Shopen, 57–149. Cambridge: Cambridge University Press.

———. 2000. *Toward A Cognitive Semantics, Vol .1: Concept Structuring Systems*. Cambridge, MA: MIT Press.

Tamori, Ikuhiro. 1980. "Cooccurrence Restrictions on Onomatopoeic Adverbs and Particles." *Papers in Japanese Linguistics* 7: 151–71.

———. 2002. *Onomatope Gion • Gitaigo-o Tanoshimu* [Joy of Onomatopoeia]. Tokyo: Iwanami Shoten.
Tamori, Ikuhiro, and Lawrence Schourup. 1999. *Onomatope* [Onomatopoeia]. Tokyo: Kurosio.
Tanaka, Hitoshi. 2021. "Yume-o Mita" [I Had a Dream]. Nichibundayori [Nichibun Newsletter], May 11, 2021. https://content.swu.ac.jp/nichibun-blog/2021/05/11/夢を見た/.
Tanizaki, Junichiro. 1933. "In'eiraisan" [In praise of shadows]. (Originally published in December–January issue of *Keizaiōrai*). https://www.aozora.gr.jp/cards/001383/files/56642_59575.html.
Tanno, Megumi. 2010. "Oranda Doitsu Ryokōki Sono San" [Records of My Travels to the Netherland and Germany]. Beyond the Skies, March 31, 2010. http://megumitanno.net/blog/2010/03/post-95.html.
Tohoku Bunkyo Daigaku Tanki Daigaku Minwa Kenkyu Senta. 2006. "Mujinamukashi." Minwa Ākaibu [Folktale Archive], March, 2006. http://www.t-bunkyo.jp/library/minwa/archives/torinomizi/text/46.html.
"Tomizawa Kakio." n.d. Waka-to Haiku [Waka and Haiku]. http://www5c.biglobe.ne.jp/~n32e131/haiku/kakio03.html.
Tonomura, Shigeru. 1961. *Ikada*. Tokyo: Shinchosha. Quoted from "Nihongo Hyōgen Info" [Information on Japanese Expressions]. n.d. https://hyogen.info/content/999120524.
Toop, David. 2004. *Haunted Weather: Music, Silence and Memory*. London: Serpent's Tail.
Toratani, Kiyoko. 2006. "On the Optionality of to-Marking on Reduplicated Mimetics in Japanese." In *Japanese/Korean Linguistics*, edited by Timothy J. Vance, and Kimberly Jones, 415–22. Stanford, CA: CSLI Publications.
———. 2017. "The Position of *To/Ø*-Marked Mimetics in Japanese Sentence Structure." In *Grammar of Japanese Mimetics*, edited by Noriko Iwasaki, Peter Sells, and Kimi Akita, 35–72. London: Routledge.
Torigoe, Keiko. 2004. "'Oto-no Hūkei'-to Tomo-ni Sumau" [Living with "Soundscape"]. *Bosei* 9: 25–31.
Toyama, Susumu. 1997. "Bashō-to Semi" [Basho and Cicada]. *International Buddhist University Bulletin* 30: 1–10.
Tsujimura, Natsuko. 2016. "Morphological Construction for Negotiating Differences in Cross-Stratum Word-Formation." In *Word-Formation Across Languages*, edited by Lívia Körtvélyessy, Pavol Stekauer, and Salvador Valera, 357–374. Cambridge: Cambridge Scholars Publishing.
———. 2017. "How Flexible Should the Grammar of Mimetics be? A View from Japanese Poetry." In *Grammar of Japanese Mimetics*, edited by Noriko Iwasaki, Peter Sells, and Kimi Akita, 103–28. London: Routledge.
Ulmann, Stephen. 1962. *Semantics: An Introduction to the Science of Meaning*. New York: Barnes & Noble.
Voeltz, F.K. Erhard, and Christa Kilian-Hatz. 2001. "Introduction." In *Ideophones*, edited by F.K. Erhard Voelts, and Christa Kilian-Hatz, 1–8. Amsterdam: John Benjamins.

Wakayamaken Kikakubu Kikakuseisakukyoku Bunkageijutsuka. n.d. "Amabikiyama" [Mt. Amabiki]. Wakayamaken-no Minwa [Folktales of Wakayama Prefecture]. http://wave.pref.wakayama.lg.jp/bunka-archive/minwa/15.html.

Walkerplus. 2018."Kyanpu NAVI-kara Gensen! Kawa-ya Umi-de Asoberu! Suzushii Mizube-no Kyanpujō 5-sen" [Careful Selection from NAVI! Enjoy at Rivers and Oceans! 5 Selected Cool Waterside Campgrounds], August 11, 2018. https://www.walkerplus.com/trend/matome/article/156651/.

Walton, Kendall. 1976. "Points of View in Narrative and Depictive Representation." *Noûs* 10 (1): 49–61.

Watanabe, Naoko. 2014. "Jōkamachi-no Tōhuten" [A Tofu Shop in a Castle Town]. *Kurashi-no Techo* 72: 161–67.

Webster's New World College Dictionary. Fourth edition. 1999. New York: Macmillan.

Williams, Joseph M. 1976. "A Possible Law of Semantic Change." *Language* 52 (2): 461–78.

Yamano, Yoichi. 2007. *Seijaku-to Iu Sōon* [Noise called Silence]. Tokyo: Bungeisha.

Yamaori, Tetsuo. 2004. "Seijaku-to Yutaka-na Oto-ga Nihonjin-no Kansei-o Sodateta" [Silence and Rich Sound have Fostered Japanese Sensitivity]. *Bosei* 9: 19–24.

Yamap Editorial Department. 2018. "Ningen-ga Motomeru 'Shizen-no Seijaku'-towa? Eiga 'In Pursuit of Silence'" [What is 'Silence in Nature' that Humans Look For? Movie "In Pursuit of Silence"]. Yamap Magazine. https://yamap.com/magazine/movie_silence.

Yoshimoto, Banana. 2002. *Amurita* II. Tokyo: Shinchosha. Quoted from "Nihongo Hyōgen Info" [Information on Japanese Expressions]. n.d. https://hyogen.info/content/321628545.

———. 2006. *Kanashii Yokan*. Tokyo: Gentosha. Quoted from "Nihongo Hyōgen Info" [Information on Japanese Expressions]. n.d. https://hyogen.info/content/680076691.

Yoshino Trading. n.d. Interspace Jr. https://www.yoshinotrading.jp/notthingham-analogue-page/interspace-jr/.

Yuzuki, Asako. 2013. *Amakara Karutetto*. Tokyo: Bungeishunju.

Index

Abe, Hideko, 64
adaptation vs. rationalization, 93
aesthetic value, 51, 122, 135
aesthetic view, 49, 82n10; recycled, 50, 83n12
Akita, Kimi, 141n29
American Sign Language (ASL), 10–11
Armstrong, Robert Plant, 92–93
ASL. *See* American Sign Language

Baba, Akiko, 123–25
Bahan, Benjamin, 68
Basho, Matsuo, 38, 42–44, 58–61
Bowler, Margit, 137
Buddhism, 46, 49, 68

Childs, Margaret H., 3
Clark, Eve, 97–99
Clark, Herbert, 92, 97–99
coda nasal. *See* mora
Cole, Janis, 68–69
contextuals, 98–99
crickets: in popular culture, 69–70
culture: Deaf, 10–11, 37, 68–69; Japanese, 37. *See also* cultural pattern; cultural practice
cultural pattern, 50–57, 61, 144

cultural practice, 37, 39–40, 50, 144, 145n2
cultural variation, 38, 63–70

depiction vs. description, 92, 115
Diffloth, Gérard, 90
Dingemanse, Mark, 92

Endo, Nachiko, 62
expressives, 87, 92

Feld, Steven, 93
figure. *See* figure-ground relation
figure-ground relation, 4–5, 35, 70–72, 128
Fujimura, Makoto, 49–50
Fujishima, Hidenori, 10, 123
Fujita, Makiko, 105
Furukawa, Juri, 53–56

geminate consonants, 85, 88–89, 138n2
Gerrig, Richard J., 92
gijōgo. *See* mimetics; psychomimes
giongo. *See* mimetics; onomatopoeia; phonomimes
giseigo. *See* mimetics; onomatopoeia; phonomimes

159

gitaigo. *See* mimetics; phenomimes
Gluckman, John, 137
Goodall, Hollis, 145n2
ground. *See* figure-ground relation

Hamano, Shoko, 89–90, 139n10
Hinton, Leanne, 90, 139n12
Hiraga, Masako, 58–61
hiragana. *See* kana syllabary
Hirai, Takashi, 50
Hobsbawm, Eric, 83n12
Horikiri, Minoru, 38, 52, 82n5
hurigana. See *rubi*
hushed tranquility, 7, 32, 143

Ichihara, Satoshi, 124–25
ideophones, 87, 90–92, 135–38, 139n12; in Gbaya, 136–37; in Kisi, 136; in Llogoori, 137; in Pastaz Quichua, 137; in Siwu, 137
immediation vs. mediation, 93, 95, 100
"in-it" feeling vs. "of-it" feeling, 93, 95, 100, 140n17, 145
Iwai, Shigeki, 50

Jacobsen, Wesley M., 141n25

Kadooka, Kenichi, 120
Kagawa, Susumu, 131
kana syllabary, 120, 138n2, 138n6
katakana. *See* kana syllabary
Kawabata, Yasunari, 49–50, 83n11
Kita, Sotaro, 91
Koren, Leonard, 83n14
Kuwako, Toshio, 56–57

lexical/vocabulary strata, 87, 104, 120–21
Lippit, Yukio, 145
Lodge, David, 118, 139n16
long vowels, 85, 114, 120

McCawley, James, 87
McVeigh, Brian, 138n5, 140n18
mediation vs. immediation, 93, 95, 114, 118

metaphor, 57–61, 74–82, 129–35; global/conceptual, 58–61; personification, 79
metonymy, 61
mimetics: accentuation pattern of, 141n29; conventionalized, 95, 100; evoked images of, 8–10, 91, 97, 100; imagination-arousing and memory-search functions of, 10, 123; innovation of, 99–100, 133, 139n11; morphological patterns, 89–90, 103–4, 119–20, 138n7, 139n11; in poetry, 10, 105, 122–26, 128–31, 133, 137; semantic properties of, 90–101; sensual and affective reactions of, 9, 86–87, 97, 100, 108, 113; subjectivity of, 9, 97, 100, 141n32
mimetics of silence, 7–10, 101–18, 121–26, 136–37, 140n20, 140n22, 144
mora, 141n30; moraic nasal, 88
Moriyama, Harumi, 124
motion vs. stillness, 55–56
music: Japanese (traditional), 51–53; Western, 51–53

Nakazato, Michiko, 104–5, 119–21
Noss, Philip A., 137

Ogura, Ro, 51–53
Ohno, Junko, 133
Ono, Masahiro, 119–20
onomatope, 138n4; *giji-onomatope*, 119, 141n28; *kango-onomatope*, 119–20, 141n29
onomatopoeia, 7, 18, 27, 31, 88, 138n3. *See also* mimetics; phonomimes
Otsubo, Heiji, 85

Padden, Carol, 10–11
Peek, Philip M., 95
phonomimes, 88, 97, 124, 126–32, 138n5. *See also* mimetics; onomatopoeia
phenomimes, 88, 91, 97, 124, 131, 138n5. *See also* mimetics

presentation vs. representation, 93, 95, 114
prosaic (non-mimetic) expressions, 87–88, 90–95, 139n11
psychomimes, 88, 91, 138n5. *See also* mimetics

quotative particle, 88, 92, 106, 139n15

reduplication, 89, 103, 119–21
Rendaku, 121
Rhee, Seongha, 66
Ross, Haj, 58–61
rubi, 120–21
Rubin, Jay, 113

Saito, Harumichi, 100
Saito, Mokichi, 123–24
Sakai, Fumiko, 130
Sakamoto, Miyao, 129
Samarin, William, 90
Sasaki, Yukitsuna, 122
Sato, Muneo, 36
Sawaragi, Noi, 145
Senba, Hisao, 62
Senses, 68–69, 74–81, 86, 100, 133, 136; and emotions, 9. *See also* mimetics
Shinada, Yoshikazu, 124
shinshin, 119–26, 132, 141n26; diachronic origin of, 119–20; synchronic status of, 119, 121–22. *See also* mimetics of silence
silence: breaking/disturbing, 41–42; concept(ualization) of, 5–6, 9–10, 32, 35–50, 57, 61, 68–69, 144; expressions of, 1–2; figurative (non-literal) descriptions of, 57–61; intensity of, 71–82, 126–35; literal descriptions of, 57–61; in music, 51–53; in paintings, 53–57; verbal, 70

Smits, Ivo, 67–68
sound: background/secondary, 3–7, 112; imaginary (insect), 44, 82n5; man-made, 3–7, 17, 37, 40–42, 71–73; meaning of, 10–11, 37, 39–40, 62–70; of silence, 29–30, 74. *See also* sound of nature
sound and silence: juxtaposition of, 5, 15–31, 44–45; relationship of, 5–6, 15–32, 35–45, 51–57, 58–61
sound of nature, 3–7, 15–44, 52, 59, 63–68, 116, 118, 128–29, 144; undertone of, 6–7, 15–42, 49, 59, 63, 66, 144
sound-symbolic words, 87
subjectivity (vs. objectivity), 53
syllable-final nasal. *See* mora
synesthetic (cross-modal) expressions, 74–82 130–31, 133–35

Talmy, Leonard, 5
Tamori, Ikuhiro, 93–94
Taneda, Santoka, 105
-to. See quotative particle
Tokuda, Shusei, 104–5
Torigoe, Keiko, 39–40, 64–66
Toyama, Susumu, 42–43
two-dimensional analysis, 91, 95; affecto-imagistic dimension, 91, 101, 106–7; analytical dimension, 91, 106–7

Uzawa, Kozue, 131–32

vowel lengthening. *See* long vowels

wabi-sabi, 45–50

Yamaori, Tetsuo, 38–39

About the Author

Natsuko Tsujimura is professor emerita in the Department of East Asian Languages and Cultures and adjunct professor emerita in the Department of Linguistics at Indiana University Bloomington. Her authored and edited books include *An Introduction to Japanese Linguistics*, Third Edition (2014, Wiley Blackwell), *Japanese Linguistics: Critical Concepts*, Volumes I–III (Editor, 2005, Routledge), and *The Handbook of Japanese Linguistics* (Editor, 1999, Basil Blackwell). She also has published articles in journals including *Cognitive Linguistics, Journal of East Asian Linguistics, Natural Language and Linguistic Theory, Linguistics, Linguistic Inquiry*, and *Studies in Language*.

www.ingramcontent.com/pod-product-compliance
Lightning Source LLC
Chambersburg PA
CBHW061716300426
44115CB00014B/2719